The Grantseekers Guide to Project Evaluation

AF732494

Second Edition

Jacqueline Ferguson
Editor

An Aspen Publication
Aspen Publishers, Inc.
Gaithersburg, Maryland
1999

Jane Garwood, Publisher
Jo Gulledge, Executive Director
Rosette Graham, Production Manager
Jennifer Barnes-Eliot, Marketing Manager

To order: 800-638-8437
Customer service: 800-234-1660

Printed in the United States of America

ISBN: 0-8342-1760-0

Table of Contents

Introduction

As money gets tighter and grantseeking more competitive, funders are increasingly concerned that their grants go to organizations that can produce and share measurable results. A strong project idea is no longer enough; funders want to see a plan for evaluating the project.

But most grantseekers find the evaluation plan the most difficult part of the proposal to write. *The Grantseeker's Guide to Project Evaluation, Second Edition* is designed to help the nonevaluator develop evaluation plans that meet funders' requirements. This book is for you if you are responsible for any aspect of evaluation. If you have no evaluation experience at all, this book will be indispensable.

This book is a guide to evaluation for the nonevaluator. It will help if you:

- ✓ Write evaluation plans for grant proposals;
- ✓ Hire evaluators;
- ✓ Evaluate projects;
- ✓ Manage grants;
- ✓ Direct grants development or management; or
- ✓ Administer program areas with grant-funded projects.

This guide will provide you with the basics to enable you to design evaluations yourself, or collaborate with experts in doing so. Many grants are small, and often there are insufficient funds for external evaluation consultants. The lessons contained in this text will help you design a simple or a complex evaluation plan.

This easy-to-read guide provides the basics of project evaluation, walking the reader through the concepts and applications of evaluation design that every grantseeker needs to know. No longer will the jargon and math of evaluations be incomprehensible or intimidating.

The hands-on approach used in this book will enable you to design an evaluation plan for your grant as you proceed through each chapter. The book will act as a consultant, providing technical assistance and a reference guide for project evaluation in any field.

The Grantseeker's Guide to Project Evaluation has been completely updated for this second edition. It will provide you with the most up-to-date information on developing evaluation plans for grant proposals and successfully conducting the evaluation. The lessons on designing the evaluation and analyzing the data have been revised to be easier for any grantwriter to understand.

Part I features lessons on the beginning stages of evaluation in which you determine what and how to evaluate. You'll learn various evaluation techniques and the pros and cons of each. Part II includes lessons on the basic statistical tools you will need to gather and analyze data to evaluate your program. The lessons of Part III explain how to manage an evaluation and report the result.

A new section has been added on how to write a qualitative evaluation for a grant project. Funders today are expecting more from the projects they fund. They are looking for strong evaluation plans that will provide them outcome data from quantitative evaluations and additional qualitative information that can help improve the project and provide a holistic understanding of the impact of the grant project. Evaluators can use qualitative methods such as interviews, focus groups, observations and secondary data to add to the quantitative data. The actual process of conducting the qualitative evaluation can engage key stakeholders in meaningful and continuing discussions that can help significantly in institutionalizing the grant project.

The most up-to-date evaluation trends and requirements are explained. New sample evaluation plans and bibliographic entries have been added.

Each lesson includes instructions for using the methods presented, plus examples of how they are used and sample charts and forms you can adapt for your own use.

At the end of the book, you'll find a glossary of the evaluation terms used in the book. The appendix includes copies of actual evaluation plans from funded proposals so you can see how successful grantseekers have communicated their plans. Also new to this edition is an appendix of more than 35 funders that fund evaluation grants. Finally, an updated bibliography list additional resources for program evaluation, the use of statistical methods, and qualitative evaluation.

A well-conceived evaluation plan is a crucial part of a successful proposal. This book will help you strengthen your evaluation plans and improve your chances of winning grants.

Jacqueline Ferguson
Editor

Acknowledgments and Appreciation

This publication could not have been revised without the special talents of several professionals who generously and enthusiastically shared their expertise. Special acknowledgment and appreciation are extended to the following colleagues.

Beverly Mills-Novoa, Ph.D., a national expert in qualitative evaluation and premier grant evaluator. She wrote the excellent chapter on qualitative evaluation methods.

Gregory P. Ferguson, M.S., expert in statistical quality control in engineering who can translate sophisticated mathematical concepts into understandable English.

James DeAngelis, former Assistant Director of Ancillary Products at Capitol Publications, who is expert in editing, using the Internet as a grant resource and focusing on producing the best publication to meet the needs of grantseekers.

Rosette Graham, Production Director, for the page layout design.

Judy Denton, Art Director, for designing the cover.

Robin Jones, Manager of Ancillary Products; Bill Reinhard, Executive Editor of the Grants Division; and Leslie Ramsey and Mike Abshire, Contributing Editors, for assisting with the editing of this publication.

My thanks to you all.

Part I

Understanding Evaluation Basics

Lesson 1
The Purpose of the Project Evaluation

Grantmakers are taking evaluations more seriously. A strong evaluation plan is a critical part of a grant-funded project because funders usually require evidence that their grantees will be able to assess the results.

But evaluations can do even more—both for the funder and the grantee. As grantseekers, we can design and execute evaluations to obtain objective data to help us:

- Demonstrate the effectiveness of the project;
- Improve the program, services or methods;
- Document cost-effectiveness of the project;
- Support replicability of the project;
- Institutionalize the project by involving key stakeholders;
- Provide data to the funder for continued or new funding; and
- Provide evidence to future funders for new or supplemental projects.

The resulting findings from evaluations should be presented to administrators, researchers, policymakers and funders to decide if the project should continue, its results should be disseminated, and its methods are valid. Findings also can produce information to assess needs for another grant project.

So, instead of being just an "add-on," a carefully constructed evaluation can strengthen a grant proposal and improve the odds of being funded.

Some funders provide funding only for evaluation purposes. (*See Program Evaluation Grants in the Bibliography*.) Evaluations can help your organization leverage future grants.

Perspectives on Evaluation

Think through what type of evaluation would be helpful to your project and organization as you are developing plans to meet the funder's requirements for a strong evaluation plan.

Typically, we have more data than we know what to do with. But talk to your colleagues about their concerns, issues and questions that could be addressed in the evaluation design. Think of collecting information in a systematic fashion to identify strengths and weaknesses of the proposed project for *your* purposes, not just the funder. Get your staff involved in the discussions with the evaluator on evaluation design and implementation. Include staff at all levels, including administrators, service providers, staff, executives and board members. Everyone has an opinion, and asking for input into the evaluation design can strengthen the process and build ownership of the project.

A rigorous evaluation design will be a scientific experiment. It will attempt to determine the impact of your activities. To do so, an evaluator often will want to randomly assign subjects to interventions or treatment and to a control group that does not receive any intervention, and statistically compare the results. If the evaluator seeks out quantitative and qualitative information, he or she can determine project strengths and weaknesses, identify improvement strategies and monitor progress.

Evaluation is not meant to be judgmental but to understand, document and quantify the effects of our activities. Even if you are not well-versed in evaluation research and methodology, you have an important role to play in constructing the evaluation design.

The actual process of developing an evaluation design can help you improve your proposed project. A strong evaluation will be based on measurable goals and objectives, a specific target population and quantifiable outcomes. Thus, an evaluator can help you and the project staff clarify the purpose of the project in order to define how to monitor it and assess its impact.

Remember that the bottom line of the evaluation is the impact of the project. An evaluator will select measures that are linked to (and even built in to) the objectives. These measures must have validity—that is, be able to measure the outcome or concept you want to assess—and reliability—that is, the stability of the measure. Often, evaluators will look for standardized instruments that have demonstrated reliability and stability.

The Funder's Requirements

Before you submit a proposal to the funder, it's a good idea to find out what it expects in the way of evaluation. Don't make the typical mistake of including only a "plan to plan" for an evaluation. Instead, provide the funder with a detailed evaluation design.

Funders vary tremendously in the types of evaluations they expect in the grants they fund. Private-sector funders often just ask applicants how they will know if they have succeeded with the project. Foundations may simply ask grantseekers to include an evaluation plan in the proposal to assess the effectiveness of the grant.

Federal agencies tend to be more elaborate. For example, the U.S. Education Department asks applicants to consider the following points regarding quality while they are designing their evaluations:

- Extent evaluation methods are thorough, feasible and appropriate to the project's goals, objectives and outcomes;
- Extent evaluation methods are thorough, feasible and appropriate to the context within which the project operates;
- Evaluation methods examine the effectiveness of project implementation strategies;
- Evaluation methods use objective performance measures that are clearly related to the project's intended outcomes and will produce quantitative and qualitative data;
- Extent evaluation methods will provide timely guidance for quality assurance;
- Evaluation methods will provide performance feedback and permit periodic assessment of progress toward achieving intended outcomes;
- Extent evaluation will provide guidance about effective strategies suitable for replication or testing in other settings.

The National Science Foundation (NSF) places a strong emphasis on evaluation in its projects and provides several paragraphs in its program announcements on the evaluation requirements, including program performance and operations. NSF sees evaluation as a way to expand the existing knowledge base and create opportunities for projects to build on successful models. Evaluation can be of the following types: accountability, management and knowledge (Rutman, Leonard, Ed., *Evaluation Research Methods: A Basic Guide*, Sage Publications, 1984). NSF requires that grant projects have accountability and management evaluation components.

Each evaluation plan in NSF grants must include objectives and critical questions, evaluation personnel, process for collecting and analyzing information, use of information to monitor progress and timeline of major milestones. Then the results of the evaluation can be disseminated to various audiences to widen the impact of the grant.

In the grant program for Developmental Disabilities, Projects of National Significance, funded by the Administration for Children and Families, U.S. Health and Human Services Department, the word "evaluation" is not used, but the grant applicant is required to explain how the results or benefits of the project will be determined. Here is the selection criterion from the Request for Proposals (RFP) that addresses the project results.

Results or Benefits Expected (20 points)

"The extent to which the application identifies the results and benefits to be derived, the extent to which they are consistent with the objectives of the application, and the extent to which the application indicates the anticipated contributions to policy, practice, theory and/or research. The extent to which the proposed project costs are reasonable in view of the expected results."

Some federal agencies are becoming very elaborate in their evaluation requirements. The Corporation for National Service focused on evaluation in its RFP for Learn and Serve America, Higher Education, Innovative Campus-Based Programs, including qualitative and key stakeholder evaluation requirements. This RFP included three evaluation components: track progress toward objectives, use stakeholder feedback, and collect descriptive data and meet evaluation reporting requirements.

Here is the description from the Learn and Serve America RFP of what is expected of the grantseeker regarding the evaluation plan.

Evaluation

"Describe an evaluation plan that, at a minimum, includes the following three components:

- A system for tracking progress toward annual objectives. Describe each of the 'methods of measure' proposed on the objectives worksheets (see Appendix A and Part Four). Describe when, how, and by whom the evaluation work will be done. For example, an applicant may specify "case studies" as the method for assessing the degree to which program components have become institutionalized. The applicant should determine how and how many programs will be chosen for study, how the case studies will be structured, when they will be conducted, and who will conduct them.

- A system for using stakeholder feedback to improve program quality. Describe the management procedures that provide regular feedback on program operations. In particular, discuss who are the program's primary stakeholders, how the program will obtain regular feedback from them, and how the program will use that feedback systematically to improve quality.

- A system for collecting descriptive data and meeting evaluation reporting requirements. Discuss who will be responsible for collecting and reporting demographic data on participants, information on program characteristics, and information on program accomplishments. (Applicants need not elaborate on specific data collection mechanisms/instruments.)

- The Corporation invites applicants to go beyond these minimum requirements and to propose more intensive and sophisticated evaluations that will create new knowledge about service-learning impacts and practice. Evaluation is an allowable program cost."

In addition to requiring an evaluation plan for each grant proposal, some federal agencies are going a step further. They are requesting that future grantees agree to cooperate in nationwide evaluation studies in an effort to learn from the combined experiences of the grantees. Thus, in some federal proposals, the grant applicant must indicate its willingness to participate in such a national study.

Above all, make certain you understand the funder's requirements for evaluation and if continued or future funding will depend on the results of the evaluation.

The Meaning of Evaluation

Definitions of evaluation cover a broad range, from complex research to simple progress reporting. Often, you will hear the experts speak of summative versus formative evaluation. Formative evaluation monitors the project's progress as it goes along. Summative evaluation looks at the data collected and analyzed to assess the project's ultimate effectiveness and impact.

Basically, an evaluation should determine whether a given project achieved its objectives and assess its results. An evaluation should provide periodic progress reports to the project staff to enable them to modify methods during the project, evaluate the strengths and weaknesses of the operation, compare the effectiveness of the methods and report findings on the project's overall impact.

The Basics of Evaluating Grant-Funded Projects

Here are six basic guidelines for grantseekers who need to develop evaluation plans.

❶ **Evaluate your objectives.** Developing concrete, measurable objectives is the key to a viable evaluation design. If the objectives are specific and measurable and contain expected outcomes, then they can be evaluated.

Although you do not evaluate the activities, you should include a plan to assess the progress the staff makes as the project gets underway.

❷ **Use multiple measures.** An evaluation plan should explain how you will collect valid, credible information systematically to determine if the project goal has been met and objectives achieved. Evaluations should include multiple methods. By using several measures, you obtain more data and different ways of looking at what the project achieved.

Usually, funders like to see "hard data" based on empirical research as well as qualitative information. It also helps to include anecdotal or observational information to give the funder a feel for the personal impact of the project it is supporting.

❸ **Choose an expert as an evaluator or evaluation consultant.** Ask a local professor or a nationally known expert to help design and conduct the evaluation. Selecting an expert in the field will lend credibility to your proposal, impress the funder and strengthen the project.

It is better to identify the evaluator in the proposal than say that one will be selected later. Also, it strengthens the proposal to show that the evaluator was involved in project planning and that the evaluation design has been completely prepared before the project's start.

❹ **Write the evaluation early.** As you begin to plan your project, ask the evaluator to participate. Along with assessing the need for the project and determining how to meet it, the evaluator can help you build in the data collection procedures and evaluation measures you will need. The evaluator can offer many new ways of collecting evaluation data.

Developing the project goals, objectives and plan of operation simultaneously with an evaluation design can result in a strong project with clear and measurable outcomes. The proposal should demonstrate that the need for the project, the goals, objectives and evaluation measures all are interrelated. Evaluators can be helpful in refining and strengthening the goals and objectives.

❺ **Create a simple, basic evaluation plan.** All an effective evaluation plan has to do is produce reliable, objective and quantifiable data to determine the results of the project and whether they are attributable to the project itself. The plan should describe measurable criteria for assessment, data collection methods and record-keeping activities, and include a timeline for reporting findings to the project director or principal investigator for continual revision of methodology.

Data collected for measurement can include statistics, records, observations, interviews and questionnaire responses. Most evaluations use data in a summative fashion to assess overall impact of the grant as well as employ formative evaluation methods to monitor the progress of the activities.

❻ Start the evaluation when the grant begins. An effective evaluation should start as soon as the grant project begins. The project's progress should be monitored continuously, and the evaluator should be a key member of the project staff from the beginning. By continuously monitoring progress, the evaluator can help the project director keep activities on track and on time.

Evaluation Questions

To begin planning an evaluation, consider the following questions.

- Who will conduct the evaluation? Will internal staff be involved as well as an external evaluator? Is the evaluator independent of the project and the organization?
- What is to be evaluated? Have the project goals and objectives been set? What are the limits of the evaluation?
- Are the measurements for the objectives specified in quantitative terms?
- What might influence the outcome of the project?
- What information and data are needed for each evaluation measure?
- How will the information be collected? Will testing or sampling techniques be used? Are the tests valid and reliable? What qualitative information can be gathered?
- How will the data be analyzed?
- What is the timetable for the evaluation?
- What resources are available for the evaluation?
- What information will the final evaluation report contain? Who will receive the report and when?

As you plan the evaluation, you might consider including it in the proposal as a project objective, with specific activities and a budget. This will integrate the evaluation activities into the daily procedures of the project and incorporate it into the management plan of the entire grant.

Selecting the Evaluator

Very often, the project's initiator is too close to the project or lacks the background to design all aspects of the evaluation. In such cases, it helps to ask an expert in the project field, such as a college or university professor, to prepare the evaluation plan.

The evaluator's credentials are very important to winning the funder's approval; evaluators must have the expertise and objectivity to provide a valid assessment of the project. Hire the best evaluator you can; the grant usually will pay for evaluation services. Check with colleges and universities for national experts in the project field and hire them from the start of the grant. Often, the funder can suggest some experts who could serve as project evaluators.

If the project is complex, you can assemble an evaluation team or committee consisting of experts in the content area of the project. For example, in an education project, experts in the subject area and instruction methodologies featured in the project could be part of the team, as well as teachers, administrators, researchers, business or corporate representatives and university professors. The evaluation team could conduct classroom observations, interview project participants, review statistics regarding participant achievement and prepare a final evaluation report.

Whoever you choose as the evaluator, list his, her or their credentials and experience in the proposal.

Many organizations have excellent in-house research or evaluation departments. Performing an internal as well as external evaluation could strengthen the proposal. The internal staff could prepare statistics, surveys and other instruments for data collection that could expand the scope of the evaluation design. The internal staff knows the target population, has access to confidential records, and can collect data on a daily basis more easily than an external evaluator. Then the independent evaluator can use his/her time to analyze the data objectively. The external evaluator could assess the data or gather additional information to bring in more ways to assess the project.

The Responsibilities of an Evaluator

A key role of the evaluator is to construct a research design that fits the purpose of the project. Here are the types of duties that you can require of an evaluator:

- Assist in refining the project goals and objectives;
- Select or develop evaluation instruments and procedures. Provide staff with the costs of the instruments and evaluation plan. Review other instruments as requested;
- Determine what data will be collected, by whom and how often;
- Establish and manage data collection, entering and storage;
- Select statistical tools;
- Write the evaluation plan in coordination with the staff preparing the proposal;
- Integrate quantitative and qualitative data from multiple data sources;
- Provide for client consent procedures and confidentiality, if required;
- Provide ongoing support and advice throughout the project;
- Interpret findings; or
- Prepare evaluation reports.

Tips in Developing the Evaluation Plan

As manager of the development of the grant, you are responsible for producing a sound and effective evaluation plan. Here are a few tips in helping you cut through the evaluation maze;

✓ Look to other evaluation plans that were developed for similar programs and grant projects;
✓ Seek the expertise of academic and professional evaluators. Often they will direct you to the appropriate methods or suggest expert evaluators;
✓ Involve the funder in the development of the evaluation plan;
✓ Ask the program staff for their input into the project and evaluation design;
✓ Find out what evaluation instruments already exist that are valid and have been field-tested; and
✓ Form an advisory committee that will support the project and act on the evaluation findings.

Evaluation as a Collaborative Process

The preparation of an evaluation plan, like the project itself, must be a collaborative effort within your organization and not dominated by one person or a clique of individuals. This approach can produce a strong project with the input of many professionals and guard against its being criticized for political reasons.

Involve people at all levels in the evaluation process. Ask for the input of project staff, administrators, members of the target population, community representatives and other key stakeholders. Include some of these members on the project advisory committee.

Another effective approach is to assemble an evaluation team to support the chief evaluator. A team can include administrators, staff, collaborators and members of the target population. Also, a graduate student or junior staff member can collect data and act as liaison to the evaluator. In several organizations with strong research and evaluation departments, the staff have conducted the daily data collection and the independent evaluator has analyzed it.

Developing the Project Goal and Objectives

The first step in developing an evaluation plan is write the project goal and objectives. Let's consider the grant proposal as a whole. To develop a project, you first set a goal that is a "solution" to a "problem" or "need." To carry out the solution, you set and work to achieve objectives. To determine whether the project has achieved its objectives, you select and use measurement methods. These form the basis of the evaluation.

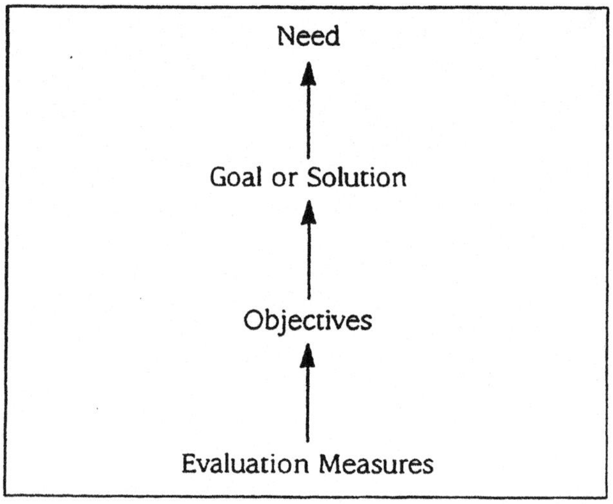

So you can see that the entire proposal is a single entity, with each part integrated with and flowing from the others (see chart at left).

Thinking of your proposal as a whole, it will be easy to develop evaluation strategies. As you begin to develop your project idea, begin with the needs that you have identified. You can outline your entire proposal from the beginning in the following way.

You can see in the chart on the next page that as you list each need, you develop one or two goals. For each goal, you set several objectives and at least one evaluation measure.

Needs	Goal	Objectives	Evaluation Measures
1	1.0	1.1	1.1.1
		1.2	1.2.1
		1.3	1.3.1
		1.4	1.4.1
2	2.0	2.1	2.1.1
		2.2	2.2.1
		2.3	2.3.1
		2.4	2.4.1

Once you have established the needs, goals, objectives and evaluation measures, you can formulate the project methodology. This is the plan of action and contains the activities that you will conduct to achieve the objectives.

You can see how each part of the proposal fits neatly together. By constructing your proposal in this way, you can show the funder the solid construction and inherent logic of your project. Not only will this form help you develop your project, but you can include it in your proposal to show the funder the project's conceptual framework.

What is a Goal? What is an Objective?

Writing clear and precise goals and objectives is crucial to developing a solid evaluation plan. Keep in mind that a grant project typically has only one or two goals. Goals state the planned outcome that will solve the problem addressed in the needs statement. The project goal should respond directly to the purpose of the grant program you are applying to.

After you establish the goals, you must develop several objectives to help meet them. Objectives must be specific, attainable and quantifiable, telling the funder who will do what, where, when, why and for how long. They can include quantitative measures of accomplishment and qualitative descriptions of progress.

Objectives should be written with action verbs, such as "to increase," "to improve," "to identify," or "to research."

Depending on the type of project proposed, you can use four different types of objectives.

- Behavioral Objectives provide information on project participants' performance. They can be classified in the cognitive, affective or psychomotor domains (*see pp. 23-25*). The objectives should state the expected behavior and how it will be measured.

Example: After attending the science education workshop, students will be able to write scientific principles represented by a formula.

- Product Objectives include the tangible results of the project, such as a publication, training materials or a curriculum.

  Example: *By the end of the project, the staff will have developed a revised curriculum and training materials for freshman college students. The curriculum will cover the criteria specified by the Education Department.*

- Performance Objectives provide criteria for project participants' performance as well as behavior.

  Example: *At the end of the training session, the participants will demonstrate their knowledge of the effects of alcohol abuse, measured by a gain of 10 points on a post-test.*

- Process Objectives describe the projects' progress and procedures, which may be as important as the outcomes.

  Example: *By the end of the first year, the project will develop new linkages between the colleges and local industries, creating at least 50 cooperative education positions for junior-year students.*

Setting Evaluation Standards

When writing objectives, you will want to include standards of measurement to show the improvement of performance or skill achievement as a result of the project. This usually is the case in education grants or any projects attempting to modify behavior or improve achievement.

To set evaluation standards, you can first call on experts. In a program to improve reading ability, for example, you might ask reading teachers to decide how well students should perform on a test before the program can be considered effective. Similarly, you might ask accounting or business experts to set the standards for a program goal of cost efficiency.

Using expert judgment sometimes is the best way—and occasionally the only way—to arrive at realistic standards for untried or experimental programs. Just be careful that the criteria set by experts don't reflect their own biases and that the standards are achievable within your project.

Another method you can use to set standards for objectives is to rely on past performance as an indicator of what you reasonably can expect. Still another way is to use the concept of statistical significance. This means that program participants are expected to show gains over time or when compared to nonparticipants. These gains must be linked to the program in some scientific way to eliminate the chances that they are caused by some outside influence. To use statistical significance as a standard, you must make sure that your evaluation design is rigorous, your sample is carefully selected and your test instruments are reliable and valid.

Finally, you can set standards by relying on established practice or norms. Just remember to take regional variations in needs and resources into account.

Sorting Behavioral Objectives into Domains

Behavioral objectives often are used in grant projects, particularly in education and training. One major objective often depends on several smaller, more specific ones called enabling, intermediate or subobjectives.

When you have a long list of objectives, it helps to sort them into various categories according to their underlying purpose. The system most often used consists of three categories or domains: the cognitive or intellectual, the affective or attitudinal, and the psychomotor or physical. By placing each objective into one of these categories, you can get a clearer picture of what the program might be expected to accomplish.

Finding Your Way around the Cognitive Domain

Any objective primarily concerned with intellectual skills belongs in the category of the cognitive domain. This domain has six levels, beginning with knowledge and moving up the scale to evaluation, the highest level.

❶ **Knowledge** At this level, the student depends largely on the ability to recall facts and figures, methods, patterns, structures and so on.

❷ **Comprehension** The student understands the message and can use the ideas it suggests.

❸ **Application** This is the level at which the student is able to use abstractions in concrete situations and under novel circumstances.

❹ **Analysis** This stage requires the ability to break a complex message down to study its parts and its organization and to determine its meaning.

❺ **Synthesis** At this level, the student is able to combine parts into a new pattern or structure that didn't exist before.

❻ **Evaluation** This level requires judgments about the value of materials and methods for certain purposes and the degree to which they meet some criteria.

Here are some objectives that fall into the cognitive domain.

- Given a paragraph, the student will identify the main idea.
- Given a set, the student will construct a subset.
- Given a paragraph in French, the student will translate it into English.
- Given a map of the United States with boundaries drawn, the student will locate and label the states.

What Belongs in the Affective Domain?

An objective primarily concerned with attitudes, values and feeling is categorized as belonging in the affective domain. This domain has five levels, beginning with "receiving."

❶ **Receiving** At the lowest level, receiving refers to the learner's sensitivity to the existence of certain phenomena. This category is subdivided into awareness, willingness to receive and controlled attention.

❷ **Responding** At this level, the student is paying attention actively.

❸ **Valuing** The learner behaves in such a way that an observer can tell he or she holds a particular value.

❹ **Organizing** At this level, the learner who holds more than one value is able to assemble them into a coherent system.

❺ **Characterization by a value or value complex** At this level, the student's actions are so consistently shaped by his or her own particular values that you actually can characterize him or her by those beliefs.

Here are some objectives that fall into the affective domain.

- Given the choice of many different foods, the student will select a well-balanced diet.

- Students in program A will indicate their improved attitude toward school by a statistically significant reduction in tardiness and absences from the previous quarter.
- Given an honor code, students will not cheat on examinations even when proctors are not present.
- After hearing an appeal for blood donations, at least half the class will volunteer.

What are Psychomotor Objectives?

Any objective primarily concerned with physical skills is categorized in the psychomotor domain. This domain has five levels, from perception to complex overt response.

❶ **Perception** Before performing a motor act, the student must become aware of conditions or surroundings through the sense organs. Perception is the main part of the situation-interpretation-action chain that leads to motor activity.

❷ **Set** This level means anticipating a certain action or experience. Set has three distinct aspects: mental, physical and emotional.

❸ **Guided response** This is an overt act by someone who is under another's guidance.

❹ **Mechanism** At this level, the learner has achieved some skill in performing an act and can do it on cue without much thought or preparation.

❺ **Complex overt response** At this level, the learner can perform a motor act that requires a complex movement pattern and can do it with a minimum of time and energy.

Here are some objectives that fall into the psychomotor domain.

- Given a pattern, the student will cut material to conform to it within a half-inch margin for error.
- The student will sink eight out of 15 baskets from the free throw line.
- The learner will demonstrate the procedure for putting a slide in place in a microscope and adjusting the view.
- With the aid of a number chart, the student will copy the numbers one through 10.
- The student will sand a board so that it is smooth to the touch.

Remember, when writing objectives, be as specific as possible, using measurable criteria and clear standards.

The Importance of Objectives in the Evaluation Plan

Often, evaluation is the weakest section of a proposal and does not receive the maximum points from the grant readers, which can cause the grant to be denied. To help you simplify the evaluation process, remember that you are evaluating the effectiveness of the proposed objectives. Determining objectives will enable you to know which evaluation questions must be asked. Let the objectives design the evaluation. If you develop the evaluation plan simultaneously with writing the objectives, the result will be a strong, integrated proposal.

As you are writing each objective, draft an evaluation measure. This exercise may cause you to rethink and refine the objective to make it more precise and measurable. Then you can determine the data that you need to collect to answer the questions posed by the objectives. The project activities then will include the types of data, sources and timetable for completion. Then the evaluator can determine the sampling, data collection and data analysis plans. The chart above can help you do this.

Objective	**Evaluation Measure**	**Data to be Gathered**	**Data Collection Procedure**
1.0	1.1	1.1.1	1.1.1.1

The evaluator should work with the project staff to agree on needs or problems identified and the proposed objectives. Only then can you begin to discuss evaluation measures. Staff must determine what is to be done and the evaluator can help in considering alternatives and suggesting how to measure program activities.

Once you have prepared objectives and evaluation measures, it will be helpful to write an evaluation action plan. This exercise will enable you to plan the staffing and budget needs of the evaluation plan.

Evaluation Action Plan					
Objective	**Evaluation Measure**	**Responsible Individuals**	**Data Collection**	**Methods**	**Budget**

Funders are increasingly looking for the outcomes of the projects they fund. This increases the importance of grant evaluations, particularly the summative evaluation. A new approach to grant funding, proposals and evaluations was proposed by Harold S. Williams, Arthur Y. Webb and William J. Phillips in *Outcome Funding: A New Approach to Targeted Grantmaking*. In this book, the authors see the grant process in an entirely new light. They view grantseekers as entrepreneurs who ask investors for the capital to innovate. Thus, grant applications are proposals for change, not for money to provide services or programs. The proposal document also changes. Objectives are more specific and targeted to a focused population. The evaluation plan becomes a verification that the performance targets are achieved, confirming the results. The evaluation methods focus on the customers and the accomplishments of the project. This turns the evaluation approach from measurement to verification of outcomes. To entice investors who are looking for a return on their capital, the evaluation or verification is key. It focuses on the outcome of the project.

Trends in Grant Evaluation

Evaluations of grant-funded projects have become more comprehensive and sophisticated in recent years. Here are several new developments in the evaluation field:

- **Qualitative Evaluation:** In addition to the quantitative methods typically employed, qualitative methods are being used to complement them and provide a holistic evaluation picture. To provide you with specific qualitative methods, such as interviews, observations and focus groups, a new section has been added to this book, Part IV, The Use of Qualitative Methods in the Evaluation of the Grant-Funded Projects. These methods gather in-depth information, uncover hidden issues and involve key stakeholders in the project.

- **Cultural Competency:** This refers to the need to increase the knowledge and skills of professional staff and evaluators in understanding the customs, beliefs, values, behaviors and mores of ethnic and racial groups that are the target population of the grant-funded project. In some grant programs, such as substance abuse prevention and intervention, funders are requesting that the cultural competency of the evaluators be addressed in the proposal. This may include identifying a set of skills that allow individuals to increase their understanding of the individuals they are serving and evaluating in a project. An awareness of one's own and other cultures is necessary when designing evaluations that are sensitive to other groups.

- **National Evaluation Studies:** A number of federal agencies are conducting national evaluation studies of the impact of its multiple grant-funded projects. In Request For Proposals, grantseekers are asked to address whether they would be willing to be involved in such a national study if funded and selected for study. This participation needs to be taken into account when designing the individual project evaluation for the grant and staffing the project to respond to the federal agency's request for information.

Using the Internet for Evaluation

There are a number of websites that can help the evaluator design evaluations, obtain data, communicate with other professionals and tap into databases. Seek out websites in the program area of the evaluation, such as technology education, substance abuse treatment or environmental protection.

Support and technical assistance in evaluation in general is available from the American Evaluation Association at http://www.eval.org. This is an international, professional association of evaluators that can help you in many ways. Its website can link you to federal sites and databases such as the U.S. Census Bureau Home Page, a List of World Wide Web Sites for the federal government and the American Statistical Association. You can also reach other evaluation sites, such as the American Educational Research Association at http://www.aera.net; the ERIC Clearinghouse on Assessment and Evaluation to download documents and publications on evaluation; and other related sites. The American Evaluation Association also provides information on its Evaluators' Institute, which features short courses for evaluators.

Lesson 2
How To Plan An Evaluation

Whether you're doing your own evaluation or trying to make sense of someone else's, you probably need help deciding the critical elements that make an effective plan.

The following guidelines can help you conduct an evaluation that accurately describes what your program is, what it does and how well it does it. You can use them to design your own evaluations or to judge the credibility of evaluations done by others.

Guideline 1: An evaluation must ask specific questions or test hypotheses about a program.

Always state the evaluation questions or hypotheses in advance. This will limit the scope of the evaluation and help people understand what kind of information they can expect to get and what kind they cannot expect to get. Here are some typical questions.

- How well did the program achieve its goals?
- Were the objectives of the project met?
- Were the program's activities implemented as planned?
- How effective were the activities in achieving the goals?
- For which groups was the program most/least successful?
- How did social and political factors influence the program's development and impact?
- What social and political effects did the program have?
- What did the program cost?
- How well was the program managed?
- What are the merits of the program compared with alternative programs?
- Were there unintended outcomes?
- Should the methodology be revised?

Example:
Living Healthfully is a curriculum designed to make adolescents aware of common health hazards and how to avoid them. Special emphasis is placed on the effects of diet, smoking and alcohol. A national evaluation of the program asked the following questions.

1. How satisfied are teachers with Living Healthfully?

2. Compared to students in the control program, do students who participate in Living Healthfully have better health habits relating to diet, smoking and alcohol?

3. Do students feel more able to control their health after participating in Living Healthfully than they did before?

4. What is the per-classroom cost of Living Healthfully compared to other major health curricula?

Guideline 2: Limit evaluation questions to those that will provide useful information for the people who expect to act upon it.

The evaluator may help formulate and clarify the evaluation questions, but the final choice of questions should be left to those who will use the data and make policy decisions regarding the program.

The evaluator, however, should assist the staff by designing an evaluation that provides a variety of data. The project director, who is in charge of the grant, should make the final decision about what will be included in the evaluation plan.

Example:
A neighborhood association asked a consultant to develop an evaluation design for a community health center project for which it was seeking a grant. The consultant drafted an evaluation that included comparative studies of the impact of the health center with efforts of other communities outside the state. The association did not agree with this approach and requested the evaluation instead use a longitudinal study of clients using the health center.

Guideline 3: Every evaluation should ask questions about outcomes.

Programs are designed to achieve certain purposes or objectives, and an evaluation must determine the extent to which these have been met. It also should identify any unintended effects.

Questions about process are important primarily because they illuminate the reasons for certain outcomes.

Example:
The staff of the Independent Study Program wanted to ask questions about the number of students who participated and their characteristics (ethnicity, gender, age, etc.), how long they stayed in the program and the content of their projects. The evaluator pointed out that answers to these questions alone wouldn't tell whether the
program met its goal, which was to enable students to complete a research project on their own.

Example:
The director of the Municipal Domestic Violence Center would like to evaluate the effectiveness of its crisis services to victims of domestic and relationship violence. She requested that an evaluator design questions for each client served to inquire about the impact of crisis and support services, including continuing or new incidents of violence. The director wanted to determine whether the services provided to victims had short- and/or long-range impact, if ongoing support is needed and the elements of such service, and whether there were differences in the needs of victims according to their racial and ethnic backgrounds. The evaluator had to develop questions that addressed all of these concerns in order to provide useful information to the director regarding effectiveness of services.

Guideline 4: Evaluations of large-scale programs always should ask questions about cost and adaptability.

Large programs usually are costly and can affect the lives of many people. It's important to know how much it will cost to produce any observed results and whether the program can be reproduced in other places.

Although evaluators of smaller programs may ask the same kinds of questions, sometimes they aren't interested in whether or not the program can be duplicated.

An evaluator also can compare the cost and results of the grant project with other available programs. And in some projects, the cost-effectiveness of each program method can be evaluated.

Example:
Sponsors of the Quit Smoking Program for adolescents wanted to show that it was worthy of adoption nationwide. They commissioned an evaluation to find out how many teenagers quit smoking for at least three years after involvement in the program and how many smoked fewer cigarettes than before. The evaluation contractors suggested additional questions about how much the program cost for each participant and how much it cost for each successful graduate.

They also suggested questions about the characteristics (age, gender, length of habit) of those who benefited most so they could report the conditions under which the program might be duplicated most successfully. The staff agreed that these questions were important, and they were included in the evaluation.

Guideline 5: Standards of program merit should be set for each evaluation question.

Standards are your criteria for judging how well the program is working. They may be stated in terms of levels of success, comparisons among groups and changes over time.

Example:
The evaluation of the School Library Assistance to Teachers (SLAT) project asked, "How satisfied are users of SLAT with the service they received?" These standards set for interpreting the information collected are stated in terms of levels of success: At least 80 percent of the teachers will indicate that:

1. Information given to them on the phone was helpful and easy to understand;
2. The person who handled their inquiry was courteous and well-informed;
3. All their questions were answered;
4. Additional information promised was received and useful; and
5. They took some action as a result of help from SLAT.

The SLAT evaluation also asked, "Does the SLAT training program give student volunteers the skills and knowledge needed to assist teachers?" The standards set for this questions are based on changes over time. At the end of their training:

1. Students will show mastery of 75 percent of the library skills considered important by their trainers;
2. Students will answer the phone and complete the phone logs with 80 percent accuracy;
3. At least 80 percent of the students will feel prepared to assist teachers; and
4. No more than 2 percent of the students will be dissatisfied with the scope, content or pacing of the training they received.

Guideline 6: Standards of merit must be set before any data collection begins.

Once you begin collecting data, it's easy to be influenced by what you've learned. If most participants like the program, you may overlook other important aspects of the evaluation.

Another reason for setting standards in advance is to help you select the evaluation design, sampling methods, instruments and data analysis techniques that will produce the information needed to answer the questions and compare with the standards.

Example:
XYZ school district wanted to evaluate the effectiveness of its public relations campaign to encourage parent participation in school activities. To do this, the evaluators tabulated the number of parents recruited in the six-month period before the campaign and the six-month period after the campaign. Before analyzing the data, the evaluators asked school staff how large an increase it would take to convince them the program was successful. The evaluators pointed out that a 20 percent increase was generally considered evidence of success in similar programs.

To everyone's surprise, the school staff said their sole standard was whether they had done at least as well as the ABC school district's campaign, which the local press had hailed as the most effective program of its type.

At this point the evaluators were trapped. Their evaluation design (which was adopted before standards were set) didn't call for a comparison group, and ABC had no readily available statistics to use for comparison.

Guideline 7: Evaluation standards must have scientific validity.

Standards with scientific validity can be based on expert judgment, past experience and empirical data. Empirical data come from experimental designs in which one or more groups are systematically selected and observed over time.

Statistically significant differences over time or across groups are not synonymous with scientifically valid standards. Statistical findings are valid only when viewed along with education and program standards. A statistically significant outcome is one that is unlikely to occur by chance, and an educationally significant outcome is one that makes a meaningful difference in meeting program goals.

Statistical significance usually is determined as part of the data analysis process and it's not necessarily the same as programmatic significance. When you have a large number of people, it's possible to observe statistically significant outcomes that don't represent real gains in performance or any other changes that are truly important.

Students in program A, for example, may learn, on the average, seven more vocabulary words than students in program B, and this difference might be statistically significant when observed in a sufficiently large population. The educationally significant question is whether the difference is sufficient to justify the cost of the program.

Guideline 8: Select a design suited to each evaluation question.

Each evaluation question may use different independent and dependent variables and different standards. Choose a design that respects these differences.

Each of the major designs—case, time-series and comparison group (both quasi- and true-experimental) —has certain strengths.

- Case design examines a single, cohesive group. Questions about new or exemplary programs for which comparisons are not yet available almost always require case designs.

- Time-series design compares a group's current performance with its past performance. Time-series designs are useful in measuring for lasting effects.

- Comparison group design measures the performance of an experimental group by comparing the performance of a control group. For the design to be true-experimental rather than quasi-experimental, the group members must be randomly selected.

Example: Case Design
The Education Department commissioned an evaluation of its seven-week public first aid classes. One of the evaluation questions asked how satisfied participants were with the program. An 80 percent satisfaction rate was set as the standard, based on the experience of several similar programs.

The evaluator chose a case design in which all participants were asked to complete a 10-item questionnaire at the conclusion of the classes. The evaluator decided that history, maturation and instrumentation were unlikely to be problems, although mortality might be. (Testing and selection were not pertinent to this design.) The evaluator therefore accepted the case design as probably adequate for the evaluation question.

Example: Time Series Design
The University Junior High School was evaluating its Balanced Living Program, which was designed to enhance the students' understanding of the relationship among the intellectual, social, physical and psychological aspects of their lives. One evaluation question asked how the program affected the students' attitude toward school. The standards stipulated that the students' school approval rating must improve by at least 1/3 standard deviation over two years and then sustain that level for at least six months.

The evaluator used a time-series design. Students were tested every six months beginning one year before they started the program and ending three years after they finished the program. The evaluator decided that testing and mortality were threats to the design but stayed with the time-series because it was easy to implement and responsive to the evaluation question.

Example: Comparison Group Design
The Department of Employment would like to substantially revise its support services to clients receiving unemployment compensation to be more effective in assisting them in securing permanent jobs. The director asked an evaluator to compare the effectiveness of a self-empowering employment support program to a group of 50 clients with a control group of 50 clients receiving minimal support in the existing system. The evaluator conducted lengthy interviews with the director and staff to design an evaluation that would compare a randomly selected, experimental group with a control group in order to assess the effectiveness of the new employment program in achieving its goals.

Each design has features that guard against certain biases. True-experimental design is the most trustworthy.

The evaluator should be confident his or her design ensures maximum internal validity (that is, observed changes must be due to the program and not to outside events). Not all biases affecting validity are equally likely in a given situation, nor are all evaluation questions equally important.

Factors that affect validity will vary with the design you choose. To avoid biased results, be aware of the following factors.

- History: Will events occurring outside the classroom affect your results?
- Maturation: People's attitudes change naturally over time. Will such changes affect your results?
- Instrumentation (tests, questionnaires, interviews, etc.): If a questionnaire is used more than once, are the same instructions given each time?

Is the same amount of time allowed? Are the instruments you use standardized?

- Mortality: People who complete a program may differ from those who drop out. Will attrition affect results?

- Testing: Will students remember and repeat correct (or incorrect) answers they gave in a previous test?

- Selection: Are the subjects assigned at random? Does your design allow for differences in groups?

(More information on selecting and using an evaluation design is included in Lesson 3.)

Guideline 9: For evaluation questions dealing with important issues or large-scale studies, use an experimental design that establishes causality.

A good evaluation design controls many if not all of the likely threats to internal validity. However, this control alone does not insure that the program causes the observed changes. The only way to establish causality is with a true-experimental design that compares two or more programs and assigns subjects randomly to treatment or placebo groups.

The next best alternative to the true-experimental design is the quasi-experimental design, in which the groups compared are very similar, though not technically equivalent.

Scientific proof of a program's merit is needed especially when large sums of money or many people are involved or when a program is controversial. Here is an example of such a program and the use of both a time-series design and an experimental design.

Example :
School ABC's philosophy is that students learn best when they contract to learn at their own speed. To test theory, the school created a demonstration project. One evaluation question was whether at least 60 percent of the students were performing at the national norm.

The evaluator first considered a time-series design, with all students in the project monitored for five years. Although the design was compatible with the evaluation question and its standards, an expert panel argues that because the school's philosophy was controversial, better evidence was needed to prove it was the program that caused the performance. Most of the students were from families that encouraged education; a 60 percent standard, although better than average, could conceivably appear without any special program.

Guided by the panel's advice, the evaluator randomly assigned students to a traditional program or the demonstration project and monitored the students in both groups for five years.

Guideline 10: For each question, select a sample representative of the population to which the findings will be applied.

In evaluating national programs, use samples that reflect the nation's population in terms of geography, gender, age, ethnicity, socioeconomic status and so on. In evaluating relatively restricted programs, it is valid to use samples that reflect only the composition of that specific population.

Example:
One question in a statewide evaluation of a school hotline program was whether people knew more about high school graduation requirements after the hotline was established. The standard required a statistically significant gain of 1/5 of a standard deviation over two years for the program to be considered successful.

The evaluator used a time-series design in which a sample of citizens was interviewed both years in June. The sample was chosen to be representative of the state's population. Using census data, the evaluator divided the state according to geographic areas, urban and rural populations, and high- and low-income groups. A random stratified sample then was drawn.

Guideline 11: Determine sample size by the importance of the question.

For important or controversial evaluation questions, large samples are needed if administrators or policymakers are to be convinced that the findings are trustworthy. A large sample also is helpful in detecting unanticapted but significant program consequences. Given the size of the effect considered meaningful (which should be stipulated by the standards) and an estimate of the standard deviation for the dependent variable in the population, it is possible to complete a sample size adequate to detect untended changes with statistical precision.

It is not always possible to obtain a sample large enough to be convincing.

To make up for small samples, repeat observations several times with different (but equivalent) samples. Such repetition provides support for generalizing a program's results. Repetition with equivalent samples also increases the reliability of a program evaluation.

Example:
The First School District was evaluating its five-week first aid program for parents, teachers and students. One of the evaluation questions was whether the new program worked better than the old program.

The evaluator used a true-experimental comparison group design. Each week, new participants were assigned at random to the new or old program. After 12 weeks, the participants were tested. The test was scored on a scale from one to 10. The evaluation standards stipulated that a one-point (10 percent) difference must be observed between the two groups. The standard deviation in the population (Vx1-x2) was 0.788 in studies with similar populations. Using this statistic and a one-point difference (X1-X2 = 1) the evaluator calculated a sample size of 626 for each group.

To obtain a sample 1,252 (two groups of 626), the evaluator estimated that all people new to the program over a period of 34 weeks must be included in the study, with individuals randomly assigned to groups at the end of each week.

The evaluator estimated that 56 people would start the program each week, and 83 percent would meet the criteria of being willing to remain in the program five weeks. Even with this commitment, the evaluator assumed a 20 percent dropout rate:

56 participants each week
83 percent eligible = 0.83 x 56 = 0.4648
80 percent likely to remain in study = 0.80 x 0.4648 = 0.3718

The evaluator could expect 37 participants each week, or 1,258 participants in 34 weeks. Thus, the evaluation design included repetitive sampling to make the results more reliable.

Guideline 12: Use instruments that are reliable, valid and suited to the evaluation question.

Data collection techniques should provide consistent and accurate information. Most standardized instruments have been pilot-tested and usually are reliable. If, however, the evaluator has created a new instrument, or if the statistics on the standardized measure are from an inappropriate sample, then systematic pilot-testing and validation are necessary. Be sure to state in the grant proposal the instruments you intend to use, explaining their validity and why you selected them. It would be helpful to the grant readers to include the instruments in the proper appendix.

Instruments should be designed specifically to obtain the information called for by an evaluation question. Collecting extraneous information is costly, bothersome to the respondent and obscures the real focus of the evaluation.

Example:
One question for an evaluation of the Pediatric Psychosocial Support Unit asked whether the program helped children adjust to school after they left the hospital. The evaluator found three possible tests to measure adjustment.

The first, the Beck Adjustment to School Inventory, had high content validity, asked only pertinent questions and was easy to administer and interpret. Unfortunately, no reliability and validity statistics were available. The second, the Rappaport School Assessment Scale, had been validated only on a population of healthy children. The third test, the Grosse Attitude to School Test, was longer and more costly than the others.

The evaluator chose the Grosse test despite its drawbacks because it had been validated on both healthy populations and special populations (including handicapped and chronically ill children) and had higher test-retest reliability statistics for healthy children than did the Rappaport Scale.

Guideline 13: Use more than one method of collecting information when assessing important issues.

The instruments used in an evaluation always can be challenged. One person may complain that a particular test doesn't measure something he or she considers important; another might not like the test's format; still another might argue that unless the test has perfect validity, it cannot be credible.

Therefore, when dealing with important issues, use more than one instrument or technique for collecting the same information.

You should use professionally developed instruments to assess interest, values, attitudes or psychological states. Unfortunately, these instruments are not always available. In such instances, rely on two or more different instruments that, taken together, provide more convincing data than would any single measure.

Example:
The most controversial question raised by the Arleigh School District concerned the costs of athletic programs. The evaluator used the Newhouse Marginal Costs audit procedure, a true-experimental design that compared the costs per student in a variety of programs. This procedure had been used reliably in similar situations, but the evaluator noted that some economists had claimed the procedure was too innovative.

The evaluator therefore decided also to use a second, very conservative technique to provide supporting data.

Guideline 14: Keep data collection as unobtrusive as possible.

In collecting data, the evaluator should avoid using people's time and talents when there are other alternatives. Data collection should not infringe upon privacy. Obey privacy laws. Adhere to grantor and institutional policies and procedures regarding the involvement of human subjects.

Example:
An evaluation question asked which students used after-school facilities most often. The school staff considered the evaluator's proposed case design interviews bothersome and suggested the evaluator obtain his information from the school's records or from observation.

Guideline 15: Use analysis techniques that are technically sound and suited to the quality of the data.

Information collection may produce data of varying quality. Sometimes, instruments of questionable validity are used; at other times, good instruments are used incorrectly.

Sophisticated and costly analytic techniques often are wasted on questionable data. The evaluator is responsible for the supervision of all data collection and analysis. Remember, sound technique and reliable data go hand in hand.

Example:
The evaluation of the Teacher-Parent Interaction Workshop asked if teachers had changed their opinions about the value of parent aides after working with them for one year. The evaluation standards required a statistically significant change

of two points on a 20-point evaluation scale administered at the beginning of the program and one year later. The evaluator planned to use repeated measures analysis of variance for data from this time-series design. Unfortunately, the person hired to make the surveys produced a response rate of 30 out of a possible 130 at the beginning of the program and 122 out of 130 one year later. The evaluator had to abandon the time-series design and repeated measures analysis in favor of a case design and descriptive statistics.

Guideline 16: Interpret analysis results in terms of the evaluation questions and standards.

Evaluations typically provide a great deal of information, not all of which is relevant to every question. Do not interpret results as a whole, but in terms of each question and its associated standards. Do not extrapolate beyond the limits of the analysis results.

Example:
An evaluation question asked how satisfied English teachers were with their inservice program. The standards stipulated that at least 80 percent of the respondents state that the program met their needs and that what they learned could be of use in their classes.

The evaluator used a case design in which each teacher filled out a questionnaire at the end of the program. A descriptive statistics analysis showed that 89 percent felt the program met their needs and 75 percent found the information from the inservice program useful in their classes. The evaluator reported these data and concluded that because the standards had not been met, the answer to the evaluation question was no.

Guideline 17: Report techniques and results so they are meaningful to both the layperson and the professional.

It is an evaluator's responsibility to communicate clearly what was done, how it was done and why it was done. A statistic should be able to follow the analytic discussions without feeling the need to question the logic or fill in the details. Others should be able to understand your methods and results without consulting a statistician. If necessary, provide summaries of technical data.

Example:

One of the questions asked in the evaluation of Omega Mathematics Program was, "Has there been a statistically and educationally significant increase in the students' knowledge of algebra?"

Using the Knowledge of Algebra Test (KAT), the evaluator tested all students one month before and three months after their participation in the pilot program. The 20-item test had been shown to have test-retest reliability of 0.91 and validities of 0.80 to 0.89. The standard required a 1/2 standard deviation gain in students' knowledge for the program to be judged successful. The evaluator collected data on 126 students and conducted a dependent t-test to find whether their knowledge had increased. The independent variable for the analysis was time of testing, pre- and post-instruction. The dependent variable was students' knowledge as represented by their KAT scores. The hypotheses tested in the analysis were as follows:

Null hypothesis: Pre-test mean score = Post-test mean score

Alternative hypothsis: Pre-test mean score < Post-test mean score

The evaluator tabulated the results as follows:

Time of Testing	*Mean*	*Standard Deviation*	*No. of Cases*	*Correlation*	*t-value*	*Degrees of Freedom*	*One-Tailed Significance*
Pre-Instr.	*9.25*	*4.32*	*126*	*0.75*	*20.38*	*125*	*0.01*
Post-Insr.	*14.72*	*4.26*					

To answer the original evaluation question: Yes, there has been a statistically and educationally significant increase in the students' knowledge of algebra. The test of hypothesis disproved the null hypothesis (i.e., that no change occurred) by demonsrating that the students' knowledge increased from the pre-test to the post-test.

(For explanation of statistics terms used in this example, see Part II)

Guideline 18: An evaluation report should answer the evaluation questions and explain how it arrived at each answer.

The evaluation report is the official public record of the evaluation. If interested people don't have access to the report or don't understand it, then the evaluator has failed to fulfill a major responsibility.

A good report clearly and logically describes each evaluation question and the procedures used to get each answer. The report should include:

- An introduction to the evaluation, the evaluation questions, the evaluation standards and the limitations on the scope of the evaluation;
- The design strategy and sampling procedures for each evaluation question and the limitations on internal and external validity;
- The information collection techniques and instruments and the limitations on their reliability and validity;
- The methods used to analyze the evaluation information, the limitations of each method and the results of each analysis;
- The answer to each evaluation question, including interpretation of findings and recommendations;
- Administrative details, such as schedules and staff assignments; and
- An executive summary that condenses your findings.

Guideline 19: Offer recommendations only on those aspects of a program the evaluation is specifically designed to study, and then only if asked to do so.

Recommendations technically are not a part of an evaluation study because they do not provide data. Sometimes, however, the evaluator is asked to make recommendations. In such a case, suggest how to improve or certify the effectiveness of a program. Avoid recommending whether a program be funded or discontinued. Funding decisions often involve organizational, programmatic and/or political considerations that an evaluator may not be fully aware of.

Example:
An evaluation examined the relative merits of programs X, Y and Z in terms of total program costs and staff attitudes. Staff attitudes were reported on a five-point scale, with five being good and one being poor. Yearly costs per student were reported for each program.

The data analysis found that program X, with 11 staff and 200 students, was the most economical ($310 per student per year) followed by program Y with 15 staff and 200 students ($352 per student), and program Z with 18 staff and 47 stu-

dents ($409 per student). Staff attitudes were best in program Z (4.2), followed by program Y (3.2) and program X (2.1).

When asked to make recommendations, the evaluator pointed out that the poor attitudes of the staff in program X could be related to the program's relatively small size and recommended an investigation of this possibility.

Lesson 3
How To Choose An Evaluation Design

Once you have written your objectives for the grant project— including quantitative measurements—and you know the critical elements of evaluation, you can select an evaluation design strategy.

A design strategy describes how you will group people and select variables to answer evaluation questions. Sometimes, a single design can be used to answer all the questions in an evaluation; sometimes, you will need several designs. A classic example of a design strategy is when you separate people into two groups, giving an experimental program to one group and a placebo program to the other.

Evaluators use internal and external validity as the criteria for deciding how accurately a design strategy will answer the evaluation questions. When a design has internal validity, you can distinguish between changes caused by the program you're evaluating and changes resulting from other causes. If an evaluation is comparing two reading programs, for example, and if the students in those two programs were not alike at the start, then it will be hard to tell whether any differences in reading ability were due to the programs or to differences that already existed between students. The design may lack internal validity.

External validity is the criterion for deciding whether an evaluation's findings will hold true for other people in other places. If participants perform better simply because they are excited about taking part in an innovative program, then the evaluation design may lack external validity.

Questions to Consider

All designs must be internally valid. External validity is important whenever your findings are going to be applied to people or settings that were not included in your evaluation or when findings based on current participants will be used to make decisions affecting future participants.

Here is a checklist to help you select the right design strategy for your particular evaluation. To use it, you must study each evaluation question to determine how many groups are being compared, how may times is each measure administered and whether the groups be considered equivalent at the beginning of the evaluation.

Following are descriptions of important design strategies to help you choose the most appropriate model for your organization.

Evaluation Design Selection Checklist			
How Many Groups Are Being Compared?	**How Many Times Is Each Measure Administered**	**Are The Groups Being Compared Equivalent At The Beginning Of the Evaluation?**	**Design Strategy To Use**
Just one group is involved	Just one time	Does not apply	Case
	Two or more times	Does not apply	Time series
Two or more groups	Just one time	Not equivalent groups	Quasi-Experimental comparison
		Equivalent groups	True Experimental comparison group
	Two or more times	Not equivalent groups	Quasi-Experimental comparison group and time
		Equivalent groups	True Experimental group and time Series

Case Design

A case design is used to examine a single, cohesive group. Evaluators typically use case designs to answer questions that ask for a description of a program's participants, goals, activities and results. Questions about new or exemplary programs for which comparisons are not yet available almost always require case design strategies. Case designs have been used, for instance, in evaluating alternative schools.

Most evaluations ask some questions that call for case designs and some that do not. Case designs are sometimes called pre-experimental, since they often are used to establish the existence of certain factors that, if confirmed, can be examined in more controlled situations.

Example 1: A Case Design

The state transportation department began an equal employment program on a trial basis to help minorities and women get better jobs. At the end of the year, an evaluator was called in to answer questions about the job rank of minority and female employees. To do this, the evaluator used a case design, interviewing all employees and reviewing employment records. The sequence of activities is depicted in the following diagram:

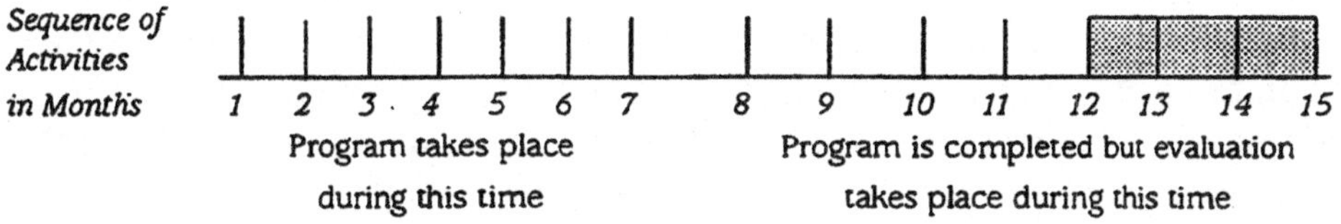

Does this design have internal validity? Consider these possibilities:

- An event that changes employment opportunities may occur at the same time as the program;

- Employees may change job ranks naturally over the course of a year;

- The people who remain employed and in the program may be inherently different from others who are fired or move away. (They might be more skilled, for example.)

Does this design have external validity? In the excitement of the program, employers and employees may temporarily abandon their prejudices toward women and minorities. Always be alert to possible threats to the internal and external validity of your evaluation design.

Time-Series Design

Time-series evaluation designs involve collecting information about the same group or groups over several periods of time. These designs are especially appropriate when an evaluation question asks you to compare a groups' current performance against its past performance. This evaluation design usually is included when a grant project includes a training component. Then, pre-and post-testing of participants provides a standard to measure the net effect of the grant project's activities.

One example of the time-series design is a longitudinal evaluation of the education achievement of students who participated in remedial programs. By comparing students' achievement from grade to grade, you can determine the extent and direction of changes. You also can use time-series designs to answer questions about whether a program has lasting effects. This might be done, for example, by testing students every year to find out how well they have retained knowledge each year for five years after they left the program.

Time-series designs help the evaluator guard against the possibility that some unusual event, such as losing records in a fire, will unduly influence the evaluation findings. But this design is difficult to implement because it's hard to keep track of students and staff over long periods of time and because problems arise when you administer the same measures repeatedly.

Most time-series designs are called quasi-experimental because they provide only partial control over threats to internal validity.

Does this design have internal validity? Consider these possibilities:

- An external event, such as a bilingual television series, might change student attitudes and affect reading achievement; or
- You might find changes in the way the tests were administered from one time to another.

Does this design have external validity? Consider this:

- Students may be reacting to the tests and not to the program;
- Students may learn because of their excitement about participating in an experimental program; or
- Students participating in the evaluation may not be representative of other fourth-grade students.

Example 2: A Time-Series Evaluation Design

The state education department is conducting an evaluation of elementary bilingual education programs. The evaluation employs a time-series design in which participating students currently in the fourth grade have their attitudes and reading achievement measured twice a year for three years. The evaluation design is depicted in the following diagram:

Time 1 (September, Year 1)	*Time 2 (June, Year1)*	*Time 3 (September, Year 2)*	*Time 4 (June, Year 2)*	*Time 5 (September, Year 3)*	*Time 6 (June, Year 3)*

Comparison Group Design

The strategy most often used to answer evaluation questions is the comparison group design. This strategy divides people into two or more groups, with one group participating in the program being evaluated. The others may take part in another program or may not participate in any program. In this example, the first group is the experimental group and the second is the control group.

Some evaluation questions require a combination of time-series and comparison group designs. If the various groups included in a comparison group design are each measured several times (say every two months for two years), the result is both a time-series design and a comparison group design.

Comparison group designs are frequently divided into two categories: quasi- and true-experimental design. Both categories include comparison groups, but membership in the groups is determined in different ways. In quasi-experimental designs, individuals are assigned to experimental and control groups in such a way that differences may exist between the groups before the program begins. That means any observed differences between them after participation in the program can't be conclusively linked to the experimental program.

In true-experimental designs, on the other hand, assignment of individuals results in groups that are initially as similar as possible, and any observed differences can be linked to participation in the experimental program. To guarantee the similarity of the groups for a true-experimental design, you usually have to assign individuals at random to the various groups.

Here are examples of how the comparison group design can be used alone or in combination with other designs.

Example 3: A Quasi-Experimental Comparison Group Design

You have been asked to evaluate two elementary school programs for children with special learning disabilities. Parents can choose either program for their eligible children. One of the questions asked by the evaluation is whether parents are satisfied with their children's progress. To answer this question, you ask parents in both groups to complete a questionnaire at the end of the school year. The evaluation design strategy for this question can be depicted as:

Program 1	*Program 2*

Is the quasi-experimental comparison group design used in the example above internally valid? Consider these possibilities.

- Students in two groups may be different from one another at the beginning of the program. For example, parents of more severely disabled children may choose one program over the other.

- Children who did poorly may have dropped out of the program.

The external validity of the design in Example 3 could be threatened, for example, because the participating students are not representative of all children with learning disabilities. You could try using the comparison group design along with a time-series design to obtain data on participating students' achievement, as in the following example.

Example 4: A Quasi-Experimental Comparison Group And A Time-Series Design

Another question posed for the evaluation for the two elementary school programs for children with special learning disabilities (Example 3) is whether students' basic skills achievement improved. To answer this question, you gave students in both programs the same achievement test three times: at the beginning of the school year, at the end of the first semester and at the end of the school year. This evaluation design strategy can be depicted as:

	Program 1	*Program 2*
Time 1		
Time 2		
Time 3		

The internal validity of the quasi-experimental comparison design and a time-series design may be threatened if parents with less severely disabled children volunteer more often for one program than the other. The design's external validity can be threatened if the tests themselves influence the achievement of students in one of the programs, for example, or if students get so excited about the evaluation or the program that they improve their skills.

Example 5: A True-Experimental Comparison Group Design

The government commissoned an evaluation to determine which of three programs for blind children costs the least. The evaluation used a comparison group design in which children at a particular institute for the blind were randomly assigned to one of the three programs and the costs of the three programs were compared. The evaluation design is depicted in the following diagram:

	Program 1	*Program 2*	*Program 3*
All costs are measured at the conclusion of the programs			

The design used in Example 5 has no realistic threats to its internal validity. Because children were randomly assigned to each program, any sources of change that might compete with the program's impact would affect all three groups equally.

Its external validity may be threatened, however, because the evaluation findings do not necessarily apply to blind children other than those at the particular institute used. Another possibility is that program administrators and staff may not spend as much money as usual because they know the evaluation involves comparing the cost of their program to its competitors.

Example 6: A True-Experimental Comparison Group And A Time-Series Design

Programs 1 and 2 in Example 5 proved to be equally cost effective. The government then commissioned an evaluation to determine which program provided the best learning experience. To answer this evaluation question, a comparison group design was selected in which achievement test scores from the beginning and end of the program for children in Programs 1 and 2 were compared. The evaluation design is depicted in the following diagram:

	Time 1 (beginning of program)	*Time 2 (end of program)*
Program 1		
Program 2		

The design used in Example 6 is probably internally valid. For external validity, you should consider the possibility that the children may react to the tests more than to the programs; that other blind children may not react to the program in the same way as the children at the institute studied; and that some children may perform better because they are excited about being involved in an innovative program.

The evaluation designs in Example 6 provide the most reliable data regarding the effect of the programs or the participants.

Lesson 4
How To Collect Evaluation Information

Once you have selected your evaluation design, you are ready to determine what evaluation information you and your organization will need.

You can collect evaluation information in many different ways. For example, if you need information to find out whether an innovative elementary school reading center has actually improved student reading ability, you probably would ask, "Have students' reading skills improved and, if so, by how much?"

To provide a credible answer to the question, you could use any of the following information collection techniques:

- Give parents a rating scale to assess their children's reading performance;
- Send questionnaires to teachers to get their opinion about student reading performance;
- Interview students to ask their opinions about student reading performance;
- Observe students as they read and rate their reading ability;
- Have students keep a diary of their progress;
- Give students a nationally normed achievement test that assesses reading performance;
- Have students take a teacher-developed test; or
- Review student records for achievement test scores, report card grades and teachers' comments.

Factors to Consider

As you choose the most appropriate technique for collecting information to answer an evaluation question, consider the following four factors.

❶ Is the method agreeable to your client and colleagues? For example, if the staff prefers interviews, but you believe questionnaires will provide substantially more information, can you use both methods?

❷ Is the method technically sound and will the data collected be reliable, valid and targeted to the evaluation questions?

❸ Will the method provide the best data the evaluation budget can afford? Can you buy or develop your own measures and use more than one technique for each evaluation question?

❹ Do you have sufficient time and resources to gather and analyze the data for the methods you choose?

Above all, the methods you select for gathering evaluation information must provide the most accurate, objective and measurable data possible.

Should You Use Paper-and-Pencil Tests of Ability?

In grant projects that provide training or education, the most commonly used technique for measuring participants' knowledge and skills is the paper-and-pencil test.

Achievement tests, one of the most popular paper-and-pencil tests, measure competency in a given subject. They can be developed by the program or evaluation staff or you can buy them from publishers. Achievement tests can be used to measure a student's knowledge of basic English usage or a class's ability to solve quadratic equations.

The advantages of achievement tests are that they can be administered to large groups at relatively low cost and that carefully developed and validated tests are available in many subject areas. Often, proposal reviewers and funders expect grantees to use such tests, including pre- and post-testing of the target population.

One disadvantage is that achievement tests must be properly validated to provide accurate information, and this can be a costly procedure. Another is that having high scores on a test of factual knowledge doesn't always mean that the student can apply that knowledge. You can obtain a more complete evaluation by using standardized achievement tests as well as other measures, such as interviews, observations and record review.

Aptitude tests, which measure potential, are another popular type of paper-and-pencil exam. The most common measure of aptitude is an IQ test. Aptitude tests have the same advantages and disadvantages as achievement tests.

What About Paper-and-Pencil Self-Report Measures?

Paper-and-pencil self-report measures ask people to explain their attitudes, beliefs, feelings and perceptions. You also can use questionnaires, rating and ranking scales, the semantic differential, the Q-sort and diaries. Results from these self-report measures will provide qualitative information.

- Questionnaires are self-administered survey forms that consist of a set of questions. Answers to questionnaire items can require free responses (short answers) or they can be structured into "forced" choices (multiple choice items).

Questionnaires are used frequently in large-scale evaluations to obtain participants' reactions and opinions. They are less expensive to construct than most measures, but the kind of information you can get from them is limited and people don't always answer the questions truthfully. Don't forget that you will have to follow up on those who do not respond, and that's an expensive undertaking.

- Rating scales can be used for self assessment or for appraisals of other people, groups, events or products. Residents' satisfaction with rural healthcare delivery, for example, can be rated on a five-point scale from one for low satisfaction to five for high satisfaction. Rating scales are particularly useful when you need to reduce judgmental data to a manageable form. They are relatively easy to complete and they produce objectified data.

Unfortunately, they are subject to many types of bias. Some who rate projects are lenient and others are not, and sometimes raters let their personal feelings influence their ratings (a halo effect). Further, the amount of information you obtain from rating scales is limited because the rating categories are never perfect.

- Ranking scales involve putting a set of items into a hierarchy according to some value or preference. Asking individuals which recycling methods they would find convenient to use on a daily basis is one example. Like rating scales, ranking scales are easy to complete and produce objectified data.

But remember that rank ordering a long list of items is no fun and it takes a lot of time. Ranking scales sometimes ask people to make distinctions among things in which they can't really see any difference.

- Semantic differential is used to measure attitudes by relying on the indirect meaning of words. For example, students might be asked to rate their country using a series of seven-point scales like the following:

Example:

United States

Good	___	___	___	___	___	___	*Bad*
Passtive	___	___	___	___	___	___	*Active*
Small	___	___	___	___	___	___	*Large*
Democratic	___	___	___	___	___	___	*Undemocratic*
Rich	___	___	___	___	___	___	*Poor*

The semantic differential is relatively easy to complete, produces objectified data, and respondents usually find it more difficult to choose "socially acceptable" answers than when they use an ordinary rating scale. However, the differential can be difficult to score.

- Q-sort requires individuals to place a series of items or statements into rating categories so that some minimum number of items is assigned to each category. For example, you could ask commuters to sort various transportation options, such as mass transit or carpooling, into "acceptable" or "not acceptable" categories so that at least one option appears in each category.

Q-sorts produce objectified data and they force respondents to establish priorities among items that are being compared in an evaluation. But the Q-sort requires people to make very difficult distinctions, the directions are often hard to follow, and the resulting data can require complex analysis methods.

- Diary techniques ask people to keep daily or weekly accounts of specific behaviors, attitudes, thoughts or events. The critical-incident technique asks people to record only those things that are particularly important, unique, useful or revelatory. For example, you could ask patients involved in a new skin cancer screening project to create a journal of their past and current behaviors that may place them at risk.

Diaries and critical incidents permit people to describe unique situations in their own words, but people sometimes forget to maintain them, and they often are difficult to score and interpret.

Why Not Try Observations?

Another information collection technique frequently used in evaluations is the eyewitness account of individual behavior or program activities. You could use observations, for example, to find if neighborhood violence has changed as a result of a project to reduce gang activities. The information collected by observers can be reported by checklists, rating scales, field notes and summary reports. Observation can be conducted by the evaluator, project director or others connected with the project, and the appropriate observation method must be selected by the evaluator.

- Standard observations require careful planning so the information obtained will be accurate. Observations can give information collectors first-hand information about a program, and they often are the only feasible and economical way to gather certain kinds of information. But it is costly to train observers, and several may be needed to get reliable results. Another drawback is that people who know they are being observed may not behave normally.

- Time-sampling observations involve repeated observations of a given situation. For example, observers may note how many students and which ones ask direct and indirect questions during 10 consecutive five-minute intervals.

Time sampling allows first-hand observations of a program, and the many observations make it possible to identify unusual events that you might otherwise think were routine occurrences. When all the observations are made one after the other, however, they are likely to depict only one particular situation and not the program as a whole.

Are Interviews Feasible?

An interview is an information collection technique in which one person talks to another or to a group. Interviews can be completely unstructured and spontaneous, or you can decide ahead of time the kinds of questions to ask. If you use multiple choice questions, even the response categories are predetermined.

- Face-to-face interviews might be used, for example, to find out why participants dropped out of a program, and might consist of three basic questions, with a series of two or more in-depth questions for each basic question asked. The best thing about the face-to-face interview is that it permits you to probe sensitive subjects, such as attitudes or values. But these interviews usually are time-consuming and expensive, and you will have to give interviewers special training.

- Telephone interviews also permit in-depth probing of sensitive issues and are less costly than face-to-face interviews. They still are expensive when compared to questionnaires, however. You also should remember that not everyone has a telephone, and some people are reluctant to reveal their feelings or give personal information over the phone.

Are Performance Tests the Answer?

- Performance tests require people to complete a task or make something so the evaluator can assess the quality of the performance or product. An example of a performance test is the typing test, when a typist is asked to type a letter, and the evaluator counts the number of words typed correctly in a set amount of time.

The major advantage of performance testing is that it relies on tasks that are close to "real world" activities. It often is very time-consuming and expensive, however, because performance tests often must be administered individually and they require special equipment.

Would Record Reviews be Enough?

- Record reviews consist of collecting evaluation information by going through program-related documents. In a program in which older pupils tutor younger ones, for example, you might review attendance records to see if either the tutors or the children they taught came to school more regularly after the program began.

Record reviews are "unobtrusive" in the sense that they do not interfere with the activities of the program being evaluated. They also can be relatively inexpensive because no new data collection is required. One drawback is that program documents may be disorganized or unavailable.

When deciding what information you intend to collect in the evaluation and how you will collect it, be sure to ask the funder and project staff the type of information they expect to see. Find out the evaluation methods used for grant projects similar to yours. Then write an evaluation plan that is as comprehensive as you can afford and are able to conduct. To do this, use as many information collection methods as possible to provide the most complete picture of the project's impact.

Here is a summary of the information collection techniques described in this lesson.

Information Collection Techniques

Information Collection Alternatives		Advantages	Disadvantages
Paper-and-Pencil Tests of Ability	Achievement Tests	Can be administered to large groups at relatively low cost	Expensive to develop and validate
	Aptitude Tests	Many published standardized tests are available	High scores do not necessarily imply that the tested knowledge can be applied
Paper-and-Pencil Self-Report Measures	Questonnaires	Can be administered to large groups at relatively low costs	Can be difficult to obtain sensitive information Respondents may not always be truthful Must follow up to obtain adequate numbers of respondents
	Rating Scales	Easy to complete Produces objectified data into a manageable form	Responses may be biased because some raters are lenient and others are strict Amount of information obtained is circumscribed by the rating categories Halo effect

Information Collection Techniques (Cont.)

Information Collection Alternatives		Advantages	Disadvantages
Pencil-and-Pencil Self-Report Measures (Cont.)	Ranking Scales	Easy to complete Produces objectified data	Difficult to rank a long list of items Distinctions are called for that are not perceived
	Semantic Differentials	Easy to complete Produces objectified data More difficult to give "socially acceptable" responses	Difficult to score
	Q-Sorts	Produces objectified data Forces respondents to establish priorities among items	Distinctions are called for that are not perceived Directions can be too elaborate Can require complex data analysis methods
	Diaries and Critical Incidents	Permits people to describe unique situations in their own words	People don't maintain them Difficult to score and interpret
Observations	Standard Observations	Can observe events at first hand	Observers can change the environment Inter- and intra-observer reliability can be difficult to obtain
	Time-Sampling Observations	Can observe events at first hand More opportunities to observe	Observers can change the environment Inter- and intra-observer reliability can be difficult to obtain

Information Collection Techniques (Cont.)

Information Collection Alternatives		Advantages	Disadvantages
Interviews	Face-to-face Interviews	Permits in-depth probing	Costly
		Sensitive issues can be discussed	Inter- and intra-rater reliability can be difficult to obtain
	Telephone Interviews	Permits in-depth probing	Costly
		Sensitive issues can be discussed	Some people may not have telephones
		Less costly than face-to-face interviews	More difficult to probe or discuss sensitive issues
Performance Tests		Close to real world situations	Costly
			Generally must be administered individually
			Can require special equipment or apparatus
Record Review		Unobtrusive	Documents may be organized or unavailable
		Can be inexpensive	
		No new data collection required	

Lesson 5
The Use of Qualitative Methods in the Evaluation of Grant-Funded Projects

by Beverly Mills-Novoa

In addition to the traditional, quantitative evaluation approach, qualitative methods are being used to increase our knowledge of the total impact of grant projects. Some qualitative data collection techniques have been discussed in Lesson 4 and include self-reports, observations and interviews. But there is much more to qualitative assessment and it can have a profound impact on the success and continuation on the project.

Qualitative research methods have been around for decades and have their roots in many disciplines, including anthropology, sociology, history and feminist studies. It has only been in the past several years, however, that the use of qualitative methods has begun to crop up in grant proposals as part of the grant evaluation plan.

Qualitative Versus Quantitative Methods

Whereas quantitative methods frequently focus on questions of "How much?" and "How frequently?" qualitative methods are concerned with questions of "Why?" and "How?" They help evaluators preserve the significance of the context in which people behave and permit a more holistic examination of grant-related processes and outcomes. They provide insight into how participants in a given setting understand or make meaning of their experiences.

Whereas quantitative methods strive for objectivity and as much distance as possible between the evaluator and what is being evaluated, qualitative methods require greater personal involvement by the evaluator. Qualitative methods are much more dependent on the personal skills of the evaluator for the integrity of data than are quantitative methods given that the evaluator, him/herself, is often the primary means of data collection.

The Use of Qualitative Methods in Evaluation

Qualitative methods are used to capture understanding and context, but are not, generally, effective methods for determining cause and effect relationships. They are, however, effective means of gathering in-depth information, uncovering hidden issues and surfacing beliefs, attitudes and behaviors within organizational and societal contexts. Qualitative methods also answer questions about quality: why a grant program works or does not work and how to improve performance. They can prevent parts of the program from being neglected, enable the program to use resources in the most efficient, effective manner and provide information needed to streamline or enhance program activities. Qualitative methods allow evaluators to move beyond the quantitative inquiry, "Did we do what we said?" to, "How well did we do it?"

Qualitative methods also allow evaluators to track changes in culture within an organization, community or group through tracking critical incidents and anecdotes that illustrate these changes over time. Use of a common language or terms in the "public conversation" about an issue and greater stakeholder involvement regarding an issue, project or program can signal changes in an organizational environment or community over time.

Multiple qualitative methods are generally used simultaneously in an evaluation effort to obtain data from a variety of sources and construct a more complete picture for the evaluator. Each qualitative method adds a different piece of information to the puzzle. For maximum diversity and effectiveness, qualitative methods are used in a cooperative, mutually informative way with quantitative methods. They each provide different data and perspectives and together, paint a clearer picture than either might in isolation.

Qualitative Data Collection Methods

The most common qualitative data collection methods are the following:

- **Interviews.** Patton (1990a) has stated that the purpose of the qualitative interview "is to find out what is in and on someone else's mind" (p. 196). Although time-consuming, one-on-one interviews can provide in-depth data. They also allow the evaluator to establish a relationship with the interviewee, increase visibility of grant-related efforts and aid project staff in establishing key stakeholder networks. Telephone interviews have also gained popularity in recent years in areas in which geography prevents personal interaction.

- **Focus Groups.** This qualitative method is one of the best known and popular in both business and nonprofit organizations. The focus group is actually a group interview. It is generally more cost-effective than individual interviews, has the benefit of interactions among group participants who build on each others ideas and is more amenable to observation. It requires a well-trained facilitator to control the interview process, which can range from a structured interview format to an open-ended one.

- **Observations.** This method allows greater objectivity and reveals insight into actual behavior. It provides a more "realistic" view of what participants do or say as long as they do not modify behavior if aware of the observation. This can involve observation of meetings. sidewalk activities, classrooms, etc.

- **Secondary Data.** Review and analysis of relevant documents and physical evidence (e.g., public records, memos, handbooks, newspaper clippings, critical incidents, anecdotes, journals, scrapbooks, posters, surveys, etc.) helps provide a cultural context for qualitative findings. This qualitative method provides information that is usually readily available and inexpensive. This method also allows the evaluator to track trends over time.

Qualitative Data Analysis

Whereas the analysis of quantitative data is derived deductively from a prior hypotheses, or categories, qualitative data analysis proceeds inductively from the data. The qualitative evaluator uses small units of information to develop larger categories and themes. This analysis goes on concurrently with data gathering and is an iterative process requiring flexibility on the part of the evaluator. Preconceived hypotheses or explanations can inhibit the evaluator's consideration of other possible explanations and prohibit him/her from exploring new lines of inquiry.

As the evaluator gains a greater understanding of what he/she is evaluating, the qualitative data gathering and analysis process adapts to fill in gaps in the evaluator's knowledge. For example, the evaluator might be striving to understand college students' reaction to a college course on HIV through requiring the students to keep a journal throughout the course. After performing a content analysis on the student journals, the evaluator may decide that focus group interviews are necessary to substantiate themes derived from the journals. The evaluator allows the data he/she uncovers to help guide the next steps of the data gathering and analysis process.

Qualitative evaluators also draw on their intuition and knowledge about people, organizations and programs to guide data collection and analysis. Some familiarity with what they are evaluating is, therefore, necessary so that they can ask questions that lead to greater understanding of the program, project, etc., they are evaluating.

Qualitative evaluators often influence the very context they are studying. For example, in conducting individual interviews with key stakeholders in an organization, they give greater visibility/credibility to the program being studied and, as a result, can often increase stakeholder investment in the program or project. This increased stakeholder involvement can even be tracked over time via the collection of critical incidents and anecdotes. Because qualitative evaluators often influence what they are studying through their values, insights and interactions and are, in turn, influenced by the context they are studying, the collection of data from multiple sources becomes important to offset these biases by obtaining the broadest range of information possible. This allows the evaluator to look at what he/she is evaluating from several different perspectives and vantage points in addition to his/her own.

Although some computer programs are available to assist with content analysis, qualitative data analysis remains an intensive, time-consuming and "messy" process which relies heavily on the evaluator to derive order out of the chaos of data collected.

Reporting of Qualitative Data

Qualitative data can be reported in any number of ways, ranging from narrative to the use of tables to indicate themes extracted from the data. How the data is reported depends largely on the audience for the data and how the information is to be used. Of greatest importance is reporting the data in such a way that the context in which a program or project functions is represented and understood by the audience.

The feedback of qualitative data can become, in itself, a change strategy since this information, especially stories of people's experiences, can be powerful when presented to key decisionmakers in an organization. For example, a qualitative report that highlights observations from a Homecoming celebration, coupled with stories extracted from individual or group interviews with Homecoming participants who relate incidents of alcohol-related risky behavior during Homecoming, may convince administrators in a college-setting to re-examine campus alcohol policies and expand drug prevention efforts on campus. The administrators may be influenced by the number of alcohol-related violations during Homecoming (i.e., quantitative data), but the qualitative data helps to put a human face on those numbers. It also provides the administrators a better understanding of the context in which these alcohol-related incidents occurred (e.g., Homecoming was on an extremely hot day and participants tried to quench their thirst with alcoholic beverages, vendors did not card underage students, there was an extended period before the late afternoon football game in which drinking was the primary activity for most Homecoming participants, etc.). If well-written, the qualitative report can help the administrators experience the campus as the participants do and view Homecoming from their perspectives. They will then be able to interpret numbers within a broader context.

Quantitative and qualitative data, when considered jointly, enhance each other by providing different pieces to the evaluation puzzle. They inform one another and help guide the evaluation process so there is a clearer sense of which evaluation questions have or have not been answered in the present evaluation design.

Qualitative data is also used extensively as process feedback for a project or program by indicating what is or is not working well at a given point in time. This process data can then be used to make changes to the program or project to increase its effectiveness and efficiency. For example, in a community-based program for teenage mothers, focus groups with program participants indicate that they feel "talked down to" by the program staff. An observation of program staff may indicate that one program employee, in particular, is condescending in his interactions with participants. Steps can then be taken to talk with the staff member about this issue.

Qualitative evaluation reports most often contain recommendations from the evaluator by him/herself or in consultation with project staff, program participants, and/or key stakeholders. These recommendations may discuss ways to improve aspects of the project or the project as a whole. They should be written with the prospective audience for the report in mind, be realistic, doable and take into account their impact on the project, organization and/or community as a whole.

Suggestions for Incorporating Qualitative Methods into an Evaluation Plan

❶ Define the evaluation questions that need to be answered prior to implementing a project. Consider qualitative methods for questions such as "Why?" "How?" and "What does this mean?" Also, consider using qualitative methods to capture environmental/cultural changes through interviews, critical incidents/anecdotes and the collection of other data.

❷ Design the qualitative evaluation plan as flexibly as possible, realizing that the data collected will help to guide the qualitative data collection and analysis process. Ensure that multiple data collection methods from a variety of sources are utilized so that a holistic picture can emerge.

❸ Consider keeping a "Documents Notebook" for the grant project in which documents such as memos, newspaper clippings, announcements, pictures, minutes from meetings, physical artifacts (e.g., samples of "give-aways" used to promote project), relevant legislation, etc., are kept. This notebook will ensure that there is a historical record for the project and will provide important secondary data for the qualitative analysis.

❹ Select an evaluator who has experience conducting qualitative research/evaluation, who has familiarity with the project/program being evaluated and who exhibits the following skills.

- Ability to ask clear, concise questions.
- Capability as an attentive listener, experienced in the techniques of active listening, such as paraphrasing, probing for clarity, etc.
- Flexibility as an evaluator to alter the qualitative evaluation design, as needed, to pursue new, promising lines of inquiry.
- Intuitive grasp of the issues being studied. Much of qualitative analysis relies on the evaluator's intuition and natural inquisitiveness regarding whatever is being studied.
- Lack of bias. The evaluator must recognize his/her own biases and perspectives and be committed to using multiple methods from a variety of sources to ensure that his/her own biases do not unduly sway the data analysis.
- Creativity. The evaluator may need to think "outside the box" when it comes to capturing qualitative data in specific populations. For example, he/she may need to be creative in recruiting individuals for focus groups, developing a telephone interview protocol that entices individuals to participate, or determining the most effective way to report data to a specific audience.
- Knowledge of organizations, people and projects. The evaluators' familiarity with these topics will save time, allow him/her to ask perceptive, important questions and also make action-oriented recommendations.

❺ Ensure that qualitative data collection and analysis are integrated, on a timely basis, with quantitative data collection and analysis so that data from each can inform the other.

❻ If cultural change is a project goal, ensure that key stakeholders in the project and its outcomes are identified early in the project life cycle. Involvement of these key stakeholders in qualitative evaluation efforts through individual/group interviews and the recording of critical incidents/anecdotes can both promote culture change and also help to capture this change over time. Involvement of key stakeholders in the qualitative evaluation process and the feedback of data to key decisionmakers in an organization can help to institutionalize a grant-funded program/project.

❼ Lastly, recognize that the goal of evaluation ultimately is action. Qualitative data, like quantitative data, is of little use if the report in which it is presented is simply stuck into a drawer and forgotten. Ensuring that the information is used in a meaningful manner to improve the project, impact the larger culture, capture cultural changes/influences or add to understanding regarding what individuals/groups involved in the project or program experience is key.

Lesson 6

Some Useful Tools — A Short Course On Statistics Introduction To Statistics

You learned to collect evaluation data in Lessons 4 and 5. Now that the data has been collected, what do you do with it?

There are tools to help you extract information from data. These tools are called statistics. That term may sound complicated or even frightening if you have not had much math in recent years. Don't be scared. What follows is a simple and intuitive approach to the world of statistics. Readers who are confident that they understand what the average and standard deviation are may want to skip this section. For those to whom it is new or who could use a review, what follows is a plain and pictorial explanation of the two most important statistics in mathematics.

An intuitive understanding of the standard deviation will help you understand almost all the other concepts in statistics.

The first concept we are going to start with is a number line. You already are familiar with one kind of number line, the thermometer.

A thermometer is a device for measuring temperature. It has both positive and negative numbers, although in Tucson, we seldom use the negative numbers. A number line is like a thermometer lying on its side. As you move to the right the numbers get larger, just like the temperature gets hotter as you move up the thermometer.

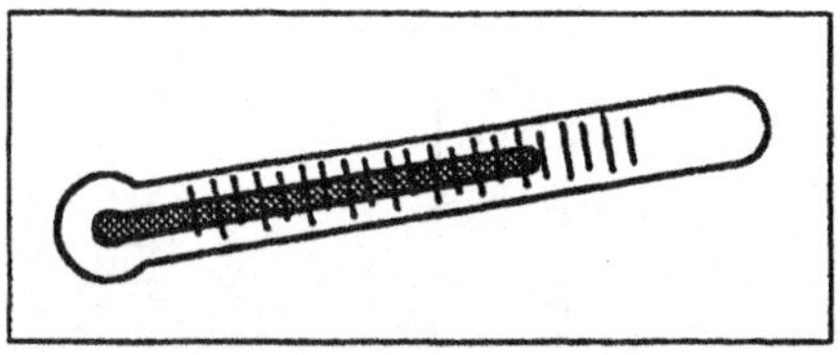

Like the thermometer, the number line also can have negative numbers. As you move to the left on the number line, the numbers get smaller. First, they get smaller, as from 20 to 10, then they reach zero and finally they become negative numbers. In this example, the number line runs from a positive 50 on the right to a negative 50 (-50) on the left, a spread of 100.

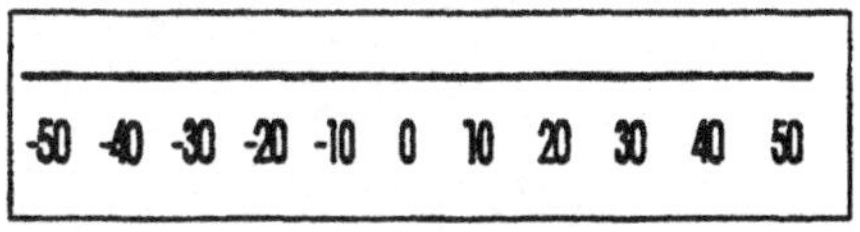

This introduces an important concept. Sometimes, we are not interested in the absolute value that a number has, but, rather, in the displacement between two numbers.

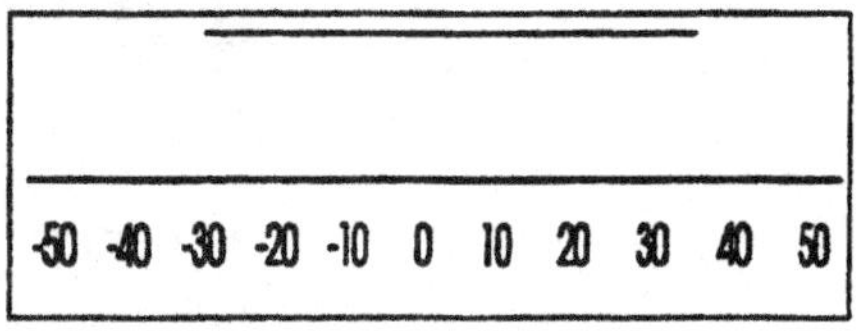

In the example illustrated to the right, the line runs from a negative thirty (-30) to a positive thirty-five (+35). What is the displacement between those two numbers? In other words, how far is +35 from -30?

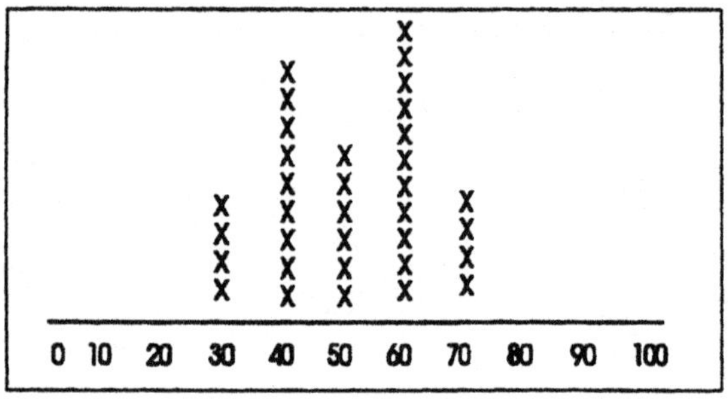

The answer is 65. It is just as far from -30 to +35 as it is from 0 to 65.

If we kept track of the high temperature every day for a month we could use a tally sheet like the one shown above. Each day, we would note the high temperature and then make an x above that number on the number line.

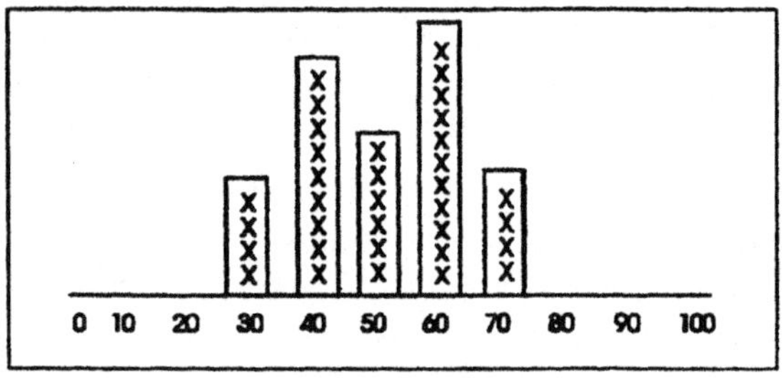

If we drew a box around each set of x's, we would have a diagram like the one illustrated above.

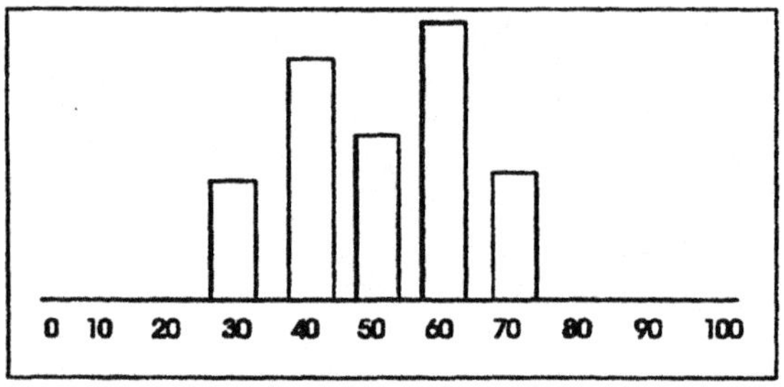

If we erased the x's, we would have a histogram.

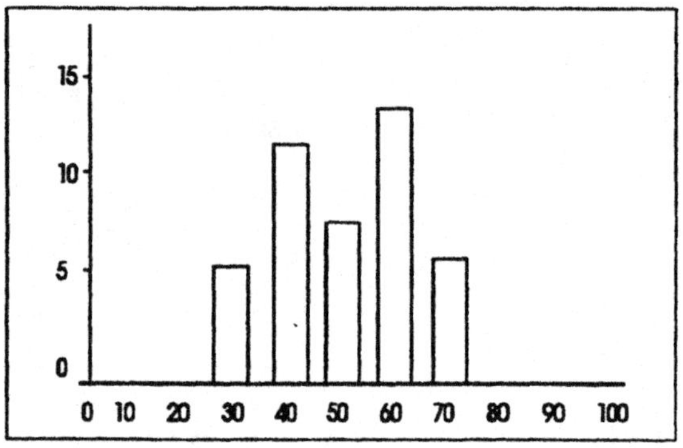

Adding a vertical scale makes the histogram easier to read. The height of each bar represents the number of times that value was observed. For example, a temperature of 60 degrees was observed about 14 times.

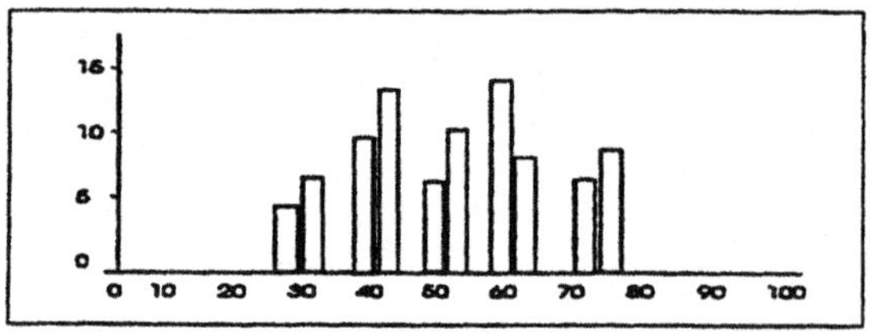

When measuring temperature, we generally do not use fractions of a degree. For example, it would be very unusual for someone to say that it was 65.765 degrees in Tucson on Oct. 8. However, there are times when temperatures are measured very precisely and other information, such as dimensions, are measured very accurately. For dimensional measurements with a micrometer, it is common to measure to the fourth decimal place, that is, to ten thousandths of an inch. To display such small numbers, our histogram uses bars that are more and more narrow. The top of each bar becomes smaller as the bar becomes more narrow.

If the bars get small enough, then the top of each bar becomes a single point, and rather than displaying the data as individual bars, a continuous line is used. This is called a continuous distribution.

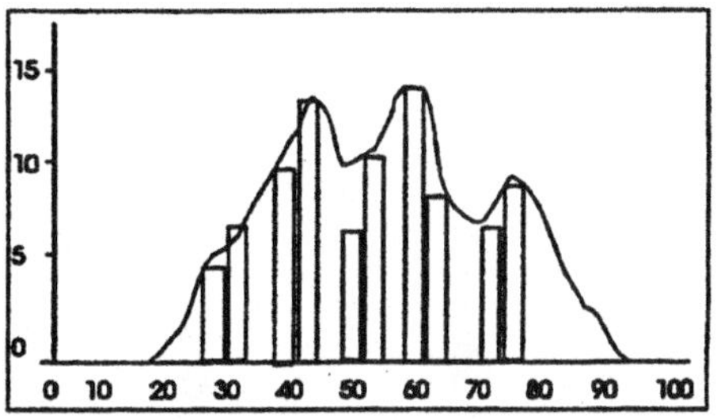

The most famous continuous distribution of all is illustrated at right. This is the Normal Distribution.

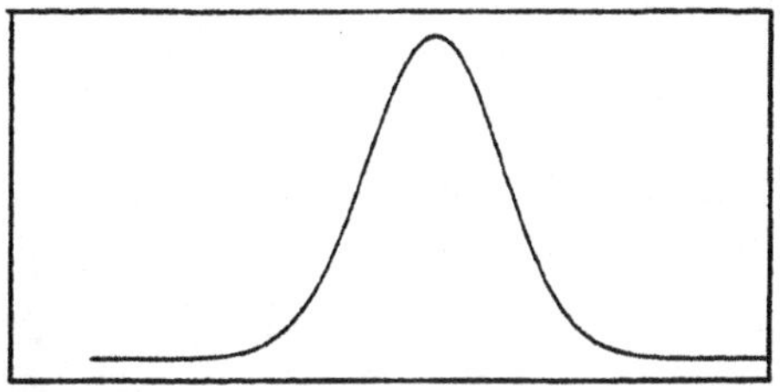

Adding a vertical scale and a number line on the bottom completes the diagram. Notice that the horizontal scale has both positive and negative numbers. Now the height of the continuous line above the horizontal scale is used to represent the number of times a value was observed.

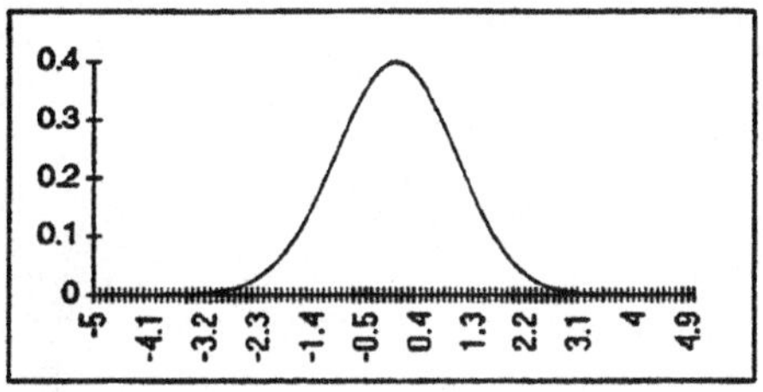

Depending on the data, the Normal Distribution will look different. For example, this distribution is rather tall and narrow.

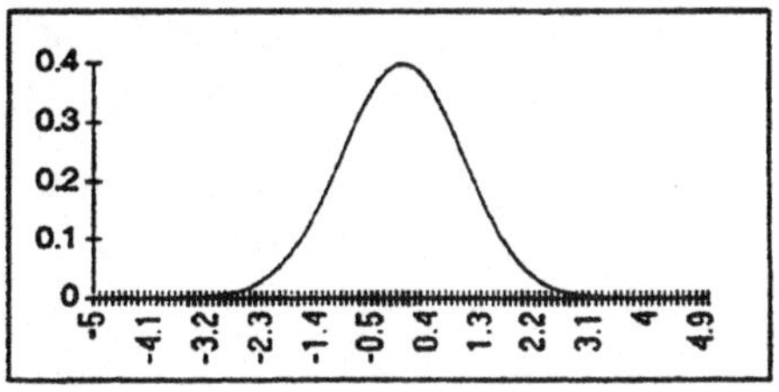

The distribution below is shorter and wider. We are going to learn some new vocabulary to describe these qualities.

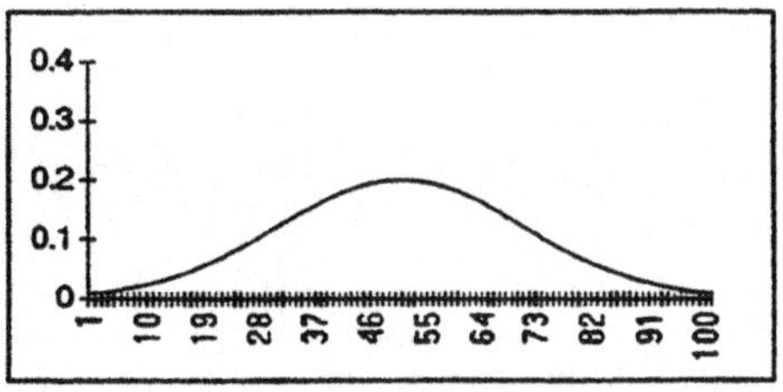

But before we learn the new vocabulary, let's go back to the number line.

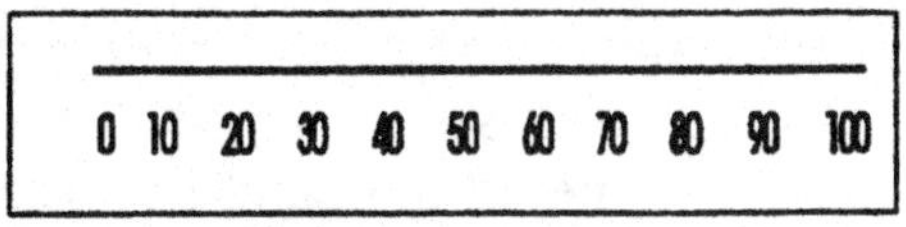

Imagine a balance beam on which we place weights at locations that correspond to the locations of the numbers on the number line.

If we place a weight on the beam, it will tilt in that direction.

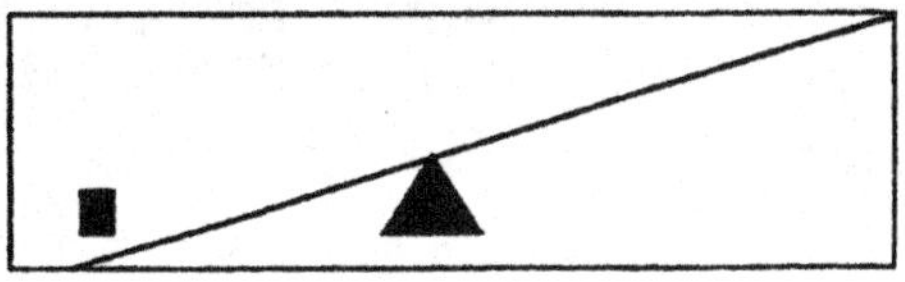

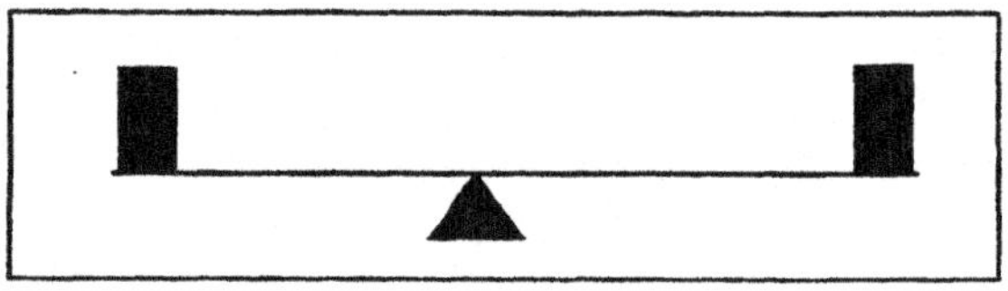

If we place an equal weight on the other side, the beam will balance. The place where it will balance is called the center of gravity. The weights can be stacked.

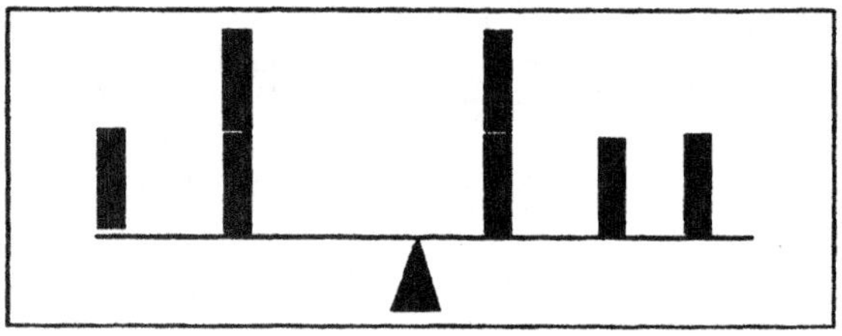

If a weight is placed far out on one end of the beam, it can balance much more weight near the center of gravity.

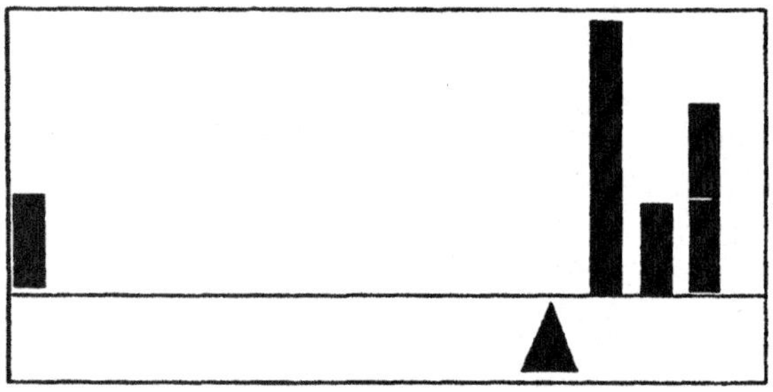

The location of the weights corresponds to the location of the numbers on the number line. The distance of the weights from each other corresponds to the displacement between two number on the number line. The balance beam begins to look like a histogram.

The loading on the beam will determine two things. First, it will determine the point at which the beam will balance: the center of gravity. The center of gravity in the physical system corresponds to the mean in statistics.

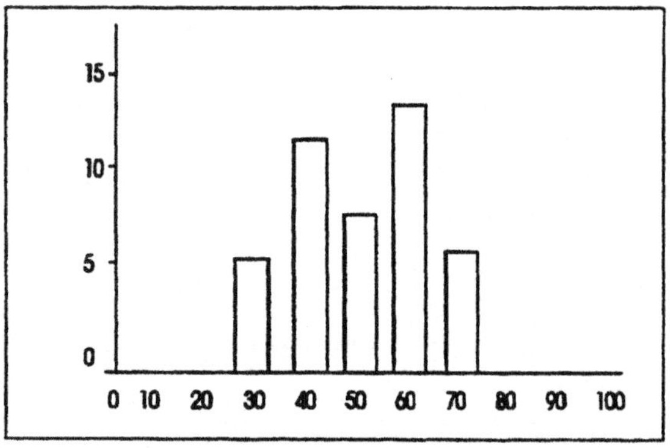

In this data set, the mean is at the point where the data set would balance if it were a physical system.

The second aspect of the beam loading is the way the load is distributed across the beam. This loading is measured in the physical system as the center of inertia. In the statistical system, this quality is called the standard deviation. It is a measure of how the data are dispersed in the distribution in the same way that the center of inertia measures how the weights are distributed across the beam in the physical system.

At this point, perhaps, a numerical example will help clarify things. Consider the following data set: 1,2,3,4,5.

Now sum the numbers

$$1 + 2 + 3 + 4 + 5 = 15$$

$$15 / 5 = 3.0$$

The average, or the mean, of the data set is 3.

Subtract the mean from each data point and square the result.

1 - 3 = -2	-2 x -2 = +4	+4
2 - 3 = -1	-1 x -1 = +1	+1
3 - 3 = 0	0 x 0 = 0	0
4 - 3 = 1	1 x 1 = +1	+1
5 - 3 = 2	2 x 2 = +4	+4

Now sum up the squared differences from the mean. 10

Now divide the sum by one less than the number of data points:
10 / 4 = 2.5.

Finally, take the square root of the result: the standard deviation. The square root of 2.5 is 1.58, and that is the standard deviation of this data set.

$$\sqrt{2.5} = 1.58$$

Let's look at another numerical example:

$$1+3+5+7+9 = 25$$

$$25 / 5 = 5.0$$

1 - 5 = -4	-4 x -4 = +16	+16
3 - 5 = -2	-2 x -2 = +4	+2
5 - 5 = 0	0 x 0 = 0	0
7 - 5 = 2	2 x 2 = +4	+2
9 - 5 = 4	4 x 4 = +16	+16

36

$$36 / 4 = 9.0$$

$$\sqrt{9} = 3.0$$

Let's look at a third numerical example:

3 + 4 + 5 + 6 + 7 = 25

25 / 5 = 5

3 - 5 = -2	-2 x -2 = +4	+4
4 - 5 = -1	-1 x -1 = +1	+1
5 - 5 = 0	0 x 0 = 0	0
6 - 5 = 1	1 x 1 = +1	+1
7 - 5 = 2	2 x 2 = +4	+4
Now, sum up the squared differences from the mean.		10

Now, divide the sum by one less than the number of data points:
10 / 4 = 2.5
The square root of 2.5 is 1.58 and that is the standard deviation of this data set

$$\sqrt{2.5} = 1.58$$

1 2 3 4 5

The mean is a measure of central tendency. Remember, it corresponds to the center of gravity in the physical system.

On the other hand, the standard deviation is a measure of dispersion, of how spread out the data is along the number line. Consider our first and third data sets:

1 2 3 4 5

3 4 5 6 7

They both have the same standard deviation (1.58) but the data set on the bottom has a different mean (5.0) than the one on the top (3.0).

On the other hand, these the second and third data sets have the same mean but different standard deviations.

1 3 5 7 9

3 4 5 6 7

In this example, the mean is 5.0 for both data sets, but the standard deviation of the upper set (3.16) is twice as large as the standard deviation of the lower data set (1.58).

To summarize how to compute the mean and standard deviation of a data set:

1. Add the numbers;
2. Divide the sum by how many numbers are in the data set to compute the mean;
3. Subtract the mean from each number in the data set;
4. Square the differences between the mean and each number;
5. Add up the squared differences;
6. Divide the sum of the squares by one less than how many numbers are in the data set; and
7. Take the square root of this number to compute the standard deviation.

In real life, no one computes the average and standard deviation by hand. They would use a calculator or even a computer. These examples were computed by hand to show you what's going on. Many calculators have keys for the average and standard deviation.

Here is an example of computing the average and standard deviation of the test scores of six students. See if you can compute the average and standard deviation by hand. Then, find a calculator or a computer and see if you can do it that way.

The scores of the six students are as follows:

Student	Score
1	9
2	8
3	4
4	10
5	9
6	2

Average = 42 / 6 = 7.0

Standard Deviation (SD) = 3.22

How to Use the Normal Curve

Evaluators often analyze and represent the distribution of data they have collected using the normal, or bell-shaped curve. This tool allows them to standardize and illustrate the variability of data: for example, test scores in a training project.

Earlier in this chapter, the words standard deviation and normal distribution were introduced.

Here are some examples of how you might hear them used.

- Student: "My score was 650, which means I'm one standard deviation above the mean on the verbal test."

- Evaluator: "My data are not normally distributed and don't resemble a bell-shaped curve, so I will rely on a nonparametric statistic."

The normal curve is the basis for deriving percentiles, standard scores and stanines, and is a requirement for using statistical techniques, such as analysis of variance (ANOVA) *(see Lesson 8).*

Here are 115 math test scores from a 10th-grade class:

Table 1: Math Scores

8	26	37	48	55	62
9	27	38	49	56	63
9	28	38	49	56	63
11	29	39	42	56	64
12	30	39	43	57	65
13	31	41	43	57	65
15	31	41	44	58	67
17	32	41	45	58	68
19	32	42	46	59	68
21	33	42	46	59	70
21	33	43	50	53	72
22	33	43	50	53	73
22	34	44	51	54	76
23	34	45	51	55	85
23	35	46	51	56	89
24	35	46	52	60	
24	35	46	52	60	
25	36	47	53	61	
25	36	47	53	61	
26	37	48	54	62	

We can group the scores in sets of 10 points as shown in table 2.

Table 2: Frequency Table of Math Scores (N = 115)

Interval of Scores	Midpoint	Frequency
1-10	5.05	3
11-20	15.5	6
21-30	25.5	16
31-40	35.5	20
41-50	45.5	25
51-60	55.5	25
61-70	65.5	14
71-80	75.5	4
81-90	85.5	2
95-100	95.5	

Starting with Frequency Distributions

Table 2 on page 79 shows the frequency counts for scores on the math test given to 115 10th-grade students. The first column gives the range of possible scores on the test, divided into intervals of 10 points. The next column gives the midpoints: for example, the middle point between a score of 1 and 10 is 5.5. The third column gives the frequency: for instance, three students had scores between 1 and 10 points.

To see how the scores on the math test are distributed among students, it's helpful to construct a histogram or frequency plot. A histogram looks like a bar graph, showing the number of scores for each interval (see Figure 1).

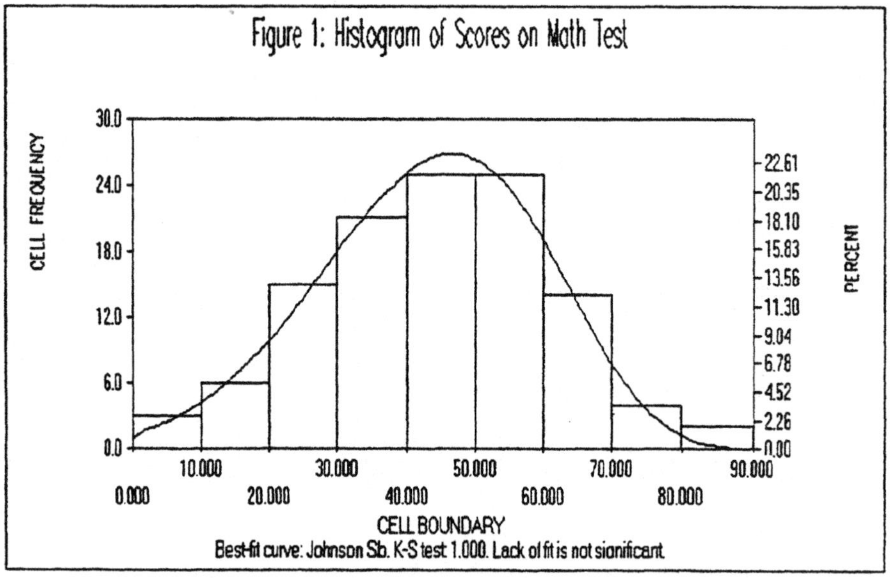

Figure 1: Histogram of Scores on Math Test

A frequency plot is similar to a histogram, but with a line connecting the midpoints of adjacent intervals, as in the example.

Now, suppose you gave the same math test to thousands of students and summarized the data just as in Table 1 on page 79, except that you used smaller and smaller intervals. This would produce more refined information, and the frequency plots would begin to resemble a continuous curve. Such a curve is called a frequency curve or frequency distribution (see figure 2).

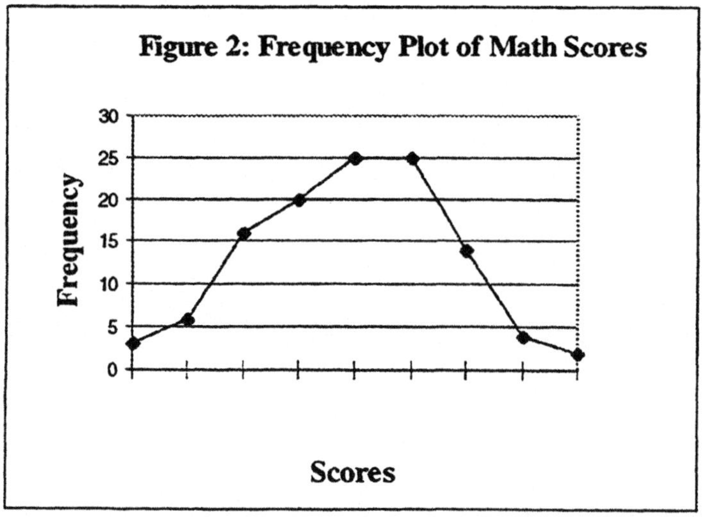

Figure 2: Frequency Plot of Math Scores

Mathematically, it helps to approximate or describe the distribution of scores by using frequency curves. One advantage of frequency distributions is that you can obtain various areas or proportions under the curves from mathematical tables. Another is that if scores fall into some well-known frequency curves, many characteristics of the distribution are known immediately.

Characteristics of the Normal Curve.

It is not necessary to understand the mathematics behind the normal distribution to be able to use it. It is possible to think of the curve itself as defining the distribution.

To say that a variable, such as math test scores, is normally distributed only means that an infinite population of math scores would have a frequency curve that is symmetrical and bell-shaped.

The normal curve has two statistics that describe it completely: the mean and the standard deviation. These were explained in detail earlier in this lesson.

Example:

Suppose your instructor told you that the average score in the class was 70.0 and the standard deviation was 10.0. What would this mean to you? If you're like many people, not too much. But earlier in this lesson, we learned that the average (or mean) describes the center of the data and that the standard deviation describes the dispersion, or how spread out the data are. One very useful tool in statistics is called the Normal Distribution. As it turns out, grades in school often follow the Normal Distribution. Perhaps your teacher called it the "bell shaped curve."

The nice thing about the Normal Distribution is that we know a great deal about it. For example, the area in the middle of the Normal Distribution has 68 percent of the data. This just turns out always to be so. The formal way of saying this is that 68 percent of the area under the Normal curve lies between plus one standard deviation and minus one standard deviation, as shown in the following illustration.

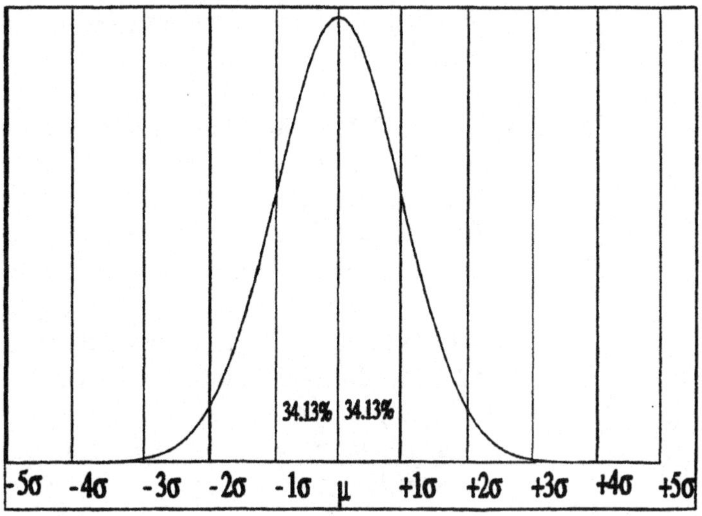

So, if there were 30 students in the class, 68 percent of them (or about 21 students) would score in this range. Now, the instructor said the average was 70.0. So one standard deviation, which is equal to 10 points, below the average is a test score of 60.0. One standard deviation above the average is 80. Therefore, approximately 21 students scored between 60 and 80 points on the test. A few scored higher and a few scored lower. This makes sense. You would expect this sort of a result since all the students are in the same class. They took the same test on material that they all had studied. Therefore, most of them received about the same score. There were a few exceptions who got high scores and a few more who received low scores.

This is the way the Normal Distribution is used. The mean and standard deviation are really just ways of summarizing information. You could list every score individually, but this would be tedious. There is much more economy in saying that the mean, or average, was 70.0 and that the standard deviation was 10.0. Many things in life follow the Normal Distribution. Furthermore, there is a rule in statistics that says that your data do not follow the Normal Distribution pattern. There is a way to make them follow it, known as the Central Limit Theorem. It says that if you take averages of many points in your distribution, then the averages will start to look "normally distributed." A good rule of thumb is that if you take averages of five readings and plot the averages, the plot will look fairly Normal. If you're really curious about this, there are tests that will tell you how well your data fit a given distribution. These are called "Goodness of Fit" tests and are covered in any textbook on statistics.

It is quite common for someone to ask: "Did the program make any difference?" Another way to say this is to ask: "Were the results different after the program was implemented?" And, of course, the results probably were different. But the important question is were the results *significantly* different? And, more importantly, were the results different in a way that is statistically significant?

The way this is often determined is by measuring the two results on some sort of scale. For example, let's say the average test score was 67 before the grant program was funded and it increased to 71 after the program had finished. These two results are different. But are they significantly different? The way to determine that is to measure the difference in the average test scores in terms of how many standard deviations they are apart. Let's say the test scores before the program had an average of 67.0 and a standard deviation of 4.0. Let's also assume that the test scores after the program had an average of 71.0 and a standard deviation of 4.0. In this case, the two averages are one standard deviation apart. As the two averages get farther and farther apart, it becomes obvious as some point that you are dealing with two different populations. As the following pictures illustrate:

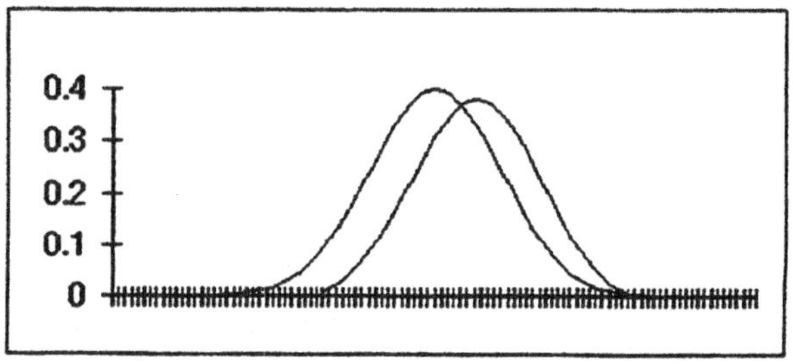

Here, the two distributions overlap so completely that you would conclude that you really have just one.

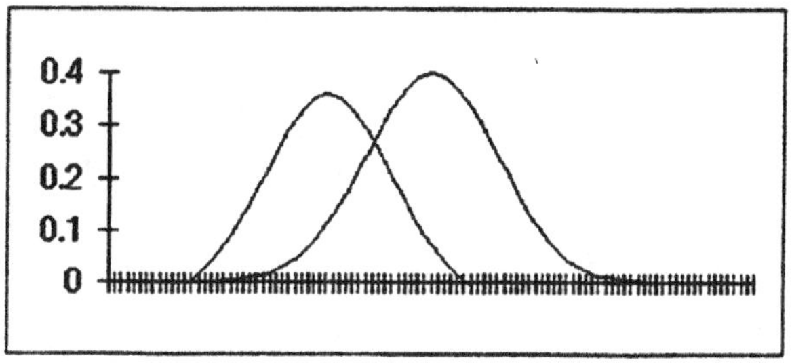

Here, they are beginning to move apart, but it would still be difficult to say if there are two.

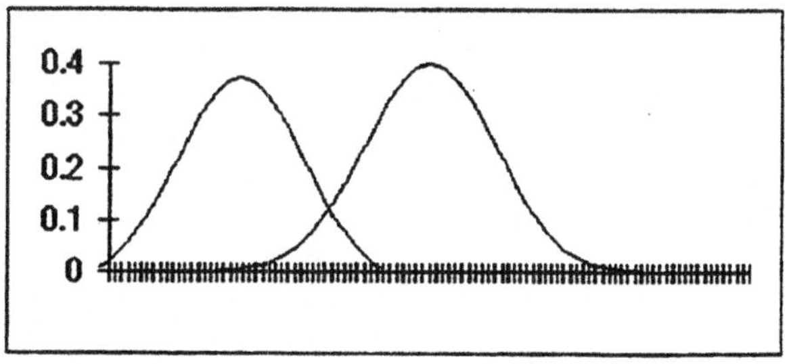

And here, they are far enough apart that you can safely conclude there are two distinct distributions.

The formal way of determining whether you have one distribution with a large standard deviation or two different distributions is called a "Test of Hypotheses on the Equality of Two Means, Variances Known." You can find a mathematical explanation in any good textbook on statistics. But it will probably be somewhat obscure.

But conceptually here is what is being done. First, they make an estimate of the standard deviation. Then, they see how many standard deviations the two averages are from each other. Once the two averages become about 1.2 standard deviations apart, there is a good chance (90 percent) that they are significantly different from each other. Once they are 1.6 standard deviations apart, there is an almost certain (95 percent) chance that they are different. A good rule of thumb then is that once the two averages become two or more standard deviations apart, you almost certainly have two different distributions. And, in the case of a grant program, if you can show that your test scores (or whatever you were measuring) moved two standard deviations or more, then your program seems to have had a significant effect. In our example, where the test scores shifted from 67 to 71, or one standard deviation, we cannot claim that there is a statistically significant difference in these before and after scores. There is only about an 85 percent chance that they are different. Most statisticians like to see a 95 percent chance or better before they conclude that the averages are different.

The point here is that you can speak with some authority about whether or not your grant program had any effect on the subject population. If you tested your subjects somehow, then the average test scores before the program can be compared with the average test scores after the grant program was in effect. If the two averages are two or more standard deviations apart, it is fair to conclude that the program had a statistically significant effect. If many different groups were tested, then ANOVA can tell you if any one group had a significantly different average score than any of the others. (For more information on ANOVA, see Lesson 9.)

Part II

Analyzing Evaluation Data

Lesson 7
How To Use Parametric And Nonparametric Statistics

After you have collected your evaluation data, you can begin to analyze it using statistical methods. These methods provide formal rules and procedures for testing hypotheses and drawing conclusions about evaluation data. Such procedures are used, for example, to find out if a group taking part in a program is different from its population of origin or whether one or more groups, some of which took part in a program, are different from one another.

Statistical methods fall into two major categories: parametric and nonparametric. When evaluators have very small samples or data not drawn from normally distributed populations, they usually rely on nonparametric statistics.

Parametric statistical tests are more powerful than nonparametric tests and are based on certain important conditions about the parameters (values) of the population from which the sample comes. Parametric tests use measures from an interval or ratio scale.

Nonparametric tests make very minor or no assumptions about the parameters of the population. You can apply such tests to quite small samples using data from any measurement scale: nominal, ordinal, interval or ratio.

The Mann-Whitney U Test

The Mann-Whitney U test is one of the most powerful nonparametric techniques. It is used to test for differences between two independent groups. It is similar in purpose to the parametric test, but can be used with ordinal data or when other assumptions of the t test cannot be met.

Here's how one evaluator used the Mann-Whitney test for a small (fewer than 20) sample:

Example

Barstin Elementary School had 10 fourth-grade students with severe hearing impairments. Four of the students were in a special program to teach them to speak more clearly. At the end of one semester, the students in the special pro-

gram (the experimental group) were compared with the six students in the traditional program (the control group).

A special education expert rated each child's ability to speak on a scale from 1 to 20, with 20 representing normal speech. The evaluator tabulated the resulting ratings as follows:

	Student					
	#1	*#2*	*#3*	*#4*	*#5*	*#6*
Control	*4*	*7*	*9*	*10*	*12*	*13*
Experimental	*8*	*11*	*14*	*15*		

If more students had been available, the evaluator might have chosen a t test; but after considering the smallness of the sample size and his unwillingness to make assumptions about populations, the evaluator decided to use the nonparametric Mann-Whitney U test.

How To Compute U

Using the previous example, let n1 be the number of cases in the smaller of the two groups and let n_2 be the number of cases in the larger of the groups. In this case, $n_1 = 4$, and $n_2 = 6$.

The evaluator tested the null hypothesis that the students in the experimental and control groups received equal ratings. The alternate hypothesis was that the performance of the experimental group students exceeded that of the control group students. (Note that the evaluator used a one-tailed test in which higher performance would have come from only the experimental group. A two-tailed test also would have been possible: for example, the alternate hypothesis that either exceeded the other.)

The statistic the Mann-Whitney test computes is called U. It represents the number of times a person in the larger group of size n_2 precedes a score in the smaller group of size n_1. For our example, the student ratings line up as follows:

Rating

4	7	8	9	10	11	12	13	14	15
C	C	E	C	C	E	C	C	E	E

where E = Experimental group student ($n_1 = 4$)
C = Control group student ($n_2 = 6$)

As you can see from the table, the first control group score (4) is not preceded by any scores from the experimental group. The same is true of the second control group score (7). The third control group score (9) is preceded by one experimental group score (8). The same is true for the fourth score in the control group (10). The last two control group scores (12 and 13) are both preceded by two scores from the experimental group (8 and 11). The U statistic in this case equals the sum of $0 + 0 + 1 + 1 + 2 + 2 = 6$.

Once you have calculated the value of 11, you can use a standard table to find out if that value is statistically significant. (You can find tables for nonparametric statistics in some statistical textbooks, such as *Nonparametric Statistics for the Behavioral Sciences*, by Sidney Siegel.)

For our example, with $n_1 = 4$, $n_2 = 6$ and $U = 6$, the tables will show a statistical significance of $p = 0.129$. Since most evaluators use $p < 0.01$ or $p < 0.05$ as their criterion of significance, the evaluator probably would conclude that the data do not suggest significant differences between the groups.

Another Way To Compute U

The method used above to compute U is particularly effective when the number of cases in the larger group (n_2) is 8 or fewer. The statistical tables for n_2 between 9 and 20 are presented in slightly different form than those for n_2 less than or equal to 8; for values of n_2 up to 20, you may find the following technique more useful.

First, assign ranks to each score in the combined groups. The lowest score gets a rank of 1, and the next lowest score 2, and so on. For tie scores, assign the mean ranking (for example, if two subjects both scores 7, and this represents spots 2 and 3n your ranking scale, assign both scores a rank value of 2.5). You then compute the U statistic as the smaller of the following:

$$U_1 = n_1 n_2 + \frac{n_1 (n_1 + 1)}{2} - R_1 \quad \text{or} \quad U_2 = n_1 n_2 + \frac{n_2 (n_2 + 1)}{2} - R_1$$

where R_1 = the sum of ranks assigned to the smaller group size n_1
R_2 = the sum of ranks assigned to the larger group size n_2

The following table shows the ranked values, R_1 and R_2, for the data from our examples:

Experimental Scores	Rank	Control Scores	Rank
8	3	4	1
11	6	7	2
14	9	9	4
15	10	10	5
	R_1 = 28	12	6
		13	7
			8
			R_2 = 27

Plugging these data into the preceding equations, you get the following:

$$U_1 = (4)(6) + \frac{(4)(4 + 1)}{2} - 28 + 6 \quad \text{or} \quad U_2 = (4)(6) + \frac{(6)(6 + 1)}{2} - 27 = 18$$

In this case, the smaller of the two is $U_1 = 6$, which is the same value arrived at with statistical tables.

Statistics and Scales

Once you have collected the statistics, you need to determine which ones you can use for different purposes. The way you collect the data will determine how you should analyze it. The scaling methods below give examples of how data can be collected and the appropriate statistics to use to analyze it.

The four common statistical scaling methods are as follows.

- **Nominal scales** give you scores for classifying individuals, objects or characteristics. Examples include classification according to gender, political affiliation, color of hair or medical diagnosis. This scale provides only groupings for your information.

The only meaningful statistics you can compute from nominal scales result from counting and include modes, frequencies and percents. Only nonparametric statistical methods can be applied to nominal scale data.

- **Ordinal scales** classify individuals or objects that stand in some kind of relation to one another, such as relations of preference or quality. Examples of ordinal scales include military ranks and grades of meat.

The median is the most appropriate statistic derived from ordinal scale data; nonparametric statistical techniques therefore apply.

- **Interval scales** have all the characteristics of ordinal scales, but the distance between any two points is known. The zero point and the unit of measurement are arbitrary. These scales rank statistics in equal internals.

Take for example the measurement of temperature, for which there are two scales, Fahrenheit and Centigrade. The unit of measurement and the zero (freezing) point are different for each scale. Since both scales are linearly related and give the same information, you can use a mathematical formula to convert from one temperature scale to the other. But look at these scales:

Definitely agree	Probably agree	No opinion	Probably disagree	Definitely disagree

Excellent	Satisfactory	Average	Fair	Poor

Such scales sometimes are considered ordinal scales, sometimes interval scales. In practice, the evaluator intuitively decides which.

- **Ratio scales**, such as height and weight scales, are interval scales with a true zero point. All parametric techniques can be applied to ratio scale data. These scales give you the most information since you will know exactly where the data is in relation to zero.

Lesson 8
How To Use Pattern Analysis

Evaluating a large grant project that involves several measures is not a simple process. Pattern analysis, a technique that helps determine if the data collected support trends for more than one measurement, may be the key for tackling large project evaluation.

For example, did you ever have to choose between two pints of strawberries at the supermarket? Either one pint is clearly better and the choice is easy, or they look about the same. Then you either count the green and the rotten strawberries in each pint or, more likely, squint your eyes and pick the pint that is the reddest overall. Evaluators often face the same problems, only on a much larger scale.

Large evaluation projects usually involve data from many different measures. A statewide evaluation of the comparative merit of two compensatory education programs, for example, might use reading comprehension, vocabulary, arithmetic and social studies tests. How can you interpret all this information and decide on the merit of each program? One way is to find statistically significant results consistently favoring one of the two programs. A less reliable, but still acceptable procedure is to find whether most of the differences favor one program — to squint your eyes, so to speak — and then see if this pattern of differences is itself statistically significant. This is called pattern analysis.

RZA: A Hypothetical Case Study

The RZA research firm conducted a statewide evaluation of two vocational education programs, each of which sought to help students enter the job market. Program A, a new program, emphasized eliminating gender biases and expanding students' career horizons. Program B offered the traditional job training curriculum. RZA had to answer three evaluation questions:

- Is Program A better than Program B at improving students' cognitive skills?
- Is Program A better than Program B at enhancing students' work-related activities?
- Is Program A better than Program B at promoting positive attitudes and values in students?

In the course of RZA's evaluation, students entering vocational education programs in the state's high schools were randomly assigned to the new or old program. In 1976, when students were in the 12th grade, and again in 1980, RZA put each participant through a complete battery of tests of cognitive skills, work-related activities, and attitudes and values. Each of the tests had several subscales.

The basic design for the evaluation was a time series in which males and females were separately tracked, primarily because they often participated in classes predominantly of one gender. The design looked like this:

Females		**Males**	
1976	1980	1976	1980

After successfully administering all the measures and getting a 98 percent response rate in all groups, the RZA evaluators began to analyze the 20 different measures (the cognitive skills and the work-related activities test batteries each had eight subscales and the attitudes and values battery had four). When the evaluators compared Program A with Program B across all the measures in each group (1976 females, 1980 females, 1976 males, and 1980 males) they found very few statistically significant results, although in most cases Program A seemed to work better than Program B. Since neither program could meet the criterion of consistent statistically significant differences for each measure, RZA decided to conduct a pattern analysis.

Terms And Tables

In using pattern analysis, you must understand the basic terms and tables evaluators use.

Single-Group Differences — Again, the evaluators had four groups for which they could compare any single measure used in Program A (the new course) and Program B (the traditional course). For the pattern analysis, RZA used summary tables to show the "direction" of single group score differences, rather than to give means and standard deviations. "Direction" was represented by A > B, B > A or A = B. This way of presenting findings was less time-consuming and also was intuitively meaningful. In addition to showing the differences, RZA's summary tables also showed, with asterisks, whether each difference was statistically significant at the 0.05 and 0.01 levels of confidence. For example, a typical table might look like this:

Sample Table

	1976 Females		1980 Females		1976 Males		1980 Males	
Measure	Direction of Difference	Signifi-nance	Direction of Difference	Signifi-nance	Direction of Difference	Signifi-nance	Direction of Difference	Signifi-nance
Composite score	A>B	**	A=B		A>B		A>B	*
Score x	A=B		B>A		A>B		A=B	
Score y	A>B		A=B		A=B		A=B	

*p<0.05 **p<0.01

Trends — For each of the 20 measures, the evaluators computed differences for each of the four groups (1976 females, 1980 females, 1976 males, 1980 males). The evaluators defined a trend as follows:

- At least three of four groups must show the same direction (i.e., at least three of the single differences show A>B, or three show B>A); or

- Two groups have the same direction and the other groups do not show the opposite direction (i.e., at least two of the single differences show A>B, or two show B>A, and the others show A=B); or

- One group shows statistically significant differences and none of the other groups shows the opposite (i.e., at least one of the single group differences show A>B or B>A, this difference is statistically significant at $p<0.005$ or $p<0.01$, and the other differences show A=B).

As you can see in the sample table, there was one trend supporting Program A (composite score).

The Sign Test

The sign test is used in pattern analysis to represent group score differences. (In this description, the test is applied to a situation in which there are fewer than 30 single group differences or matched pairs.)

The sign test gets its name from its use of plus and minus signs rather than quantitative metrics. In RZA's evaluation, the evaluators used a plus sign when A>B (i.e., A + B = N) and a minus sign when A<B (i.e., A - B = x). No signs are assigned to ties.

The null hypothesis tested by the sign test is that the number of plus signs is equal to the number of minus signs. That is, the sign test assesses whether $A > B$ as often as $A < B$. The null hypothesis is rejected when too few differences of one sign occur.

There are statistical tables for interpreting sign test data. To use them, you need to know only the total number of plus and minus signs (called N by statisticians) and the number of minus signs (called x). The columns of the table are arranged by increasing N's and the rows by increasing x's. For any given N and x, the entries of the table give the probability, or p-value. For example, if $N = 14$ and $x = 5$, a sign test table will show $p = 0.212$. This p-value is not significant at $p < 0.05$.

But very few statistics texts give a sign table. Fortunately, computing the p-value is not too difficult, and you can do it with a hand calculator. The probability of having a certain number of pluses and minuses is based on a mathematical concept called binomial distribution. The sign test assumes that the probability of getting a plus or minus is equal. In this situation, the formula for the binomial distribution can be written as follows:

*** Put mathematical equation here...(will scan in)**
ROBIN -- WHEN YOU SCAN THIS CHART SAVE AS A .TIFF OR .EPS

Consider the evaluation question on work-related activities. Evaluators could make 32 single group comparisons between Program A and B (eight measures times four groups). RZA found that out of 32 comparisons, 20 favored Program A (20 pluses), four favored Program B (four minuses), and eight were ties. They then tested the null hypothesis that the number of pluses and minuses were equal, with the alternative hypothesis that there were more pluses. In this case, $N = 24$ (the ties are not counted) and $x = 4$, and the binomial formula (24/4) (1/2) 24 — or a table — gives $p = 0.001$ (significant result). RZA therefore rejected the null hypothesis and suggested that the pattern of differences significantly favored Program A.

RZA's Findings

The first evaluation question RZA need to answer was, "Is Program A better than Program B at improving students' cognitive skills?"

The evaluators had information from eight measures of cognitive skills: reading, writing, vocabulary, abstract reasoning, science, social science, mathematics and a composite score.

Overall, students in Program A scored better in cognitive skills than did students in Program B. In the 32 possible comparisons between the groups, Program A students scored higher in 25 cases, lower in three cases and the same in four cases (see Table 1).

Table 1: Cognitive Skills

	1976 Females		1980 Females		1976 Males		1980 Males	
Measure	Direction of Difference	Signifi-nance	Direction of Difference	Signifi-nance	Direction of Difference	Signifi-nance	Direction of Difference	Signifi-nance
Composite score	A>B	**	A=B		A>B		A>B	*
Reading	A>B	**	A>B		A>B		A>B	
Writing	A>B		A>B		B>A		A>B	
Vocabulary	A>B		A>B		A>B		A>B	
Abstract reasoning	A>B		B>A		A+B		A>B	
Science	A>B		A=B		A=B		A>B	
Social Science	A>B		A=B		B>A		A>B	
Mathematics	A>B	*	A>B		A>B		A>B	

*$p < 0.05$ **$p < 0.01$

As you can see from the table, the evaluators found trends favoring Program A in all measures except social science and abstract reasoning. Only four of the differences were statistically significant: 1976 Program A females scored significantly better than did Program B females in reading, vocabulary, mathematics and composite scores.

To test the significance of the pattern of differences — which seemed to favor Program A, even though most differences were not statistically significant — the evaluators computed a sign test, which showed students in Program A did indeed perform significantly better than those in Program B ($p < 0.01$).

The second question was, "Is Program A better than Program B in enchancing students' work-related activities?"

There were eight measures of work-related activities: adjusted hourly earnings, hours working for pay each week, definiteness of occupational plans, expected earnings at 40 years of age, job satisfaction, number of household chores performed, employer satisfaction and a composite score (see Table 2).

Once again, the evaluators found new significant single group differences between programs but many patterns. Out of 32 tests, 20 differences favored Program A, and this overall trend was proved significant by the sign test ($p < 0.01$).

Table 2: Work-Related Activities

	1976 Females		1980 Females		1976 Males		1980 Males	
Measure	Direction of Difference	Significance	Direction of Difference	Significance	Direction of Difference	Significance	Direction of Difference	Significance
Composite score	A>B	**	A=B		A>B		A>B	*
Adjusted hourly earnings	A>B		A>B		A>B	*	A>B	
Hours worked for pay each week	A=B		A=B		A=B		A=B	
Definition of occupational plans	A>B		A>B		A>B		A>B	
Expected earnings at 40 years of age	A>B	**	A>B		A>B	**	A>B	
Job Satisfaction	A>B		B>A		A=B		B>A	
Number of household chores performed	A>B		A>B		A>B		A=B	
Employer satisfaction	A=B		B>A		B>A		A>B	

*$p<0.05$ **$p<0.01$

In all, the evaluators found five trends. Students in Program A had higher adjusted earnings, more definite occupational plans and higher expected earnings, performed more household chores and had higher composite scores. The evaluators found four statistically significant single group differences that favored Program A.

All these differences related to two measures:

- Adjusted hourly earning (1976 and 1980 Program A males had significantly higher earnings); and
- Expected earnings at 40 years of age (1976 Program A males and females had higher expected earnings).

The third evaluation questions was, "Is Program A better than Program B at promoting attitudes and values?"

RZA studied four measures of attitudes and values: plans for future education, community involvement, self-esteem and a composite score. The evaluation findings suggested little difference in attitudes and values between students in the two programs (see Table 3).

Table 3: Attitudes And Values

	1976 Females		1980 Females		1976 Males		1980 Males	
Measure	Direction of Difference	Significance	Direction of Difference	Significance	Direction of Difference	Significance	Direction of Difference	Significance
Composite score	A>B	**	A=B		A>B		A>B	*
Plans for future education	B>A		A=B		B>A	*	B>A	**
Community involvement	A>B		A=B		B>A		B>A	
Self-esteem	A=B		A>B		B>A		A>B	

*p<0.05 **p<0.01

Of the 16 possible differences (four measures times four groups), students in Program A scored higher in five cases, lower in six cases and the same in five cases. There are two trends in the table, but they are in opposite directions, and a sign test sowed that the overall pattern of differences was not significant. The only subpattern the evaluators could discern in Table 3 was a tendency for Program B males to report more positive attitudes and values than their Program A counterparts in 1976. This tendency is a vertical subpattern — not a trend — that encompasses all four measures of attitudes and values.

Lesson 9
How To Use Analysis Of Variance

Many decision problems require that more than two parameters be considered. For example, a university might be investigating the effects of a program to reduce substance abuse among students. Suppose there is a program underway to reduce the use of tobacco, alcohol, marijuana and cocaine. The first-cut question that might be asked is: Did our program reduce the use of any of these substances? The formal, statistical way of stating this question is to test the equality of the four means before and after the prevention programs were implemented. Did we reduce substance abuse in a statistically significant way?

We might initially think that this problem could be solved by performing a test of hypothesis on each of the four means independently. However, testing each pair would lead to a distortion of an effort due to uncertainty. Suppose that all four means were equal before and after the program. Moreover, suppose that there is a 95 percent chance of coming to that conclusion. Then the probability of coming to the right conclusion in all four cases is 95 percent raised to the fourth power, or 81 percent. There is a chance that one or more tests of hypothesis would indicate at least one pair of means were different when they really were not.

The appropriate procedure for testing the equality of several population means is the analysis of variance. The one-way analysis of variance (ANOVA) is a fairly complicated form of analysis and is difficult to explain it intuitively. Mathematical explanations are available in most statistics' textbooks, but those may not be of much help. One way to think about it is this: You are going to use something called an F-value. In a sense, the F-value is analogous to the standard deviation. It is a measure of how far apart things are. As the F-value gets larger, it becomes more likely that one or more of the averages are statistically different from the others. We said that if two averages are two or more standard deviations apart, then you probably have two different distributions. In ANOVA, once the F-value gets large enough, then you know that at least one of the means is significantly different from the others. Beyond that limited explanation, it is necessary to rely on mathematics.

In this lesson, we will examine the one-way ANOVA used by evaluators to compare two or more groups or to trace a single group's progress over time. If you want to compare different groups or study changes that take place in the same group from one time period to the next, then analysis of variance is a method you should consider. ANOVA can allow you to evaluate the effect of three or more variables simultaneously.

Here's how we proceed:

Step 1: Take a careful look at the evaluation questions to be sure ANOVA is appropriate.

Remember, ANOVA is used to make comparisons among groups or across times. Here are examples of questions that could be answered using one-way ANOVA:

❶ Do students in the experimental program have different attitudes toward school than students in the traditional program?

❷ Do students in the experimental group change their attitude toward school from the beginning to the end of the school year?

❸ Do male and female students have different attitudes toward school?

❹ What percentage of male and female students in the experimental and control groups have a satisfactory attitude toward school?

Question 3 could be answered using ANOVA because it asks about differences in attitude between male and female students. Question 4 cannot be answered with ANOVA because it only requires tallying students in each group according to how satisfactory their attitude is but it does not ask for comparison between the groups or across time.

Step 2: Decide which comparisons to make and state your hypotheses.

Once the evaluation questions are posed, you are ready to decide which comparisons you want to make. For example, in Question 1 ("Do students in the experimental program have different attitudes toward school than students in the traditional program?"), you will compare students in the experimental and the traditional programs in terms of their attitude toward school.

To evaluate comparisons, you must restate the question as a proposition or hypothesis to be accepted or rejected. You could rephrase Question 1 in two ways:

Hypothesis 1 — On the average, students in the experimental Program And students in the traditional program have different attitudes toward school; or

Hypothesis 2 — On the average, students in the experimental Program And students in the traditional program have the same attitudes toward school.

Because of its mathematical structure, ANOVA cannot prove directly that there are differences between groups. It can prove only that they aren't the same. To use ANOVA properly, you must test hypotheses about the sameness or equality of behavior and not the differences. For Question 1, for instance, you would have to use Hypothesis 2. This is called the null hypothesis.

To use ANOVA, how should you state your hypothesis to be tested (the null hypothesis) for Questions 2 and 3?

Null hypothesis for Question 2: The experimental students' attitudes toward school are the same at the beginning and end of the school year.

Null hypothesis for Question 3: On the average, male and female students have the same attitude toward school.

Step 3: Make sure you have the data you need in the form you need it.

ANOVA depends on the use of arithmetic averages and standard deviations. You can't use ANOVA to test a hypothesis about the equality of two groups' achievements unless you have a way to determine their mean performance. For achievement, averages are typically based on test scores. For other behaviors, averages may be based on observations or ratings.

Step 4: Test the hypothesis and report the results.

Hypotheses are tested with an F-statistic, the probability of the difference in measurements, which is derived mathematically using the ANOVA formulas. In general, if the F-statistic resulting from the ANOVA is a small number, then the hypothesis cannot be rejected. For Question 1, a small F-value would mean that you could not disprove the hypothesis that experimental and traditional students are the same.

To test hypotheses, first compute means and standard deviations. Apply the ANOVA procedure to these descriptive statistics to get an F-statistic. You will find formulas from analysis of variance in standard statistics texts, but canned computer programs usually are available and probably should be used. ANOVA is not a procedure that readily lends itself to hand calculations.

There are statistical tables that list the smallest value that an F-statistic can take in order to reject a hypothesis. These tables provide F-values for different degrees of freedom (df) and significance levels (p). Degrees of freedom are the number of independent scores (or observations) entering into the computation of the statistic. The level of significance refers to the probability of falsely rejecting the hypothesis. Evaluators usually use the 0.05 or 0.01 significance level, which means that there are either five chances in 100 or one chance in 100 that the hypothesis will be rejected unintentionally.

The results of a one-way ANOVA frequently are displayed in the following way:

One-Way ANOVA Table

Source of Variation	Degrees of Freedom (df)	F-Value	Level of Significance (p)

The source of variation column names the hypothesis being tested (e.g., male and female students' attitudes toward school are the same) and the error term for the analysis (a mathematical result).

The following is a typical report of the use of a one-way ANOVA to answer one evaluation question for an experimental mathematics program. Based on what you have already read and the content of the report, complete the missing portions of the text.

Example: One-Way ANOVA

Program Description: *A new compensatory mathematics program, unlike the traditional compensatory mathematics program, has as one of its purposes helping students apply their knowledge of math to daily life. The two programs are being compared to see whether they have influenced students' ability to tell time, count money and measure distance.*

Step 1: Evaluation Question

Are students who participated in the new program more able to apply their knowledge of mathematics than students who participated in the traditional program?

Step 2: Comparisons and Hypothesis

A comparison-group design strategy was used for the evaluation in which students' ability to use mathematics to tell time, count money and measure distance was contrasted in the new and traditional programs. Ninety-six second-grade students at a particular elementary school participated in the evaluation. A random sampling plan was used to assign them to groups so that 48 students were assigned to each group.

New Program	*Traditional Program*
48 Students	*48 Students*

The null hypothesis tested by the analysis was: ______________________

____

____

____

Step 3: Getting the Data

At the end of the school year, all students who participated in the evaluation were given a nationally normed mathematics achievement test accepted as valid and reliable for second-grade students. The highest possible score on the test was 75 points, and the lowest possible score was zero.

Step 4: Test the Hypothesis and Report Results

Descriptive Statistics

New Program	*Traditional Program*
X = 46.36	*X = 45.33*
SD = 3.46	*SD = 3.78*
N = 48	*N = 48*

ANOVA Table

Source of Variation	*Degrees of Freedom (df)*	*F-Value*	*Level of Significance (p)*
New and Traditional Programs	*1*	*3.22*	*ns (Not significant)*
Error	*94*		

This test of the null hypothesis resulted in an F-value of 3.22, which is not statistically significant (because the value in the F-statistic table is 3.93552 for 1 and 94 degrees of freedom at the 0.05 level). Consequently, the hypothesis that students' mathematics ability in the new and traditional compensatory education programs is equal can/cannot (circle one) be rejected.

This result was recorded in the evaluator's final report in the following way:

A one-way ANOVA was conducted to answer the evaluation question. The analysis was unable to uncover significant differences in average daily mathematics ability between students in the new and traditional programs. This suggests that students who participated in the new program were/were not (circle one) better able to apply their knowledge of mathematics.

ANSWERS:

***Step 2** — Null Hypothesis: The average ability to apply knowledge of mathematics of students in the new and traditional mathematics programs is equal.*

***Step 4** — Cannot be rejected; were not better able to apply.*

Lesson 10
How To Choose Data Analysis Techniques: Descriptive Statistics, Correlation Statistics And Regression Analysis

After collecting data, analyzing it is one of the most important tasks an evaluator has to perform. Even if you don't have to do it yourself, you should understand enough about the basic principles to know what the statistician is doing.

The evaluation questions shape the entire evaluation, and you should choose analysis methods that will permit you to answer the questions directly.

This lesson will first explain simple descriptive statistics and examine correlation statistics and regression analysis, which are used to establish the relationship between variables.

Will Descriptive Statistics Answer the Question?

Descriptive statistics are among the most useful analysis techniques for evaluations because they are inherently meaningful and easily understood. They are the units for more complex statistical procedures.

Here's one way descriptive statistics can be used to analyze evaluation information:

Example: Sample Descriptive Statistics

Program Description: *The goal of the program is to teach college students interpersonal communication skills. To accomplish this goal, students view videotaped conversations between two persons and are trained to distinguish between what speakers say and what they mean by observing content, tone, context and body language.*

The program is judged to be successful if students learn to adequately use content, tone, context and body language to interpret conversations.

Evaluation Question: *Are students able to use content, tone, context and body language to interpret conversations?*

Design Strategy: *Evaluators used a case design in which all students who enrolled in selected undergraduate communication courses participated in the interpersonal communication skills program during three weeks of the fall semester. The dependent variable was an ability to interpret conversations as measured by an achievement test. The independent variable was studied at only one level: participation in the interpersonal communications skills program.*

Information Collection Plan: *A test was given to all participating students at the end of the course. The highest possible score on the test was 100 points, with adequate performance defined as a score of 70 or better.*

Analysis Plan: *Descriptive statistics were computed from students' total test scores at the end of the three-week program.*

Analysis Results

X	*SD*	*N*	*Range*	*Number of Students Who Achieved a Score of 70 or Better*
78.8	*13.6*	*130*	*44-96*	*71*

Interpretation: *One hundred and thirty students (N = 130) completed the program. Their average score (X) was 78.8 points, which is above the criterion, and 71 students demonstrated an adequate ability to interpret conversation. The relatively small standard deviation (SD) and range indicate that each student's ability is similar to the others.*

Should You Use Correlation Statistics?

Correlations measure the relationship between two variables, a dependent variable and an independent variable, for example, number of years of schooling and salary. They are reported within a range of + 1 (perfect positive correlation) to -1 (perfect negative correlation).

When high values on one variable occur simultaneously with high values on another, the two variables are said to be positively correlated. When high values on one variable occur with low values on another, the two variables are said to be negatively correlated.

Correlations can be used to answer evaluation questions such as:

- What is the relationship between self-concept and the number of visits to the school nurse?
- Can scores on college entrance examinations be used to identify people who are likely to succeed in the new management training program?
- Is vocational preference correlated with parents' jobs?

Warning: You can use correlations to identify relationships between variables but you cannot use them to establish causation. A correlation analysis can show that people who have completed many years of schooling usually earn high salaries, but it cannot show that people earn high salaries because they had many years of schooling.

Here's one way correlation statistics might be used to analyze evaluation information:

Example: Correlation Statistics

Program Description: *The goal of the program is to improve fourth-grade students' reading ability. Program directors selected teachers who have at least three years of teaching experience and master's degrees in reading education. The program takes place throughout the school year and occupies one hour a day of each student's time.*

The program is considered successful if, at the end of the year, students' reading levels are above the national norm.

Evaluation Background: *Preliminary evaluation findings indicated that some students did very well with the program, while others did poorly. The evaluator was asked to identify factors that distinguished among them. One of the factors studied was birth order.*

Evaluation Question: *Is there a relationship between birth order and success in the program? (Birth order refers to whether a child is the first-born, second-bond, etc.)*

Design Strategy: *Evaluators used a case design that included all students who participated in the program. The dependent variable was success in the program as mesured by students' scores on an achievement test. The independent variable was students' birth order.*

Information Collection Plan: *A 500-point, nationally normed achievement test was given to all participating fourth-grade students at the end of the school year. Students' birth orders were determined from school records.*

Analysis Plan: *Students' raw scores on the reading-achievement test and their birth orders were correlated.*

Analysis Results: *A correlation coefficient (r) of -0.89 was obtained based on dta from 206 students.*

$$N = 206$$
$$r = -0.89$$
$$r^2 = 0.79$$

Interpretation: *A high negative correlation ($r = 0.89$) was found between students' reading scores and their birth orders, indicating that 79% ($r^2 = 0.79$) of the total variation in students' reading scores could be accounted for by their position of birth.*

This finding suggests that first- and second-born students are more successful with the program (have higher reading scores) than the others. (It canot be concluded that first- and second-born students are necessarily smarter.)

Is Regression Analysis the Technique You Need?

Regression is a method for examining the relationship between a dependent variable and two or more independent variables. If there is only one independent variable, the regression is the same as correlation statistics.

Regression can be used to predict the value of a dependent variable based on values of one or more independent variables. Regression analysis can also be used to answer the question, "What is the relationship between students' mathematics performance (the dependent variable) and the number of hours of instruction received, grade level and gender (the three independent variables)?"

You can express the answer to that question mathematically as an equation of the following form:

y	=	w_1x_1	+	w_2x_2	+	w_3x_3	+	c
Dependent Variable		weight #1		weight #2		weight #3		Constant
		Independent Variable #1		Independent Variable #2		Independent Variable #3		
(Students' Mathematics Performance)		(Number of Hours of Instruction Received)		(Grade Level)		(Sex)		

This equation shows the relationship between a dependent variable (y) and three independent variables (x_1, x_2 and x_3). The weights (w_1, w_2 and w_3) or regression coefficients, are computed as part of the analysis and reflect the contribution of each independent variable in explaining the dependent variable.

That is, if w_1 is greater than w_2 and w_3, then x_1 is the independent variable that contributes most to an understanding of y, the dependent variable. (For such interpretations to be made, x_1, x_2 and x_3 must be measured using the same metric, or alternately, w_1, w_2 and w_3 must be normalized or standardized as part of the computations for the regression analysis.)

Here's an example of how you might use regression analysis if you were evaluating a high school program for disruptive students:

Example: Regression

Program Description: *The purpose of the program is to teach stress management and self-discipline skills to high school students with behavior problems so they can be placed in a regular classroom.*

Specifically trained teachers instruct students and their parents in how to recognize the early warning signs of behavioral outbursts, how to treat them and when to seek assistance. Teachers and students together decide how many hours students should be counseled. Fewer classroom disruptions is considered evidence of the program's merit.

Evaluation Background: *Preliminary evaluation data showed that some students received only five hours of counseling, while others received as many as 25 hours. The average was 10 hours per student.*

Since counselor salaries represent the major cost of the program, you have been asked to investigate the relationship between the number of classroom disruptions and the number of hours students are counseled, taking into account their age and the severity of their behavioral problems.

Evaluation Question: *What is the relationship between number of classroom disruptions and (1) hours of counseling, (2) severity of behavioral problems at the beginning of the program, and (3) age?*

Design Strategy: *You chose a case design for the evaluation. The dependent variable is the number of times a student caused a classroom disruption during the months of December through May. The independent variables were (1) the number of hours of counseling a student received, (2) the severity of a student's behavior problem at the beginning of the program, and (3) a student's age. The evaluation included all high school students who were identified by the district as having behavior problems severe enough to warrant being taken from the regular classroom and placed in a special one.*

Information Collection Plan: *You reviewed school records to obtain information about students' ages. You gave teachers special forms to document the nature and frequency of classroom disruptions. You asked counselors to rate the severity of their students' behavior problems at the beginning of the program using a nine-point scale, with one as "extremely mild" and nine as "extremely severe." You also asked them to keep records of how many hours they spent counseling each student throughout the program.*

Analysis Plan: *You conducted a multiple regression analysis, transforming the weights for each independent variable so that you could report them in terms of the same 10-point scale in the regression equation below.*

y	=	$5.01x_1$	-	$2.11x_2$	+	$0.07x_3$	+	25.01
Number of Disruptions		*Severity of Behavior Problem*		*Hours in Counseling*		*Age*		

$R^2 = 0.85$

Interpretation: *The results of a multiple-regression analysis demonstrated a relationship between the number of classroom disruptions and the severity of a student's behavior problem, number of hours of counseling received and age. In particular, the more severe the behavior problem, the greater the number of disruptions. With more hours of counseling, however, fewer disruptions can be expected. Furthermore, a student's age does not affect this pattern.*

These findings suggest that if a student received more counseling, the number of his or her disruptions could be reduced. For example, by increasing counseling hours from 10 to 15, the expected number of disruptions could be decreased from 14.97 to 4.43 for a 15-year-old student with a severity rating of two, and from 45.03 to 34.49 for a 15-year-old with a severity rating of 8, a reduction of 10.54 disruptions in both cases.

Lesson 11
How To Analyze Categorical And Continuous Data: Using The Chi Square Statistic

Evaluators divide the data they collect into categorical (classified separately) or continuous (classified in a hierarchy) categories. Consider the following example:

A school district in California asked an evaluator to find out if the nation's top 10 colleges were accepting the same proportion of students from Monroe High School as from Hart Township.

The evaluator's design looked like this:

College	High School Monroe High	Hart Township
1		
2		
3		
4		
5		
6		
7		
8		
9		
10		

Another evaluator in California had to find out if the proportion of state college preparatory program students being accepted by the best colleges was similar to the national average.

The evaluator's study design looked like this:

	Colleges									
	1	2	3	4	5	6	7	8	9	10
Frequencies in California										
Frequencies in Nation										

Both evaluators were working with categorical data (in this case, distribution across different colleges) as opposed to continuous, or hierarchical, data (for example, ranking in the school accepting students on a scale from 1 to 100). Variables arranged in classes that can be distinguished from one another but that cannot be arranged into a hierarchy produce categorical information. For example, classifying gender as male or female or program satisfaction as high or low will produce categorical data.

Chi Square

The chi square statistic is used to analyze categorical information. Evaluation data often call for two specific procedures that use the chi square statistic: goodness-of-fit testing and contingency table analysis.

Goodness-of-fit testing is a way of comparing empirically derived data (expressed as frequencies) with theoretically expected results. For example, one evaluation question that could be answered using goodness-of-fit testing would be, "How do participants' approval rating of program x compare with the one-third disapproval rate of previous years?"

Suppose a new demographic theory predicts a certain population will contain four ethnic groups in the proportions 9:3:3:1, and a random sample of 240 persons resulted in 120, 40, 55 and 25 people in the four categories. You can use a goodness-of-fit test to compare the theoretically expected data with the empirically observed data. The result of the test would be a chi square statistic, which could be computed with the following table and formula:

	Category 1	Category 2	...	Category n
Empirical Frequencies	o_1	o_2	...	o_n
Theoretical Frequencies	t_1	t_2	...	t_n

If the obtained or empirical data (oi) are the same as the theoretical data (t), the fit will be perfect, and the difference (oi - ti) for each category will be zero, and so will the chi square value. Consequently, the smaller the chi square value, the better the fit; the larger the chi square value, the poorer the fit. You can compare your chi square values with values in chi square tables and accept or reject the goodness of fit at the desired level of statistical significance.

Contingency tables are used in chi square analyses to compare two sets of empirical data expressed as frequencies, for example, in testing for significant relationship between two variables. The relationship between the proportion of students on probation and the students' gender might be organized in a contingency table as follows:

	Not on Probation	**On Probation**
Male	Number of Observations	Number of Observations
Female	Number of Observations	Number of Observations

You also could use contingency tables to find out if two sets of empirical data are alike or, in statistical language, whether the two sets are random samples from the same population. For example, you could use a contingency table and a chi square statistic to compare the number of children contracting polio in a sample of vaccinated and unvaccinated children:

	Not Vaccinated	Vaccinated
Polio	Number of Observations	Number of Observations
No Polio	Number of Observations	Number of Observations

The chi square statistic used for contingency tables is similar to the one used for goodness-of-fit tests. In this case, however, you compare the observed frequencies with expected rather that theoretical frequencies.

Example:

The LEGAL program is design to help students pass law school entrance examinations by giving them practice answering typical standardized examination questions. The school board will approve the LEGAL program if a significantly greater number of LEGAL as opposed to non-LEGAL graduates are accepted by law schools. The evaluation question was, "Is there a statistically significantly difference in the rate of law school acceptance between LEGAL graduates and other students?"

The evaluators used a comparison group design. They organized the data into a contingency table with two variables: program participation and admittance to law school.

The evaluators randomly selected 210 college seniors to take part in the evaluation from all the seniors who requested to enroll in LEGAL. The evaluators then randomly accepted half of the 210 students into the program and refused the other half. Two of the refused students were disqualified from the evaluation when they enrolled in another program similar to LEGAL.

Evaluation Sample

No LEGAL	***LEGAL***
103	*105*

The evaluators organized the data into a contingency table and used a chi square statistic to test the hypothesis that law school acceptance rates were the same.

	No LEGAL	LEGAL	Totals
Not Admitted	80	30	110
Admitted	23	75	98
Totals	103	105	208

Chi quare value (x^2) = 48.4
Degrees of freedom = 1
Significance = $p < 0.01$

The results of the chi square analysis refuted the hypothesis. The evaluators concluded that the chi square test value of 48.4 indicated a statistically significant difference between LEGAL and non-LEGAL students, with LEGAL students being accepted by law schools more frequently.

Lesson 12
How To Answer Evaluation Questions Using Simple And Multivariate Statistical Analysis

The preceding lessons have outlined the most commonly used methods of analyzing data for your grant evaluation. This lesson provides a brief overview of several other methods you might want to use.

To start, review the evaluation questions you will have to answer. These are the best guide for selecting an analysis technique suited to you particular study. Here are some examples:

- How does the XYZ reading program differ from the ABC reading program in promoting good reading habits in young children?

- How does the XYZ reading program differ from the ABC reading program in promoting good reading habits in young children, encouraging parental involvement and gaining teacher acceptance?

- Is there a relationship between birth order and success in the XYZ reading program?

The first two questions ask the evaluator to describe differences between programs. The first question asks only about reading habits, but the second question includes other variables as well. You may need different analysis techniques to answer these two questions, possibly using a t test for the first and a multivariate analysis of variance (MANOVA) for the second.

The third evaluation question asks about a relationship, which means you will need any analytical technique, such as correlation, that focuses on the association between variables.

Besides the technical properties of the various methods, you must weigh other important considerations. Are the data reliable and valid enough to warrant extensive analysis? Do you have the time and money to organize and coordinate raw data for the more complicated methods? Can you meet the mathematical assumptions for the data analysis techniques you choose?

The following pages present a brief overview of various techniques evaluators have found useful. Each summary ends with a hypothetical question that might be answered by using the data analysis procedure just described.

Simple (Univariate) Statistical Analysis

Descriptive Statistics: These statistics summarize and organize the important aspects of a set of data. This may be by computing the mean, median, mode, range, standard deviation and frequency. It also includes organizing data in tables and representing them graphically.

Example: What are the mean, standard deviation and range of scores on the Nobel Standardized Test of Science Ability?

Inferential Statistics: These statistics permit you to draw conclusions about a whole population from data on a sample of that population. A commonly used inferential technique is the t test.

Example: Are children in statewide Program A reading more books than children in statewide Program B?

Nonparametric Statistics: These techniques can be used with small samples and with nominal or ordinal data. A "normal" distribution is not necessary. Nonparametric techniques include chi square, the sign test and the Mann-Whitney U test (see Lesson 6).

Example: Are the health attitudes for the 10 children in classroom X different from the health attitudes of the 10 children in classroom Y?

Multivariate Statistics

Analysis of Variance (ANOVA): ANOVA is used to test hypotheses about the average performance of two or more groups or programs. Generally, only one dependent variable can be analyzed at a time. If there is a single independent variable, the analysis is called a one-way ANOVA; if there are two independent variables, it is called a two-way ANOVA, and so on.

Example: Do the test scores show that the mathematical ability of groups A, B, C and D is about the same?

Linear Regression: Linear regression analysis is a method for determining the relationship between a dependent variable and one or more independent variables. The relationship is expressed as a linear equation. If a single independent variable is involved, the procedure is called a simple or bivariate regression. If two or more independent variables are involved, it is a multiple or multivariate regression. A regression equation often is used to predict because the dependent variable is shown as a function of the independent variables.

Example: What is the relationship between school absenteeism and a student's age, gender and course of study?

Correlation: Closely related to regression analysis is correlation, the degree of association between variables. Simple correlation describes the relationship between a single dependent and a single independent variable. Partial correlation measures the relationship between the dependent variable and an independent variable, when one or more independent variables are held constant. Multiple correlation measures the relationship between the dependent variable and some "best" inear combination of the independent variables. Correlation does not prove that one thing causes another, only that the events are related.

Example: Are frequent visits to the doctor associated with self-esteem?

Path (Causal) Analysis: Path analysis uses linear multivariate regression techniques to establish a causal relationship among variables.

Example: What are the effects of certain socioeconomic variables on the job opportunities of students from different ethnic backgrounds?

Automatic Interaction Detection: This procedure involves dividing seemingly dissimilar people into homogeneous groups on the basis of a single dependent variable.

Example: What distinguishes adults who use the public library from those who don't?

Analysis of Covariance (ANCOVA): ANCOVA combines the methods of ANOVA and linear regression, making it possible to compare the average performance of different groups on one or more variables after "correcting" for the effects of some outside factor.

Example: How effective is flu control Program A compared to Program B, considering the initial level of flu in the areas in which the two programs were tested?

Discriminate Analysis: When groups of individuals are defined in advance, discriminate analysis is used to differentiate between them on the basis of variables that are presumed to account for the differences.

Example: Can high-achieving boys be distinguished from high-achieving girls on the basis of mathematical ability and parents' occupation?

Multivariate Analysis of Variance (MANOVA): Like ANOVA, this procedure is used to determine the statistical relationship between the average performance of two or more groups. In MANOVA, however, the differences are based on mean scores on a set of dependent variables instead of just one.

Example: What is the statistical relationship among three programs using different curriculum materials, based on these four factors: student attendance and achievement, parent involvement and teacher approval.

Multivariate of Covariance (MANCOVA): Just as ANCOVA uses regression to correct for a covariate within an ANOVA, MANCOVA does the same within a MANOVA. That is, multivariate analysis of covariance is simply a multivariate analysis of variance performed on a set of corrected scores or values.

Example: Taking into account students' ages, what is the statistical relationship among three programs using different curriculum materials, based on these four factors: student attendance and achievement, parent involvement and teacher approval.

Canonical Correlation: Canonical correlation offers an overall measure of the relationship between a set of two or more dependent variables and a set of two or more independent variables. This procedure also identifies the weighted linear combinations of the dependent and independent variables that will produce the maximum correlation.

Example: What is the overall correlation between certain socioeconomic variables and selected measures of verbal, mathematical and mechanical ability?

Cluster Analysis: Cluster analysis uses a series of techniques to identify structure within complex bodies of data. Typically, the data are based on a sample of individuals and their scores on selected variables. The object is to group people or objects into clusters that have a high degree of "natural association" within, but remain distinctly different from, other clusters. Unlike discriminate analysis, the categories or groups are not created in advance. The object is to discover a set of natural groups.

Example: Given a large body of descriptive data on teaching, can you identify clusters of successful methods?

Factor Analysis: Factor analysis techniques are similar to cluster analysis by concentrate on structure among variables instead of structure among individuals. In particular, factor analysis takes many variables whose values are known and reduces them to a smaller number of factors. The factors are assumed to describe the original set of variables without losing any important information.

Example: Are the most important factors underlying the XYZ measure of creativity artistic or intellectual?

Cohort Analysis: Cohort analysis is basically a nonstatistical method for investigating changes in behavior and attitude among a group of individuals linked by some common factor, such as age or grade in school. The simplest form of cohort analysis involves comparing the same cohort at different periods to detect any changes over time.

Example: Do graduating seniors have higher career aspirations than they had as sophomores?

Lesson 13
How To Create Your Own Statistical Tables

After you collect and analyze the evaluation data, you can present your work in easy-to-read statistical tables.

Readers of the evaluation report, including funding individual officials and policymakers, should be able to understand the data you collected and what it means in terms of the evaluation questions.

Here is an example of a typical statistical table. It has been labeled to indicate all the elements you should include when constructing your own tables.

Figure 1

Table number and title — NO. 215. ENROLLMENT IN PUBLIC AND PRIVATE SCHOOLS: 1960 TO 1977

Unit indicator / Headnote — [In millions of persons 3 to 34 years of age. As of October. Elementary includes grades 1-8; high school, grades 9-12. College data represent degree-credit enrollment]

LEVEL	1960 [1]			1970			1977		
	Total	Public	Private	Total	Public	Private	Total	Public	Private
Total	46.3	39.0	7.2	60.4	52.2	8.1	60.0	51.6	8.4
Nursery	(NA)	(NA)	(NA)	1.1	.3	.8	1.6	.6	1.1
Kindergarten	2.1	1.7	.4	3.2	2.6	.5	3.2	2.7	.5
Elementary	30.3	25.8	4.5	34.0	30.0	3.9	29.2	26.0	3.3
High school	10.2	9.2	1.0	14.7	13.5	1.2	15.8	14.5	1.2
College	3.6	2.3	1.3	7.4	5.7	1.7	10.2	7.9	2.3

Footnotes — NA Not available. [1] Data are for persons 5 to 34 years of age.

Source: U.S. Bureau of the Census, *Current Population Reports*, series P-20.

Labels: Footnote indicator; Stub; Spanner; Column heads; Field; Heavy rule; Parallel rule

Headnotes immediately below table titles provide information important for correct interpretation or evaluation of the table as a whole or for a major segment of it.

Footnotes below the bottom rule of the table give information relating to specific items or figures within the table.

Unit indicators ("in thousand," "in millions of dollars," etc.) usually are in boldface type as the first element of the headnotes. In tables in which several units are used, the unit indicators generally are given in the stub or unit column or in the column headings.

Parallel vertical rules are used to the right of a total column to indicate: (1) that the following components add to the total; and (2) in the case of derived figures, that the underlying data are additive to their total.

Heavy vertical rules are used: (1) in tables in which the stub is continued into one or more additional columns across the table to separate each segment of stub in its accompanying data columns from the continued segments; and (2) to set off independent sections of a table.

Rules For Reading Statistical Tables

Here are 10 rules that will help you quickly grasp the information included in a table. Use these steps to study the information presented in Figure 1.

❶ Read the title carefully.
❷ Read the headnotes or other explanation carefully.
❸ Notice the source.
❹ Look at the footnotes.
❺ Find out what units are used.
❻ Look at the overall average.
❼ See what variability there is.
❽ See how the average is associated with each of the main criteria of classification.
❾ Examine the consistency of the overall effects and the interactions among them.
❿ Look for things you weren't looking for: aberrations, anomalies or irregularities.

Steps to Reorganize Data into a New Table

It is one thing to be able to read a statistical table; it is quite another to construct a table to meet your individual needs. Suppose, for example, you wanted to know the total and the percentage of all persons in selected types of residential areas who are African American so you can compare these figures with similar information from an earlier time.

Figure 2 is an example of a table that includes necessary information but is not organized specifically to answer the reader's questions. After studying the parts of a statistical table in Figure 1, can you create a new table from the information in Figure 2 that will highlight the comparisons you want to make?

Figure 2

NO. 21. POPULATION, BY METRO.-NONMETRO. RESIDENCE AND RACE: 1950 TO 1979

[In millions, except percent. Covers 243 standard metropolitan statistical areas (SMSA's) as defined in 1970 census publications. Data for 1950–1970 as of April. Data for 1979 are five-quarter annual averages centered on April from the Current Population Survey; see text, pp. 1–3. Minus sign (-) denotes decrease. See also *Historical Statistics, Colonial Times to 1970*, series A 276–287]

RESIDENCE AND RACE	TOTAL RESIDENT POPULATION							NONINSTITUTIONAL POPULATION		
	1950	1960		1970		Average annual percent change [1]		1970, adjusted [2]	1979	Average annual percent change, [1] 1970–1979 [2]
		Total	Percent	Total	Percent	1950–1960	1960–1970			
All races	151.3	179.3	100.0	[3]203.2	100.0	1.7	1.3	199.8	215.3	.8
SMSA's, total	94.6	119.6	66.7	139.4	68.7	2.3	1.5	137.1	145.4	.7
Central cities	53.7	59.9	33.4	63.8	31.6	1.1	.6	62.9	60.6	-.4
Outside central cities	40.9	59.6	33.3	75.6	37.0	3.8	2.4	74.2	84.8	1.5
Nonmetropolitan areas	56.7	59.7	33.3	63.8	31.4	.5	.7	62.8	69.9	1.2
White	135.2	158.8	100.0	177.7	100.0	1.6	1.1	175.3	186.1	.7
SMSA's	85.1	105.8	66.7	120.6	67.8	2.1	1.3	118.9	123.1	.4
Central cities	46.8	49.4	31.1	49.4	27.8	6	(Z)	48.9	44.8	-1.0
Outside central cities	38.3	56.4	35.5	71.1	40.0	3.8	2.3	70.0	78.3	1.2
Nonmetropolitan areas	50.1	53.0	33.4	57.2	32.2	.7	.8	56.3	63.0	1.2
Black	15.0	18.9	100.0	22.6	100.0	2.3	1.8	22.1	25.1	1.4
SMSA's	8.9	12.7	67.5	16.8	74.3	3.6	2.7	16.3	19.1	1.7
Central cities	6.6	9.9	52.3	13.1	58.2	4.1	2.9	12.9	14.1	1.0
Outside central cities	2.2	2.9	15.2	3.6	16.1	2.1	2.4	3.4	5.0	4.1
Nonmetropolitan areas	6.1	6.1	32.5	5.8	25.7	1	.5	5.7	6.0	.5

Z Less than .05 percent. [1] For explanation of average annual percent change, see Guide to Tabular Presentation.
[2] 1970 census data adjusted to exclude inmates of institutions and members of the Armed Forces living in barracks and similar types of quarters for comparability with 1979 data from Current Population Survey.
[3] See footnote 3, table 1. Totals include corrections and some annexations that are not included in data by race.

Source: U.S. Bureau of the Census, *U.S. Census of Population: 1960 and 1970*, vol. I; and *Current Population Reports*, series P-20, No. 350.

Follow these instructions, which are grouped by elements of the table structure, to help you construct your new table.

Stub: Use the same residential categories (i.e., SMSAs, central cities, outside central cities, metropolitan areas) that were in the original table.

Spanner: Divide this table portion into two parts. One will present information for the earlier period (e.g., 1950); the second will give information for the later period (e.g., 1970).

Column Heads: You will need a two-level column head so you can use both the total and black population figures to calculate the percentage of blacks within each area. Label the first-level column heads (immediately below each section of the spanner) "Total" and "Black." Use "Total" and "Percent" as the titles for the second-level column heads below the "Black" column head for each year.

If you followed these instructions and drew lines to separate its parts, the rules for the spanner and column heads should be similar to Figure 3.

Figure 3

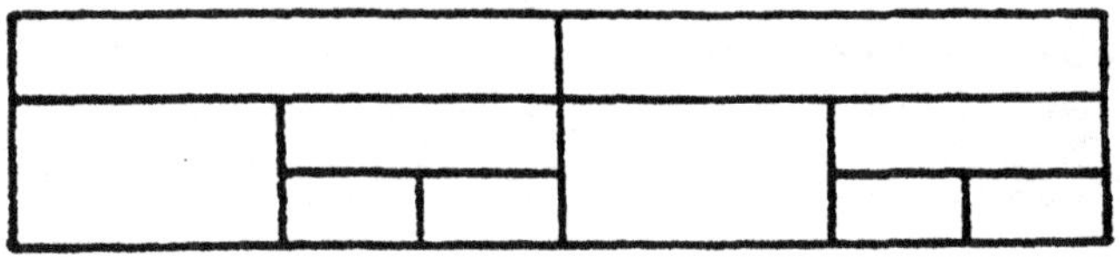

Field: You are ready to place the 24 cells (4 x 6) of information in the field. The population information to be included in the "Total" column will come directly from Figure 3 (or a more recent source). However, you should calculate the percentages after the "totals" are posted. Compute the percentages by dividing each of the totals (e.g., 1970 black population living in SMSA's divided by 1970 total population living in SMSA's x 100).

Table Title: Prepare a table title that is comprehensive but to the point. Be sure to refer to the variables displayed in the stub, the spanner and the column heads, as illustrated in Figure 1.

Headnotes: Review the information in the headnotes of Figure 2 (or its equivalent) to determine which of the numerous notes are needed for your new table. You probably should include a unit indicator (e.g., millions). But must you cite the Current Population Survey? Why or why not?

Footnotes: You have changed the original table to create your own table, so it is important to use for the footnote and source only information that is relevant to your table.

Once you are satisfied that the structure of your new table is complete, review its contents. What summary statements can you make regarding the changes that have occurred between the two periods?

In the same way that one's description of a sculpture may vary if viewed from the side rather than from the front, the information in a table may be interpreted differently if its contents are reorganized. Using the information compiled in your new table, devise a second table by reversing the location of information: What was in the spanner and column heads should be placed in the stub, and vice versa.

Analyze the two formats. Are the totals and percentages easier to read vertically or horizontally? Which table is similar? Which is more clear? Why?

Are there other ways the information could be presented to help the reader comprehend the changes that have taken place during the 20-year period (e.g., additional derived measures, such as a measure of absolute change or percent change in the total population and black population)?

Finally, when you present your information and data in tables, you should also summarize your findings in narrative form. This will help the reader understand the information you have provided and how you have used it to determine your findings.

Lesson 14
How To Analyze Evaluation Information: Some Tips

Evaluators use a standard process for analyzing information, whether it is for grant-funded projects or other purposes, that includes the following steps:

- Pilot testing the information analysis;
- Conducting the analysis;
- Interpreting the results of the analysis; and
- Making recommendations, if requested.

Pilot Testing

Information analysis techniques must be pilot tested to find out if they work. If the techniques don't work properly, they must be redesigned. A pilot test should include all the planned information analysis activities and should reveal whether:

- Needed information will be available in manageable form;
- Necessary expert personnel and special equipment, such as computers, are available; and
- Data reduction procedures are efficient and accurate.

Conducting the Analysis

Once the information analysis techniques have been pilot tested and revised, the evaluator can collect and begin to analyze the information. Sometimes, evaluation questions require more than one analysis. At other times, further analysis is unnecessary unless warranted by the results.

For example, to answer the evaluation question, "Which of the four programs is most effective in teaching subject X?" you could use a statistical method, such as one-way analysis of variance. You would test the hypothesis that there is no difference in average program effectiveness. If the results confirm the hypothesis, then no further analysis would be necessary. If, however, the results disprove the hypothesis, you would need additional analysis to find out which programs are responsible for the differences.

An ordered approach to information analysis is the most efficient, yet evaluators often have the notion that most is best. Be careful; security gained from doing all manner of analyses often is illusory. A scattered approach to information analysis is technically unsound because:

- It increases the probability of finding significant results by chance alone;
- It results in a loss of credibility as the evaluator strays from the plan specifically tailored to answer the evaluation question; and
- It is hopelessly inefficient.

Interpreting Results

Assume that data collection and analysis have proceeded smoothly. What does the evaluator do with the results?

For example, an evaluation question asked whether shoppers read price-per-pound information used by a food retailer. A survey questionnaire showed 40 percent of the shoppers said they do read the information. The evaluator now has to consider the following three questions:

❶ Is 40 percent sufficient to prove the program's effectiveness?

❷ Were the shoppers who responded representative of all shoppers?

❸ Does a positive response (reading the price-per-pound information) mean that the information influenced what the shoppers bought?

These questions are typical of problems underlying many evaluations. The first deals with standards of program merit, the second with design strategy and sampling procedures, and the third with validity of information collection and analysis methods. (The last question also points out the importance of asking the right evaluation question in the first place.) Was the evaluation trying to find out whether consumers read the information or whether they read and acted on the information?) If the evaluation is well-organized and carefully thought out in the first place, then the information gathered can be interpreted with a minimum of trouble.

Once you have interpreted the analysis results for each evaluation question, you can look at the analyses collectively to get an idea of the effectiveness of the Program As a whole. Such overall interpretation is useful in getting a feel for program dynamics or the relationship between parts of the program.

Interpreting results also involves distinguishing between statistical and programmatic significance. Statistical significance tells you how likely it is that an outcome is due to chance. Programmatic significance tells you whether an outcome makes a difference in terms of program goals, that is, whether the outcome justifies the time, effort and money spent.

Statistical significance and programmatic significance are analogous to reliability and validity. Like reliability, statistical significance is a measure of precision. Like validity, programmatic significance is a measure of efficiency and cogency.

Making Recommendations

Finally, analysis results sometimes point to obvious recommendations for improving or certifying the effectiveness of a program. The evaluator, however, is not always expected to make — and the client is never obligated to accept — such recommendations.

For the price-per-pound information evaluation, the evaluator supplied the following recommendations when asked.

"Our analysis of descriptive statistics reveals that shoppers between age 20 and 40 meet the standards set for reading price-per-pound information, while shoppers between age 40 and 60 do not. We therefore recommend that you continue to give price-per-pound information in markets serving young communities. We also recommend you give price-per-pound information for products bought primarily by young consumers."

Part III

Managing And Reporting Evaluations

Lesson 15
How To Manage An Evaluation

Because funders are placing increasing emphasis on the importance of project evaluation, it is vital that grantseekers develop strong, detailed evaluation plans and prove they will be able to manage those plans well, completing them on time and within their budgets.

Directors of grant projects should manage the evaluation carefully. Evaluation information is perishable. It's essential to coordinate activities so that the right information is ready when needed. If project staff and the funding agency don't get answers to their questions in time to make decisions, the evaluation isn't worth much. No matter how large or small an evaluation is, some of your time must be allocated to management.

The three most important management functions you will have to perform are establishing schedules, assigning staff and monitoring their activities, and budgeting, and are explained below. You might include in the grant proposal one or more of the schedules illustrated in this lesson to give the grant reader specific information about the evaluation plan.

Step One: How to Establish Schedules

Evaluations must be completed within a given amount of time. If you don't finish on time, funds probably won't be available to continue the evaluation unless you make special arrangements with the funder ahead of time by asking for a carry-over of funds or an extension of the project period.

Evaluation of a grant-funded project should never be put off to the last few weeks or months of the project. The evaluator should work with project staff from the beginning and be ready to start collecting data as soon as the project is launched. Starting from the beginning of the project also allows the evaluator to give the project director feedback as it goes along so adjustments can be made as they are needed.

To manage an evaluation effectively, it is important to know just when each evaluation activity will take place, the sequence of activities and how long each activity will last. To do this, you must set a schedule that takes the following factors into account:

- Hiring an evaluator;
- The nature of the evaluation activities themselves;
- The amount of time to be given to each activity, i.e., the actual number of professional hours, days or weeks needed, even if they are spread over a longer period of time; and
- The deadline for completing each activity.

You can combine evaluation activities, deadlines and time allocations in several ways to create schedules. The following examples illustrate some schedules for managing evaluations.

Example 1 lists a beginning and end date (or deadline) for each activity and specifies the time allocated to it.

Example 1: Overview of Activities, Staff and Schedule

Activities	*Dates*	*Total Allocation (Total Days)*
1. Becoming familiar with the program goals, activities and evidence of program merit, including • Reading all program related documents and reports; • Meeting with program director and staff; • Observing program in operation; • Meeting with internal evaluation or research development	*3/1 to 4/15*	*15*
2. Formulating evaluation questions from project objectives, including a review by program staff and Advisory Committee	*4/16 to 5/31*	*10*
3. Preparing evaluation design strategies and sampling plan	*6/1 to 6/30*	*10*
4. Preparing information collection to include field testing	*6/15 to 9/30*	*12*
5. Collecting evaluation information for analysis	*10/1 to 5/30*	*35*
6. Preparing information for analysis	*11/1 to 6/15*	*7*
7. Analyzing evaluation information and interpreting the results	*2/1 to 7/31*	*14*
8. Preparing preliminary evaluation reports	*8/30-31 to 2/27-28*	*4*
9. Preparing final evaluation report	*6/1 to 8/31*	*22*

Example 2 represents a schedule organized by month with beginning and end dates for each activity joined by an arrowed line and the number of days allocated to each activity in parentheses directly under the line.

Example 2: Evaluation Schedule

The numbers in parentheses refer to the amount of professional staff time allocated to each activity, not the period of time it takes to complete the activity.

Either type of schedule could be included as part of the evaluation plan described in the proposal itself.

The number in parentheses refer to the amount of professional staff time allocated to each activity, not the period of time it takes to complete the activity.

Step Two: How to Assign Staff and Monitor Activities

Before you assign staff to specific evaluation activities — or employ outside evaluators — you should know what skills it takes to perform each activity. Example 3 shows a convenient way to summarize staff assignments.

Example 3: Staff Allocation Chart

Staff Assignment	*Title/Role*	*Percent Time*
Dr. Leroy Samuels	*Evaluation Director*	*50%*
Dr. Susan Baker	*Instrument Development*	*15%*
Dr. Sharon Hathaway	*Information Collection*	*50%*
Ms. Gretel Burry	*Information Analysis*	*20%*
Mr. James Wardling	*Research Associate*	*100%*
Mr. Harry Vivell	*Secretary*	*25%*

Example 3 is organized to show the role each person will play in the evaluation and the total amount of time each person will devote to it. Example 4 is arranged according to activity. It is the same as Example 1 except that it has been expanded to show the specific amount of time allocated for each activity by each staff member.

Example 1: Overview of Activities, Staff and Schedule

Activities	*Dates*	*Staff Assignments*	*Total Allocation (Total Days) By Staff*	*Total Days*
1. Becoming familiar with the program goals, activities and evidence of program merit, including *• Reading all program related documents and reports;* *• Meeting with program director and staff;* *• Observing program in operation;* *• Meeting with internal evaluation or research development*	*3/1 to 4/15*	*Smith* *Ramirez* *Goldberg*	*10* *2* *3*	*15*
2. Formulating evaluation questions from project objectives, including a review by program staff and Advisory Committee	*4/16 to 5/31*	*Smith* *Ramirez* *Goldberg*	*7* *2* *1*	*10*
3. Preparing evaluation design strategies and sampling plan	*6/1 to 6/30*	*Smith* *Ramirez* *Goldberg*	*2* *7* *1*	*10*
4. Preparing information collection to include field testing	*6/15 to 9/30*	*Cheung* *Smith* *Ramirez* *Goldberg*	*3* *2* *7* *1*	*12*
5. Collecting evaluation information for analysis	*10/1 to 5/30*	*Smith* *Goldberg* *Cheung*	*3* *12* *20*	*35*
6. Preparing information for analysis	*11/1 to 6/15*	*Smith* *Ramirez*	*1* *6*	*7*
7. Analyzing evaluation information and interpreting the results	*2/1 to 7/31*	*Smith* *Ramirez*	*3* *11*	*14*
8. Preparing preliminary evaluation reports	*8/30-31 to 2/27-28*	*Smith*	*4*	*4*
9. Preparing final evaluation report	*6/1 to 8/31*	*Smith* *Ramirez* *Goldberg* *Cheung*	*7* *6* *6* *3*	*22*

Managing an evaluation also means you will have to keep an eye on how efficiently your staff performs the evaluation activities. You should collect information about the amount of time spent on each activity, how thoroughly it has been accomplished and any problems encountered. This information can be collected in several ways, ranging from highly structured reporting systems to informal meetings with staff members. A regular, structured reported schedule is most effective, and it is up to the project director to ensure that it is in place or that the evaluator has prepared it.

Step Three: How to Budget

Evaluations of grant-funded projects usually have a given amount of money and must be completed without exceeding that amount. To set a budget that will adequately fund an evaluation, you must weigh what needs to be done against what you have to do it with, juggling activities, time allocations and staff assignments according to the amount of money and time available. A good ballpark estimate of evaluation cost is about 15 percent of the total project budget.

The following sample budget includes items required by most state and federal agencies and foundations that support health, education and welfare programs. Note the distinction between direct and indirect costs. Direct costs are staff and non-staff costs related to a particular evaluation. For example, the salaries and expenses of secretaries or clerks who work for the evaluations are charged as direct costs according to the amount of time they actually spent on the evaluation.

Indirect costs are expenses that are not directly related to the particular evaluation but that contribute to the evaluation agency's continued existence. Expenses for secretaries or clerks who keep your office running would be incorporated into the indirect costs.

Funders, particularly federal agencies, often place strict limits on the kind and amount of costs you can charge to the grant. Be sure to adhere to their rules. Use the funder's budget categories and definitions.

Sample Budget

DIRECT COSTS

Divide your costs into staff and non-staff sections.

I. Staff Costs

A. Salaries and Wages

List here the salaries and wages of full-time and part-time persons employed for the evaluation at a rate proportionate to their efforts on the evaluation. For each staff position, provide the following information: number of persons at that position, their titles, daily, monthly or annual salaries, percent of time on the evaluation, what evaluation activities they will perform, the number of months employed and the total dollar figure.

Example A — Salaries and Wages:

1. Dr. Peter Korn, Evaluation Director	*$12,000*
(20% time at $60,000 per year; 2/1-1/31)	
2. Ms. Maureen Malanaphy, Information Analysis	*$4,200*
(35% time at $24,000 per year; 3/1-5/31; 9/15-12/14)	
3. Dr. Ralph Heffer, Instrumentation	*$14,000*
(35% time at $40,000 per year; 2/1-7/31)	
4. Dr. Susan Schrager, Field Research	*$8,750*
(35% time at $25,000 per year; 2/1-1/31)	
5. Secretary/Clerical Assistant	*$9,000*
(50% time at $18,000 per year; 2/1-1/31)	
Subtotal	*$22,650*

B. Employee Benefits

Show the costs of all employee benefits related to the salaries and wages of full-time or part-time staff. Benefits usually are computed as a percentage of salaries and wages and include funds set aside by the employer for Social Security, retirement, medical care, etc. Sometimes, each type of benefit is listed separately.

Example B — Employee Benefits:

1. 20% of Salaries and Wages ($57,750)	*$11,550*

C. Consultants

Consultants are persons who are hired on an as-needed basis, such as reviewers, members of an advisory panel, subject matter experts or field workers. (You might choose to hire an outside consultant to conduct all or most of the evaluation, which could take up all your evaluation funds, instead of including most of the evaluation costs as "salaries" above.)

Example C — Consultants:

1. Members of Advisory Panel (9 persons at $200 per day for 2 days each)	*$3,600*

II. Non-Staff Costs

A. Rent

Show here the cost of using facilities for the evaluation, including utilities and maintenance services. (Funds often expect the grantee to provide office rent, supplies and equipment and not charge it to the grant, or these costs may be considered part of the indirect costs.)

Example A — Rent:

1. Office space (250 sq. ft. at $1.50 per sq. ft. for 12 months)	*$4,500*

B. Office Supplies

List consumable supplies used exclusively for the project, like paper, computer disks, etc.

Example B — Office Supplies:

1. Office supplies (paper, etc.) at $100 per month for 12 months	*$1,200*

C. Equipment

Specify the cost of equipment acquired or rented for specific use on the project, such as computers, copy machines, etc.

Example C — Equipment Rental

1. Rental of computers and photocopying machines for 12 months	*$2,000*

D. Equipment Purchases

List costs for equipment purchases required for the project, such as computers.

Example D — Computer:

1. Personal Computer (give specifications) *$2,500*

2. Computer supplies (disks, printer ribbon, etc.) *$100*

E. Telephone and Mail
Show costs of telephone services, phone calls, postage.

Example E — Telephone and Mail:

1. Telephone and mail at $50 per month for 12 months *$600*
(Specify the telephone installation costs that are required).

F. Printing and Reproduction:
List costs of photocopying, word processing, report duplication, etc.

Example F — Printing and Reproduction:

1. Printing (questionnaires, observation schedules, reports) *$1,200*

2. Reproduction at $15 per month for 12 months *$180*

G. Travel
Show all travel charges incurred for the project, including the per diem expenses, gas mileage, airfare, etc.

Example G — Travel:

1. Travel to sites (9 trips at $300 per trip) *$2,700*
(Provide name of traveler, purpose of trip and itemized expenses.)

INDIRECT COSTS

You may compute indirect costs as a percent of the total direct costs or as a percent of salaries and wages. (Some grants limit the percent of allowable indirect costs; equipment and stipends often are excluded form the base figure when calculating indirect costs.)

Example — Indirect Costs:

Indirect Costs = 22 percent of Direct Costs ($87,880) *$19,334*

Now you can translate all the information recorded in your sample budget into a conventional budget format as shown here:

Detailed Budget for a 12-Month (260-Day) Evaluation Form, February 1 to January 31

Direct Costs
I. Staff Costs
A. Salaries, Wages and Benefits

Name	Title	Time (Days)	Salary	Benefits	Total
1. Dr. Korn	Director	52	$4,800	$768	$5,568
2. Ms. Malanaphy	Information Analyst	45 1/2	4,200	672	4,872
3. Dr. Heffer	Instrumentation	45 1/2	4,200	672	4,872
4. Dr. Schraer	Field Research	91	5,250	840	6,090
5. To Be Named	Secretary/Clark	130	4,200	672	4,872

B. Consultants
1. Members of Advisory Committee (nine persons at $200 per day for two days) $3,600

II. Non-Staff Costs

A. Rent
1. Office Space (250 square feet at $1.50 per sq. ft.) $4,500

B. Office Supplies
1. Office supplies (paper, etc.) at $100 per month for 12 months $1,200

C. Equipment
1. Rental of typewriters and photocopy machine at $83.33 per month for 12 months $1,000

D. Equipment Purchase
1. Personal Computer $2,500
2. Computer supplies (disks, etc.) $ 100

E. Telephone and Mail
1. Telephone and mail at $50 per month for 12 months $600

F. Printing and Reproduction
1. Printing (questionnaires, observation schedules, reports) $1,200
2. Reproduction at $15 per month for 12 months $180

G. Travel	
1. Travel to sites (nine trips at $300 per trip)	$2,700
Subtotal, Non-Staff Costs	$18,580
INDIRECT COSTS	
22 percent of Direct Costs ($87,880)	$19,334
Grand Total	$107,214

Note that the total budget for this sample evaluation includes significant staff time, office rental, computer purchases and other costs. Most evaluation budgets would not include all of these items, which are provided here for illustration. Most evaluation budgets are 15 percent to 30 percent of the total grant budget.

Lesson 16
How To Write An Evaluation Report

The final step in evaluating a grant-funded or any project is writing and submitting the report of findings.

The report is the official record of an evaluation — the document in which you make public your activities, data and findings — and state whether the project achieved its goal. It should be truthful, believable and easily understood. It's your job to communicate in a comprehensive way — without omitting any qualitative or quantitative details — what was done, how it was done and why it was done.

A credible evaluation report clearly and logically describes the evaluation questions and the procedures you used to get the answers. It should include:

- An executive summary of the evaluation;
- An introduction to the evaluation, the evaluation questions and limitations on the scope of the evaluation;
- Design strategy and sampling procedures for each evaluation question and their limitations;
- Information collection techniques and instruments, their limitation and any field activities;
- Methods you used to analyze the evaluation information, their limitations and the results for each analysis;
- Answers to each evaluation question, including your interpretation of the findings and your recommendations;
- Administrative details, such as schedules and staff assignments; and
- Recommendations, if any.

Step 1: Introduction

In the introduction, you should briefly describe the program or programs being evaluated, the group that is conducting the evaluation and your approach to evaluation. Discuss any legislation that created the program and mandated its evaluation.

Be sure to include the process you (and your client) used to arrive at statements of program goals, objectives, activities and evidence of program merit. Finally, explain your choice of evaluation questions, list the questions and describe any constraints imposed upon the scope of the evaluation.

Step 2: Design and Sampling

In this section, you should describe the evaluation's design strategy and sampling procedures and any limitation on them. For each evaluation question, explain and justify the way you grouped participants, the independent and dependent variables, the sample and any limitations on internal and external validity. A drawing of the design also is helpful.

Include the sampling procedure you used, justify any subdivisions or strata into which you divided potential participants for sampling purposes, show the final numbers of individuals in the sample and explain any problems you encountered in selecting the participants or any limitations that are inherent in the sampling plan. Again, a drawing of the final sample is useful.

Finally, discuss how well the procedures you used produced the desired sample, at least as far as you can tell with statistical methods or comparisons with tables of demographic data.

Here's an example of one way to report sample and design information:

Example:

The Sample: *The Kennedy Unified School District, the largest in the state, was selected to participate in the evaluation. In each of the district's 32 elementary schools, one third-grade classroom was selected at random for the experimental health program, and one third-grade classroom was selected at random to receive no health instruction. The remaining classrooms were allowed to continue with their regular health education program, if one existed. The sample is depicted in Figure 1.*

Figure 1: The Evaluation Sample

	School 1	School 2	.....	School 32	Total
Experimental Program	1 classroom	1 classroom	.....	1 classroom	32 class-rooms
No Program (Control)	1 classroom	1 classroom	.....	1 classroom	32 class-rooms
Total	2 classrooms	2 classrooms	.....	2 classrooms	64 class-rooms

The Design: *The sample selected to participate in the evaluation was compared to all third-grade students in the Kennedy Unified School District in terms of students' age, reading and math ability, and ethnic and gender composition, and teachers' years of experience, gender and ethnicity. The results of a series of chi square tests showed that there were no significant differences between the sample and all third-grade students.*

The design strategy used to group students is described separately for each evaluation question, for example: "Did students in the experimental program know significantly more about diseases at the end of the school year than they did at the beginning?"

To answer this question, evaluators used a time-series design. The independent variable was the timing of measures (which was studied at two levels: pre-instruction and post-instruction), and the dependent variable was knowledge of diseases. All classrooms in the experimental program were included in the design, which can be illustrated as follows:

Preinstruction	Postinstruction

The limitations on the internal validity of the design include history (some event, such as a public television series on microbe hunters, might have influenced students' knowledge), maturation (during the school year, students may have matured and learned more about their bodies, health and disease), testing (taking the pre-instruction measure may have affected students' performance on the post-instruction measure, although different forms of the measures were used on each occasion) and instrumentation (the administration procedures may have differed from time to time.)

Limitations on the design's external validity include the reactive effects of testing (the pre-instruction measure may have alerted students to their lack of knowledge about diseases, making them more attentive to the program), the interactive effects of selection bias (students in this program may not be representative of students in other districts), the reactive effects of innovation (the fact that students were in a special program might have motivated them to learn) and multiple program interference (some of the students also participated in a compensatory education program at the same time as the health education program, and it was not possible to distinguish the effects of one program from the other).

Step 3: Information Collection

Describe each instrument, the people to whom it was administered and when, and explain why you chose that particular instrument for answering the evaluation questions. Reprint the entire instrument if possible. If not, give sample items. If the instrument has been commercially published and is protected by copyright, you may provide instructions about how to order a copy and summarize its design and purpose.

Give information about the reliability and validity of the instruments. Were they pilot tested or validated? If so, with whom and by whom? What were the results? It's also a good idea to explain how the instruments were administered and scored.

Summarize all field activities, noting any irregularities in information collection that could affect the evaluation's findings. If interviewers strayed from the set procedures for interviewing, for example, you should describe what happened and what the consequences were.

Finally, state how many people participated in each information collection activity, tell how many you obtained complete data for, and explain any missing information.

Here's an example of one way to report information collection:

Example: Information Collection

For each question, the evaluation team selected one or more information collection techniques that were likely to provide answers. The proposed information collection techniques were submitted to the advisory committee for review. Figure 2 contains an excerpt from the approved list of evaluation questions and information collection techniques and summarizes any limitations.

Figure 2: Evaluation Questions and Information Collection Techniques

Evaluation Questions	*Information collection Technique(s) to Be used*	*Limitations*			
		Schedule	*Design*	*Sampling*	*Other*
1.					
2.					
3.					
4. Did students in the experimental program know significantly more about diseases at the endof the school year than they did at the beginning	*Paper and Pencil Achievement Test*		*Must have parallel forms of the achieve-ment*	*All pro-gram par-ticipants must be tested*	*Must insure confiden-tiality of responses*
5.					
6.					

One the information collection techniques were agreed on, the evaluation team began to select, adapt and/or develop the appropriate instruments. To answer the question about students' knowledge of diseases, the evaluation team used a test specifically designed to measure elementary school students' knowledge of health problems and how to manage them.

The instrument has been validated on over 6,000 elementary-school children within the past five years. Split-half reliability of 0.89 and test-retest reliability of 0.98 were reported on the average for third-grade students. Content validity was established through expert review by more than 100 educators and health professionals.

Step 4: Information Analysis

Describe the relationship of each separate analytic method to the evaluation questions, the source of information for the analysis, the design strategy (including the independent and dependent variables) and any limitations.

Give the analysis results and interpret the findings related to the evaluation questions for each analytic procedure.

Finally, although you need not explain their mathematical or philosophical derivations, you must name and justify the analyses. No matter how careful an evaluator you are, the quality of your methodology may be challenged because there are many equally appropriate procedures, each with its own advocates.

Step 5: Evaluation Findings

The most critical part of any evaluation report is the answers to the evaluation questions. You must provide a clear and succinct assessment of whether the project met its goals and objectives.

When reporting answers to evaluation questions, it's important to point out both the strengths and the weaknesses of the program. Clients who have been involved in the program are likely to reject finds that are totally negative. Others are likely to be suspicious if an evaluation report is totally favorable. Occasionally, of course, you may have only positive or negative findings to report.

It is important to explain the limitations of the evaluation. If information came from instruments whose reliability or validity is suspect, tell the reader about it when the evaluation question is answered.

You must report the limitations on your findings even if this makes the report appear noncommittal and the results more difficult to translate into action. Your responsibility is to give policymakers credible and understandable answers they can use to make decisions.

Step 6: Administration

Explain the sequence of events between defining the evaluation questions and arriving at the answers. Information about you and your staff also may be appropriate in this section of the report.

One way you can combine information about the evaluation schedule and the staff is to draw up a calendar of events. Here's an example:

Evaluation Schedule

First Year

October 19 *Meeting with Dr. ________ and others from the Office of ______*

October 31 *Proposal for evaluation of _____ submited to the Office of _____*

November 20	*Revised evaluation design submitted to Dr. _____ at the Office of _____*
Second Year	
June 30	*Sampling procedures refined and implemented*
Third Year	
July 31	*Data analysis completed*
August 15	*Preliminary draft of final report completed*
August 31	*Submission of final report to project director and funder*
September 1	*Thank you letter sent to all participants in the evaluation study*

Step 7: Executive Summary

Although the executive summary should be placed at the beginning of the report, it is helpful to write it last, after you have completed all other sections and have a clear understanding of what you are reporting.

An executive summary should distill into a few pages the activities and findings described in a relatively large evaluation report. The purpose of the summary is to give readers an overview of the evaluation that is easy to read but detailed enough to be believable and usable. The summary may be printed on a different color paper to distinguish it from the body of the report.

Because it may be more widely read and circulated than the complete report, prepare your summary carefully. Use professional writers or editors if necessary.

Step 8: Recommendations

Recommendations sometimes accompany answers to evaluation questions, but not all clients ask for or want recommendations. You should always find out in advance whether recommendations are required, and if they are, how extensive they should be.

When making recommendations, don't take on the policymaker's responsibility for deciding whether or not to continue the program. Instead, you should focus on how to improve the program, changes that might achieve better results and the people who are most likely to benefit from the program.

Step 9: Submitting the Report

The process for submitting the evaluation report will vary for each project depending on the funder's requirements and those of other parties that may need to see the report. Generally, the report goes to the project director, who then submits it to the funder and shares it with other interested parties.

It may be more effective to deliver the final evaluation report in person, and provide the project directors, staff and key administrators with a verbal summary of the findings.

Part IV

Appendices

Appendix A
Glossary Of Terms

Analysis of Variance (ANOVA): Used to compare different groups or study changes in the same group over time. For example, if you wanted to compare the scores of several groups of students participating in a project to the performance of students in a traditional program, you could use ANOVA to see if their scores were significantly different.

Chi Square Statistic: Used to **analyze categorical** information in two ways:

- **Goodness of Pit:** Uses the chi square statistic to compare empirically collected data with statistically predicted results.
- **Contingency Tables:** Compare two sets of empirically collected data to test for a significant relationship between two variables.

Data:

- **Categorical Data:** Information arranged in categories that can be distinguished from one another. For example, men, women, and children.
- **Continuous Data:** Data that can be arranged into a hierarchy. For example, good performance, better performance, best performance.

Data Analysis Techniques:

- **Descriptive Statistics:** Values computed from collected data. For example, the mean, he medan and the standard deviation.
- **Correlation Statistics:** Measurement of the relationship between two variables.
- **Regression Analysis:** Method of examining the relationship between a dependent variable and two or more independent variables. Regression is correlation for several variables simultaneously.

Domains:

- **Cognitive:** The intellectual domain that includes knowledge, comprehension, application, analysis, synthesis and evaluation.
- **Affective:** The attitudinal domain that includes values and feelings.
- **Psychomotor:** The domain that includes physical skills.

Evaluation.

- **Formative:** A review of the progress of activities conducted during a project.
- **Summative:** An assessment of the overall impact of the project, based on data and information collected during the project and analyzed at the end of the project.

Evaluation Design:

- **Case Design:** Examines a single, cohesive group.
- **Time-Series Design:** Compares a group's current performance to its past performance.
- **Comparison Group Design:** Measures the performance of an experimental group with a control group, all randomly selected.

Nonparametric Statistics: Computationally simple methods of testing data from very small or abnormally distributed populations.

- **Mann-Whitney U Test:** A nonparametric technique that tests differences between two independent groups.

Normal Curve: Data distributed in a bell-shaped curve, with about 68% of the data within one standard deviation on either side of the mean and about 96% within two standard deviations. Also called normal distribution.

Null Hypothesis: A starting point for data analysis that assumes no change has occurred from the beginning to the conclusion of the activity. It usually is compared to an alternative hypothesis that theorizes some kind of change has occurred.

Objectives:

- **Behavioral:** An objective that provides information on participants' actions and performance.
- **Performance:** An objective that provides performance criteria as well as information on participants' behavior.
- **Process:** An objective that describes the project's progress and procedures.
- **Product:** An objective that produces tangible results, such as a publication.

Observations: Eye-witness accounts of behaviors or project activities.

- **Standard Observations:** First-hand information collected by observers.
- **Time-Sampling Observations:** Repeated observations of a given situation.

Paper-and-Pencil Self-Report Measures: Requests for information from participants about their attitudes, beliefs, feelings or perceptions. They often take the form of questionnaires or participant diaries and can be analyzed using the following methods.

- **Rating Scales:** Asking respondents to make judgments based on a predetermined scale, such as highly satisfied, satisfied, dissatisfied.
- **Ranking Scales:** Asking respondents to organize their values or preferences in a hierarchy, such as rating recycling methods from one to five based on level of preference.

- **Semantic Differential:** Asking respondents to place their assessment of a certain project aspect somewhere on a multipoint scale between two extremes, for example, asking them whether their neighborhood is rich or poor and providing five or six spaces between the two extremes for them to place a check.
- **Q-sort:** Organizing items or statements into rating categories with a minimum number in each category.

Paper-and-Pencil Tests of Ability: Measurement of participants' knowledge and skills.

- **Achievement Tests:** Measurement of participants' competency in a given subject.
- **Aptitude Tests:** Measurement of participants' potential.

Parametric Statistics: The science of drawing conclusions about a population based on the analysis of sample data drawn from that population.

Pattern Analysis: Evaluating data from several different measures by determining if a pattern of statistically significant differences occur.

Performance Tests: Requires participants to complete a task or make something for assessment of skill.

Record Reviews: Collecting information by reviewing program-related documents.

Sampling-. Collecting data on part of a large population when it would be too expensive or impossible to contact each individual.

- **Stratified Random Sampling-.** Sampling of subdivisions of a population to increase accuracy by homogenizing the groups to be sampled.

Scales:

- **Nominal Scales:** Give scores for classifying individuals, objects or characteristics. For example, you could use a nominal scale to classify participants in a study of outpatient care by illness or condition treated.
- **Ordinal Scales:** Classify individuals or objects that stand in relation to one another, such as relations of preference or quality, for example, organizing military officers by rank.
- **Interval scales:** Similar to ordinal scales, but the distance between any two points on the scale is fixed, such as degrees of temperature on the Fahrenheit scale.
- **Ratio Scales:** Organize data with zero as a starting point. For example, measurement of weight is understood in terms of the number of pounds above zero.

Standard Deviation: The square root of the variance. This is a measure of dispersion or spread about the mean.

Variance: Measures the dispersion or spread of data around the mean. The variance is the standard deviation squared.

Appendex B
Sample Evaluation Plans

Migrant Home Literacy Project
New York State Education Department

Funded by the U.S. Education Department's
Migrant Education Even Start Program

Evaluation Design

The project. evaluation will provide defective information in the areas outlined below. The coordination of evaluation activities will be the responsibility of the Project Director with assistance from the Literacy Specialists, New York State Education Department personnel,
Migrant Education Project Managers and consultants.

Area 1: The Migrant Home Literacy Project will be successful in executing its objective at the 95% level. (i.e., service to 200 migrant adults, 200 migrant children 3 and 4 years old)

Methods:
- Daily records regarding visits will be maintained by Home Literacy visitors.
- Quarterly evaluation reports will be generated by the Literacy Specialists.
- A final evaluation report will be generated by the Project Director.
- The Technical Assistant Center (TAC) will be contacted for assistance in the design and implementation.

Area 2: Proposed project activities will be effective in increasing literacy skills of adult and child participants for 95% of the participants.

Methods:
- Pre and post scores on tests used to evaluate the literacy skills of project participants will be collected and analyzed by research analysts and statisticians available through he Bureau of Evaluation, State Education Department.
- Weekly directed interviews will be maintained for each enrolled adult by the Home Literacy Visitors.
- A survey of the number of migrant adults who attain a Graduate Equivalency Diploma or who enroll in a program designed to further their education will be conducted by the Literacy Specialists.

Area 3: The project inservice design will be effective in preparing professional and paraprofessional personnel as Home Literacy Visits.

Methods:
- A *Participant Survey* regarding their perceptions of the program, the Home Literacy Visitors and their own accomplishments will be conducted by the Project Director.
- A *Home Literacy Visitor Survey* regarding their perceptions of the program and their own effectaveness as Home Literacy Visitors will be conducted by the Project Director.
- The Project Director, Literacy Specialists and Migrant Educataon Managers will conduct monthly in-home supervisory visits to evaluate the effectiveness of Home Literacy Visitors.
- Home Literacy Visitors will complete monthly self-reports regarding inservice needs.

Area 4: Migrant parents recruited and trained as Home Literacy Visitors w3LU be as effective m delivering services and increasing literacy skills of project participants as are professional educators functioning m the same capaclty.

Methods:
- The pre and post scores on tests used to evaluate the literacy @ of project partacipants served by migrant Home Literacy Visitors will be compared to those of participants served by professional Home Literacy Visitors.
- The *Participant Survey* of participants served by migrant Home Literacy Visitors will be compared to those participants served by professional Home Literacy Visitors.

Area 5: The home is an effective learning environment for teaching literacy s to adults and children.

Methods:
- The percentage of adult participants who attain a GED or who enroll in a program designed to further their education will be compared to the percentage of adults who attain a GED or continue their education as a result of enrollment in migrant GRASP projects.

Area 6: The literacy activities developed by the project are appropriate for teaching literacy skills to adults and children and m giving parenting information to parents.

Methods:

- Parents and Home Literacy Visitors will evaluate each adult and child literacy activity m terms of interest, reading level and effectiveness on a scale of 1-10.

Graduation, Reality and Dual-Role
Skills Program for Adolescent Parents
Ohio State Department of Education

Funded by the U.S. Education Department's
National Diffusion Network

Evaluation Plan

A. Quality of the Plan

1. Appropriatedness of the evaluation methods. All sites will use consistent evaluation methods and instruments to measure the attainment of project objectives. The nature of the program requires adaptations to conditions on site. For example, an urban school district is likely to have sufficient numbers of prospective students for classes to meet daily; rural districts on the other hand may not. A teacher housed at a secondary vocational center may find herself traveling to several feeder-school locations to meet with a few students once a week. Reporting forms must allow this type of program variation. At the same time, the form must provide sufficient documentation indicating the adoption site is meeting minimum standards.

2. Quantifiable objectives. Each of the project objectives listed in the BLMP can be quantified. The table below estimates the attainment of each objective by year. The level of difficulty in measuring attainment of each objective varies a great deal from objective to objective.

Objective Measures	**Year I**	**Year 2**	**Year 3**	**Year 4**
1. Number of copies				
Program flier	6,000	4,000	3,000	2,000
Operations manual	750	0	0	0
Videotape	0	10	10	10
Implementation package	70	100	100	100
Training manual	10	10	10	10
Adoption agreement	750	0	0	0
Adolescent Parent Resource Guide	250	0	0	0
2. Number of certified GRADS trainers	10	0	10	0
3. Number of new adoption sites (cumulative estimate)				
Sites in Ohio	20	40	60	80

Objective Measures	Year I	Year 2	Year 3	Year 4
Sites out-of-state	4	10	50	100
Number of expanded programs*	15	20	25	100
4. Student knowledge gain (% increase)	**	10	10	10
Student retention (% increase over national norms)	20	20	20	20
Birth weight (% increase over national norms)	10	10	10	10

* Expanded programs are defined as programs serving additional numbers of students.
** Baseline measures of student knowledge will be developed this year.

B. Scope of the Plan

1. Quality and effectiveness of informational materials- training and follow-la and internal management. As indicated in BLMP tasks 1d and 4a, there will be expert review and revision of each product prior to its trial use in the field. Following this use, feedback will be solicited and changes noted for subsequent revisions of the material. Training sessions (BLMP task 4b) will be evaluated at the end of each workshop. The results will be summarized and incorporated into the annual project report. Notes from the telephone interviews will be compiled and used as a basis for estimating the degree of program adoption at each site. Certain key indicators, such as the average number of contact hours with students per week and the incorporation of GRADS as a class in the school schedule, will be used to determine full installation of the program. The BLMP will be used as an indicator of acceptable progress in the management of this project.

2. Effects of adoptions on students, teachers- and/or administrators. In addition to data collected for the annual report, using a modified version of the Ohio GRADS form, a series of in-depth studies will be conducted on critical issues associated with educational programming for pregnant and parenting teens. A panel of university professors, support agency representatives, and GRADS teachers will be convened at least once per year to review information on GRADS and recommend the pursuit of more intensive evaluations. For example, very little information currently exists on what happens to the babies of students in the GRADS program. Some instructors currently teaching GRADS in Ohio have students whose children are preschool age. A study of these children could be conducted.

   More needs to be known about the impact of GRADS on the occupational planning of its students. This is one of the primary objectives of GRADS.

Goal-setting behavior needs to be investigated particularly among those students who have so much to learn about practical reasoning and problem solving. The goal of the GRADS program is to develop proactive individuals and families who are in charge of their own lives. According to experts (Roosa, Fitzgerald and Carlson, 1981), teen parents expect too little too late from newborn babies. They expect too little cognitively and too much of them physically. A study of the knowledge gain in communication and cooperative decision-making skills is expected to be proposed as an evaluation study.

An evaluation study of the occupational preparation of GRADS students for economic independence will be conducted during the first two years of this project. Evaluation priorities will be identified by the panel; instruments will be located or developed; and data collected in response to program improvement needs. Additional research and evaluation sources will be solicited from private foundations such as, the Joseph P. Kennedy Jr. Foundation, Kellogg Foundation, Mott Foundation and government agencies such as Department of Health and the Department of Human Services. the Department of Human Services.

C. Outcomes Expected

The GRADS program is expected to keep students in school until graduation, increase their knowledge of positive parenting practices, increase the likelihood of delivering a healthy baby, prepare students for the world of work, and help them set goals for balancing work and family. The successful installation of GRADS in other states can provide benefits to pregnant and parenting teens across the country. This project will work with schools, both public and private, both directly and through state departments of education. Many secondary adoptions could be promulgated through liaisons with state departments of education. Leadership by the Ohio Department of Education is responsible for the growth of GRADS within Ohio.

Public School Emphasis Project,
Department of Speech,
University of Florida

Funded by the U.S. Education Department's
Training Personnel for Education of
Individuals with Disabilities Program

Evaluation Plan

D.I. Existing Program Evaluation Procedure

In 1975 the UF Speech-Language Pathology/Audiology program designed and implemented a formal evaluation methodology. (Appendix J) that, with minor modifications, has successfully monitored the program's strengths and weaknesses. It will continue during the proposed funding period. Analyses of 4 questionnaires (Appendix K) have yielded data used to create and/or revise courses, modify teaching procedures, establish new practicum sites, and refine evaluative protocols. Students are evaluated in: 1) academic "core" courses, seminars, and independent studies; 2) qualifying examinations; 3) terminal graduate projects, theses, and dissertations, 4) practica; and 5) classroom teaching experiences. During 1984-85, a departmental self-study was completed, involving faculty, staff, students, and an external review committee. This type of self-evaluation is conducted approximately every 5 years.

In compliance with a State University Systems requirement that students be given the opportunity to evaluate instructors and courses, at least once each year standardized forms are used to generate statistical summaries of student evaluative data on the instructor, course content, lecture presentation, and class discussion. In addition, during an exit interview with the Graduate Coordinator/Clinic Coordinator — used for verification of certification requirements and compilation of permanent records — the student is provided the opportunity for open discussion of his/her experiences within the program.

Between 1982 and 1987, a total of 104 students reported scores on the National Teacher Ex. nation (NTE) in Speech Pathology or Audiology (Table D. 1). Analysis of the raw data revealed that (45%) of the examinees received a score of 700 or better. This superior performance reflects the high admission standards and academic excellence maintained by this program.

Table D. 1. National Teacher Examination (NTE) for University of Florida Speech-Language Pathology/Audiology Students (1982-1987)

Area	Number of Examinees	Average Score	Passing No.	Scores* %	Score Range
Speech-Language	71	667	69	97.1	580-830
Audiology	33	644	31	93.9	570-730
Combined Total	104	655	100	95.5	—

*Students with passing scores on their initial attempt.

D.2. Evaluation of Objectives of PUBLIC SCHOOL EMPHASIS PROJECT

Objective 1. The primary method of monitoring the increase in number of graduate students will be collection of statistics by the Project Director (PD). Each semester data on the number of entering and graduating students will be compiled. The number of students entering from the UF and from other undergraduate programs will also be documented. A yearly report of data will be prepared for review by the Recruitment Committee and Chair. Recruitment activities will be increased or modified if increases in numbers of students do not meet projections in the objective.

In addition, student responses in exit interviews and questionnaires will be examined for possible differences in perception and satisfaction with the program between students from the UF and from other undergraduate programs. Such differences, if any, may indicate a need to review course content; graduate entrance requirements; practicum procedures.

Progress of stipend recipients will be monitored by the PD to insure that all special requirements are met: 40-hour school observation lab, 1-day visit to State offices, presentation of reports on observations to other students, completion of 3-hour seminar, completion of coursework and practica leading to State certification, maintenance of academic standing, inclusion of education personnel on research committee, attendance at "school reality training" meetings, and exit interview with PD.

Objective 2. Monitoring the increase in graduates entering and retaining public school careers will be beyond a mere counting of employment sites. These efforts will focus on feedback from 4 sources:

1) SCT and public school personnel who interact with students,
2) reactions of participating students, 3) academic progress of participating students, and
4) follow-up of graduates' career over 5 years.

The SCT will interview school personnel—speech-language pathologists, classroom teachers, and principals at schools visited by undergraduate observers and by graduate student observers and practicum participants. The PD will meet biweekly with the SCT to monitor student progress and to work out strategies for solving any problems encountered.

Undergraduates having completed the 5 hours of required observation in public schools to write brief "reaction papers" on their experiences. These will be collected by the SCT and discussed with the PD and other faculty members at clinic meetings. Graduate students in in school reality training" groups in clinicians' meetings focusing on career sites, and in the graduate Research Methods class to be asked to write briefly on their perceptions of each component and to make suggestions for modifications. Suggestions from faculty members involved will also be solicited. This feedback will be collected by the SCT and PD and used to improve each component of the project during subsequent years.

Graduate student participants in the 40-hour school observation lab and 1-day visit to State offices will prepare graded oral and written presentations to be made to groups of graduate and/or undergraduate students. The SCT will grade these efforts and provide feedback on student progress to the PD. Students in the 3-hour seminar win be evaluated a graduate course: by exams, projects, in-class discussion, etc.

All graduates will be followed by PD to document their career placement after 1, 3 and 5 years, with note made of those who were stipend recipients. These data will be used to make any needed modifications in the Public School Emphasis, e.g., alternate observation and/or practicum sites, additional course components, guest lecturers.

Objective 3. A rotating schedule of graduate courses and practica offered during the Summer-B term will be kept by the Department Chair to insure that a variety of courses is available. The PD will monitor registration in these courses to document the number of school personnel and of program graduate students enrolling in each. These data will be used to modify advertising efforts to target both populations of students, increasing interaction between graduate students and school personnel. Progress of students in these courses will be evaluated as any graduate course. However, written feedback from students on the implications of course content for school children will also be solicited by the instructors and collected by the PD.

An annual report of the results and recommendations of the PUBLIC SCHOOL EMPHASIS PROJECT will be prepared by the PD and made available to all faculty members and interested school and State education offices personnel.

Geometry Symposium
Campbell Union High School District, San Jose, Calif.

Funded by the National Science Foundation's
Teacher Enhancement Program

Evaluation

Evaluation activities for the Geometry Symposium will be conducted by an external evaluator. The evaluation plan for this training project is based upon attainment of the program's overall goal and supporting objectives. It will: 1) measure the increase in knowledge and skills of geometry teachers; 2) examine the impact of increased teacher skills on students; 3) document the development of new instructional materials. Outcomes win be examined at four levels.

Proposed Evaluation Model

Level	Evaluation Question
1. Reaction	What is the participants' evaluative response to the training process?
2. Acquisition	What knowledge, skills, and attitudes are acquired by the participants?
3. Application	Which of the learned skills/strategies are applied in the work setting?
4. Changes	What changes occur in students and/or the school as a result of the training program?

The program evaluator will assist the project staff in the development/selection of assessment instruments including questionnaires and content tests. Project documents and records of activities completed will be made available to the evaluator to assist in the process monitoring. The evaluator will observe the implementation of program activities at specified intervals and will provide ongoing feedback to facilitate improvement in program processes.

The project evaluator will be responsible for providing interim and end-of-project evaluation reports, written in accordance with NSF guidelines and will also provide a summary of findings for presentation to the project staff, advisory board, school board, and other interested parties.

Drug-Free Families with a Future
Illinois Department of Public Health

Funded by U. S. Department of Health and Human Resources
Office for Substance Abuse Prevention
Model Projects for Pregnant and Postpartum Women and
Their Infants

E. Evaluation
IDPH will contract with the Addictions Research Institute (ARI) at DASA1 to conduct the evaluation. ARI, which is described in section F, will 1 be responsible for all aspects of the evaluation including convening the 1 Evaluation Sub-Committee of the Project Advisory Council (see Figure 1), leading the evaluation team, producing the quarterly and annual evaluation reports, and subcontracting with the Center for Health Services Research at the University of Illinois to perform specific evaluation tasks.

The evaluation questions are:

- Were substance abusing pregnant and parenting women identified, assessed, and provided with appropriate services which address their substance abuse, medical and social services needs?
- What were the impacts of these services on them and their infants?
- How did the Project's integrated service system perform?
- What was learned which should be applied with this population in other communities in Illinois and across the country?

The evaluation will have five major components: orientation to the evaluation, instrumentation and data systems, process, service system impacts, and mother and child impacts. This integrated design will provide a comprehensive evaluation of this project.

Orientation to the Evaluation - As DPH convenes the FWF lead agency and-substance abuse treatment providers from the five demonstration sites and the Project Management Group (see Figure 1), ARI and its consultants will deliver sessions on:

- A common conceptual framework for the evaluation of integrated services and case management;

- The activities necessary across all five sites to allow evaluationof the Project; and

- Resolution of Project implementation questions from the evaluation perspective.

This' component will be delivered during the first four to six months of the Project.

Instrumentation and Data System - The evaluation will fully use the existing data systems developed by DPH for FWF lead agencies and by DASA for substance abuse treatment providers. In addition, a uniform evaluation data collection process will be developed and implemented for: a) assessment and case management activities; b) treatment outcomes for the women; and c) impacts upon the infant.

The existing statewide DPH FWF data system will change on July 1, 1989 from paper reporting to electronic reporting via modem using IBM compatible personal computers. The FWF system has three parts: 1) the Prenatal Services form, submitted 8-12 weeks after the end of pregnancy; 2) the Services During Infancy form, submitted 8-12 weeks after the 1st birthday or death; and, 3) a Quarterly Activity Report. The first two are client specific, capture demographic information, and are completed by the FWF case manager. The third provides aggregate information,-and is compiled by the lead FWF agency based on information from case managers and network members.

Prenatal data elements include such items as the month of pregnancy in which prenatal care began, number of prenatal visits, date pregnancy ended, whether an assessment of needed services was completed, and whether 10 discrete services - including substance abuse counseling were needed and delivered. Infancy data elements include such items as birthweight, the occurrence of well child visits, the results of an accidental injury risk assessment, and delivery of well child/EPSDT services. The quarterly report provides an overview of case managed and prevention activities, including the number of units of substance abuse services delivered.

The DASA treatment provider data system will transition on July 1, 1989 from submission of optically scanned paper forms to transmission of information via diskette using IBM compatible PC's. The counselor is the source and data is submitted on a monthly schedule. Data elements include client demographics as well as the types and amounts of services delivered to individual clients.

The Project will arrange for common client identifiers to be utilized across providers to allow information to be integrated by client. Evaluation reports will present only aggregate information, and the confidentiality requirements will be carefully followed for program evaluation.

Existing data sources will significantly assist the Project to measure accomplishment of the Project objectives. However, up to six new data collection procedures are necessary to allow all of the objectives to be assessed.

1. Comprehensive Assessment — Measurement of the ability of the FWF networks to assess the need for substance abuse, medical and social services will require that the demonstration sites utilize a common assessment instrument for the target population. This task will principally involve systematizing current practices.

2. Services Integration — A system for capturing the client specific practices of the case managers will also be developed. This system will compare needed services to delivered services, track caseloads by worker, determine the percentage of crisis and planned services, and identify changing client circumstances which require modifications to the client service plan. Information from this data system will be used to assist in the development of standards for case management services to this population.

The common assessment instrument and the case management reporting system will be developed, tested and refined during the first nine months of the Project, and in place in all demonstration sites by July 1, 1990.

3. Impacts of Treatment on Women — Measurement of the impacts of the Project activities on pregnant addicts and their infants will utilize procedures specific to this demonstration. The initial client assessment will be repeated at discharge and changes in status on each item analyzed. The alcohol and drug treatmen provider will utilize a client self-assessment instrument which collects information on drug and alcohol use, frequency, dose and route of administration during the previous 30 days. This instrument will be used at intake, every 60 days during service delivery, and at discharge. The self report data will be supplemented by urinalysis at intake and on approximately a 60 day schedule through discharge.

4. Critical Incidents Review — The staff of the substance abuse providers. and FWF case managers will maintain a client log which records critical incidents in the lives of the women in the Project as well as problems experienced with the service delivery system. The information from the critical incidents logs will assist the Project sites to more fully understand the complex life problems experienced by pregnant and parenting substance abusers, to note

changes in patterns of crisis events during treatment and recovery, and to provide important feedback to the local Project teams and the Project Management Group concerning breakdowns in services design and delivery.

5. Infant Impact Information — Failure to thrive information will be collected on the infants. Nurses making home visits will measure head circumference, length and weight on a regular schedule. Project infants will be compared against established standards. Information on obvious birth defects and gestational age at birth will be collected.

6. Comparison to Infants of Untreated Substances Abusers — Hospitals located in the demonstration areas will be asked to participate in a study of the infants of women presenting for childbirth who admit to drug and/or alcohol consumption during pregnancy and who were not enrolled in either FWF or substance abuse treatment services. The study will compare the condition of the infants of Project participants with infants born to untreated mothers. Cook County Hospital in Chicago is currently planning to collect these data, however the other hospitals will not be approached until after the Project is funded.

Process Evaluation — The process evaluation is the shared responsibility of all of the organizations involved in the Project. The IDPH Project Coordinator and ARI will have the leadership roles. The Project Coordinator will be responsible for documenting on a monthly schedule to the ongoing activities of DPH, the Project Advisory Committee, the to Project Management Group, and the five demonstration sites. These reports will compare planned activities to actual accomplishments, identify problems as they arise, and capture information concerning solutions to implementation problems.

ARI will produce a quarterly report, which documents evaluation activities from the same perspective, including the work of the Evaluation Advisory Sub-Committee and evaluation subcontractors. In the first year of the demonstration, these products will focus on data manuals and preliminary findings. As the demonstration progresses, the ARI will report summary information and outcome data.

Service System Impacts — This section indicates the analyses which will be performed and shows the connections between the evaluation and the Project objectives.

Objective I (interagency coordination): The process evaluation described above will provide information concerning Project operations at participating State agencies, the Project Advisory Committee and other groups. These data will assist in Project management and the development of a "how to" manual for use in other locations.

Objective 2 (to link FWF and substance abuse services) and Objective 3 (casefinding and case management capacities): The case management assessment, the FWF Prenatal Services forms and service tracking system will determine the extent to which clients have been screened, assessed, linked with substance abuse treatment, and are receiving the medical and social services they have been assessed as needing.

Objective 4 (improved pregnancy outcomes and reduced infant morbidity): FWF Services During Infancy forms and the client impact data system will capture information about Project infants at birth and during the first year of life. However, as treatment of the mothers substance abuse problem is a critical element in successful pregnancy outcomes and infant wellness, the evaluation will also carefully measure the relative success of the treatment interventions. The impacts of the medical and social service interventions will also be evaluated.

Sample Qualitative Evaluation Section for Grant Proposal

A quantitative and qualitative process evaluation of the intervention, including target population and staff, will be conducted from the project start-up. It will include continuous assessment of project objectives, activities and resources to enable the staff to make changes during each year and to allow the project to be replicable. The evaluation plan for this project will be "user-focused."As Michael Quinn Patton noted in *Utilization-Focused Evaluation*, "Program evaluation uses research methods for gathering information, but evaluation differs fundamentally from basic research in the purpose of data collection ... Research is aimed at truth. Evaluation is aimed at action" (p. 14).

A key component of the evaluation plan will be identifying key stakeholders through an Evaluation Advisory Board. All evaluation instruments and procedures will be selected/developed by the end of the first quarter of the grant and will be piloted and revised, as needed, during the first year. The Evaluation Advisory Board will advise this process.

The qualitative evaluation will provide information regarding the components of the model being used for this project, thus facilitating ongoing development/improvement and providing needed information for replication of the project at other sites. This component of the evaluation will use: 1) key informant (stakeholder) interviews, conducted quarterly using a standardized interview protocol; 2) observations of project events/interventions, conducted on a regular basis, *by* two to three observers using a standardized observation protocol; and 3) surveys/interviews of staff and the target audience regarding implementation of the project, conducted quarterly. The qualitative evaluation will also analyze the content of secondary data sources, such as media (newspaper articles, television stories, etc.) related to project efforts or with potential influence on the target audience, student records and critical incidents/anecdotes collected by staff on a regular basis.

The qualitative evaluator will design tools to allow self-assessment and feedback throughout the project. These tools, which include ongoing assessment of prevention efforts and needs, strategic planning aids, worksheets for monitoring organizational change and program evaluation checklists, will set up a norm of self-assessment to allow for the collection of qualitative data on an ongoing basis.

The evaluation tools designed to collect data, including interview protocols and guidelines for observing project events, will have utility for other projects funded by the sponsoring agency. The evaluation process will be documented to allow replication by future projects. The qualitative evaluator will collect qualitative information quarterly; project staff will collect such information on an ongoing and regular basis. In addition, the qualitative evaluator will meet with the quantitative evaluator for the project on an regular basis to share data.

Quarterly reports will describe: 1) the problem for which the intervention is designed; 2) project goals and objectives (whether they were met as planned, and if not, why not); 3) staff patterns and functioning (including recruitment, qualifications, training and staff perceptions of project implementation and their work environment); 4) the intervention itself (including perceptions of both staff and participants regarding effectiveness); 5) cost/benefit data; 6) preliminary indicators of campus and community impact by the project (including evidence of key stakeholder involvement in project efforts, policy changes related to the project, evidence of local and national networking, etc.); 7) the evaluation procedures and tools being used; and 8) barriers/obstacles impeding project efforts.

Appendix C
Bibliography

Program Evaluation

Bloom, Benjamin, et al., *The Taxonomy of Educational Objectives, Handbook I: The Cognitive Domain.* David McKay, New York, 1956.

Campbell, Donald T. and Julian C. Stanley. *Experimental and Quasi-Experimental Designs for Research.* Rand McNally and Co., Chicago, 1967.

Census 80, Projects for Students. U. S. Bureau of the Census, Washington, D.C.

Claudy, John G., et al., "The Consequences of Being an Only Child: An Analysis of Project Talent Data," American Institutes for Research, AIR-75501-12/79-FR, Palo Alto, Calif., December, 1979.

Fitz-Gibbon, Carol Taylor, and Lynn Lyons Morris. *How to Design a Program Evaluation.* Sage Publications, Newbury Park, Calif., 1987.

Glass, Gene V., Victor L. Wilson and J. H. Gottman. *Design and Analysis of Time Series* Experiments. Laboratory of Educational Research, University of Colorado, Boulder, Colo., 1972.

Hall, Mary. *Getting Funded: A Complete Guide to Proposal Writing,* third edition. Portland State University, Portland, Ore., 1988.

Herman, Joan L., Lynn Lyons Morris and Carol Taylor Fitz-Gibbon. *Evaluator's Handbook.* Sage Publications, Newbury Park, Calif., 1987.

Hoel, Paul G. *Introduction to Mathematical Statistics.* John Wiley and Sons, New York, 1966.

Jensen, Arthur. *Plain Talk About Mental Tests.* Free Press, Macmillan Publishing Co., New York, 1981.

Krathwohl, David, et al., *The Taxonomy of educational Objectives, Handbook II.- The Affective* Domain. David McKay, New York, 1964.

Morris, Lynn Lyons. *Evaluator's Handbook.* Sage Publications, Beverly Hills, Calif., 1978.

Ratzlaff, Leslie A., ed., *The Education Evaluator's Workbook: How to Assess Education Programs,* five volumes. Capitol Publications, Alexandria, Va., 1986-1990.

Riecken, Henry W., and Robert F. Boruch. *Social Experimentation: A Method of planning and Evaluating Social Interventions.* Academic Press, New York, 1974.

Siegal, Sidney. *Nonparametric Statistics for the Behavioral Sciences.* McGraw Hill, New York, 1956.

Simpson, Elizabeth. *The Classification of Educational Objectives, Psychomotor Domain.* Research Project No. OE-5-85-104, University of Illinois, Urbana, Ill., 1956.

Tuckman, Bruce W. *Conducting Educational Research.* Harcourt Brace Jovanovich, New York, 1972.

Van Maanen, John, "The Process of Program Evaluation," *Grantsmanship Center News,* No. 27, Grantsmanship Center, Los Angeles, 1979.

Wallis, W.A. and Roberts, H.V. *Statistics: A New Approach.* Free Press, New York, 1956.

Application of Statistical Methods

Duncan, D.B. "Multiple Range and Multiple F Tests," Biometrics, Vol. 11, pp. 1-42,1955.

Feller, W., An *Introduction to Probability Theory and Its Applications,* third edition. John Wiley and Sons, New York, 1968.

Kendall, M. G. and A. Stuart. *The Advanced Theory of Statistics.* Hafner Publishing Co., New York, 1963.

Mood, A. M., F. A. Graybill and D. C. Boes. *Introduction to the Theory of Statistics,* third edition. McGraw-Ifill, New York, 1974.

Neter, J., and W. Wasserman. *Applied Linear Statistical Models.* Richard D. Irwin, Homewood, Ill., 1974.

Owen, D.B., *Handbook of Statistical Tables.* Addison-Wesley Publishing, Reading, Mass., 1962.

Tucker, H.G. An *Introduction to Probability and Mathematical Statistics.* Academic Press, New York, 1962.

Qualitative Evaluation

Debus, M. *Handbook for Excellence in Focus Group Research.* Academy for Educational Development, Washington, D.C, 1990.

Dennison, D. *Corporate Culture and Organizational Effectiveness*, Wiley Series on Organizational Assessment and Change. Wiley and Sons, New York, 1990.

Greenbaum, T. L. *The Practical Handbook and Guide to Focus Group Research.* D.C. Heath Lexington, MA, 1988.

Patton, M. Q. *Qualitative Evaluation and Research Methods.* Sage Publications, Newbury Park, CA, 1990a.

Patton, M. Q. *Practical Evaluation.* Sage Publications, Newbury Park, 1990b.

Strauss, A. & Corbin, J *Basics of Qualitative Research.* Sage Publications Newbury Park, CA:, 1990.

Van Maanen, J., Editor. *Qualitative Methodology.* Sage Publications, Beverly Hills, 1984.

Evaluation Design

Berk, Richard A. and Rossi, Peter H. *Thinking About Program Evaluation.* Sage Publications, Newbury Park, 1990.

Fyechtling, J. ed. *User-Friendly Handbook for Project Evaluation: Science, Mathematics, Engineering and Technology Education.* National Science Foundation, Directorate for Education and Human Resources. Arlington, VA, 1994.

Scriven, Michael. *Evaluation Thesaurus.* (Fourth edition). Sage Publications, Newbury Park, 1981.

Shadish, William R., Cook, Thomas, D., and Leviton, Laura. *Foundations of Program Evaluation.* Sage, Newbury Park, 1991.

Planning an Evaluation

Brinkerhoff, R. O., Brethower, D. M., Hiuchyj, T., and Nowakowski, J. R. *Sourcebook: Program Evaluation.* Kluwer-Nijhoff, Boston, 1983.

Freeman, Howard E., Rossi, Peter H., and Sandefur, Gary D. *Workbook for Evaluation* (Fourth Edition). Sage, Newbury Park, 1989.

King, Jean A., Morris, L. L., and Fitz-Gibbon, C. T. *How to Assess Program Implementation*. Sage, Newbury Park, 1987.

Light, Richard J., Singer, Judith D., and Willett, John B. *By Design: Planning Research on Higher Education*. Harvard University ,Cambridge, 1990.

Love, Arnold J. *Inernal Evaluation*. Sage, Newbury Park, 1991.

Rossi, Peter H. and Freeman, Howard E. *Evaluation: A Systematic Approach*, fourth edition. Newbury Park, Sage, 1989.

Stecher, Brian M. and Davis, W. Alan. *How to Focus an Evaluation*. Sage, Newbury Park, 1987.

Analyzing and Interpreting Evaluation Data

Fitz-Gibbon, C. T. *How to Analyze Data*. Sage, Newbury Park, 1990.

Reporting and Using Evaluation Findings

Morris, L. L. and Fitz-Gibbon, C. T. *How to Present an Evaluation Report*. Sage, Newbury Park, 1987.

Morris, L. L., Fitz-Gibbon, C. T., and Freeman, Marie E. *How to Communicate Evaluation Findings*. Sage, Newbury Park, 1987.

Cultural Competence in Evaluation

Orlandi, Mario A. ed. *Cultural Competence for Evaluators: A Guide for Alcohol and Other Drug Abuse Prevention Practitioners Working with Ethnic/Racia Communities*. U. S. Department of Health and Human Services, Rockville, MD: 1992, DHHS Publication No. (ADM) 92-1884.

Outcome Funding

Williams, Harold S., Arthur Y. Webb, and William J. Phillips. *Outcome Funding-q: A New Approach to Targeted Grantmaking*, second edition. The Rensselaerville Institute, Rensselaerville, NY: 1993.

Funding for Evaluators

Program Evaluation Grants. The Foundation Center, New York, 1997.

Appendix D
Sources of Evaluation Funders

This section contains more than 40 funders that fund, or have funded in the past, evaluation grants.

California

California Endowment

c/o Mariane Diaz, Exec. Dir.
21550 Oxnard St., Suite 600
Woodland Hills, CA 91367
(818) 703-3311
Source Date: 2/96

Geographic Restrictions:
Limited to CA.

Restrictions:
No grants to individual health practitioners, medical, scientific, or non-applied research, overhead and administrative costs directly related to a proposed project or program in excess of 15%, overhead and administrative costs not directly associated with a proposed project or program, or activities that exclusively benefit members of sectarian or religious organizations.

To Whom:
Community Health Investment Grants: provide health care or health education to uninsured and/or medically underserved populations, including low income, children, women, seniors, disabled, and ethnic groups. This can include needs assessment, planning and program design, strengthening of existing programs, staff skill development and education, equipment and capital expenditures for necessary program effectiveness, **evaluation of program models**, health service, or public policy, **replication of tested and evaluated programs**, public education and awareness promoting personal health responsibility, collaborative efforts to improve health planning and service.

Financial info:
Giving: $31,908,100 for 145 grants.

Application info:
Applications accepted. Application form required with proposal (10 page limit, 2 copies). No deadline.

Recent Grants:

$200,000	California Public Health Foundation, Statewide. To support the planning and development phase of the proposed California Health Interview Survey (CHIS) to generate health-related data at the local level.
$150,000	California Women's Law Center, Statewide. To support the Breast Cancer Legal Clinic's capacity to provide free education and legal assistance to California women with breast cancer.
$84,438	Catholic Social Services of Sacramento, Sacramento. To support outreach to improve access to health and health-related services for the homebound elderly.
$200,000	Central San Joaquin Valley HIV Care Foundation, Fresno. To support the Women In Prison AIDS Case Management program.
$300,000	Central Valley Indian Health Inc., Fresno To support the Native American Women's Health Program's outreach, intervention, and education for rural Native American women and girls.
$350,000	CommuniCare Health Centers, Yolo and Solano. To support the Davis Community Clinic to increase access to primary care for low- income residents in Yolo and eastern Solano Counties.
$50,000	Community Health Group Foundation, San Diego. To convene a two-day forum on border health issues and to compile a resource book on border health data resources.
$186,870	Elwyn, Inc. (dba California Elwyn) Orange and Los Angeles. To establish the South Bay Clubhouse. providing a day program serving individuals with head injuries.
$272,981	EOC Health Services, San Luis Obispo. To expand the Promotoras Comunitarias (Community Health Promoters) program, a Latina woman-to-woman peer education, outreach and leadership program.
$1,000,000	Foundation Consortium for School-Linked Services, Statewide. To support the Foundation Consortium's workplan to improve health outcomes for children, youth, families by promoting comprehensive, integrated school-linked and community-based services.
$50,000	Foundation For Advancements in Science & Education, Los Angeles. To develop a study/viewer guide to enhance the utilization of the documentary film, It Ain't Love, targeting teens to help prevent date/spousal violence.
$200,000	Human Services Charitable Council of Monterey County, Monterey. To support the Children's Dental Center's capacity to provide care, outreach and education to underserved children from low-income farmworker families.
$876,553	LAC + USC Violence Intervention Program, Los Angeles. To cre-

ate a Family Advocacy Center model using collaborative service delivery for the assessment and treatment of sexual assault, domestic violence and child abuse.

$281,535 Linda Vista Health Care Center, San Diego. To expand the Adolescent Health Promotion Project to provide primary and preventive medical/health education services to high-risk adolescents.

$152,000 Los Angeles County Department of Health Services, Planning and Policy Development, Los Angeles. To expand the Los Angeles County Health Risk Assessment Survey to identify and address priority health needs of under-served populations.

$339,325 Asian & Pacific Islander Health Forum, Alameda, Fresno, San Diego. To conduct policy analysis and to provide training and technical assistance.

$61,500 Assistance League of Southern California, Los Angeles. To expand the Alzheimer's Adult Day Services and to explore feasibility of a satellite location.

$591,678 Asthma & Allergy Foundation, Los Angeles. To provide four additional Mobile Asthma Clinics, providing regular preventive asthma care to at risk inner-city children.

$251,440 Boys & Girls Club of Buena Park (The Club), Orange. To expand service capacity and develop the prevention and education efforts of the dental clinic for children.

$99,000 California Black Women's Health Project UCLA, Los Angeles. To assist the Partners in Prevention program to provide low-income Black women and girls access to healthy life-skills training and support to reduce the incidence of obesity.

$25,000 California Department of Health Services, Medi-Cal Managed Care Expansion Evaluation. To support a participatory planning process leading to the development of a plan to evaluate the Medi-Cal managed care expansion plan in 12 counties.

$25,000 National Health Foundation, Los Angeles. To expand the "L.A. Model", a computer-based tool designed to model the need for and supply of health services in L.A. County.

$95,000 Northern Sierra Rural Health Network, Nevada, Lassen, Plumas, Sierra. To implement strategies to strengthen rural health care in four-county regions.

$128,053 Olive Crest Homes & Services for Abused Children, Orange and Los Angeles. To establish the Olive Crest Residential Treatment Center for severely abused children.

$219,000 Pajaro Valley Unified School District, Santa Cruz and Monterey. To enhance an existing Healthy Start school-linked health service program for at-risk children, youth and their families.

$23,500	Peer Education Program of Los Angeles (PEP/LA), Los Angeles. To train 60 peer educators and develop PEP/LA satellite programs for the HIV/AIDS Prevention Program.
$120,000	Pilgrimage Family Therapy Center, Orange. To continue providing baseline mental health services to the medically underserved and support for short and long-term planning.
$210,605	Planned Parenthood of San Diego and Riverside Counties, Riverside. To support service expansion of a reproductive health care center serving low-income women in Indio.
$51,400	Prevent Blindness Northern California, Merced, Stanislaus, and San Joaquin. To duplicate the success of the preschool vision screening program for early detection of amblyopia.
$55,990	Redwood Coast Medical Services, Inc. (RCSM), Northern Sonoma and Southern Mendocino. To stabilize the After Hours Program and its capacity to ensure the accessibility and affordability of health care to the under- served and uninsured population.
$514,633	St. Francis Medical Center/California State University, Dominguez Hills, Los Angeles. To support improvements in primary health care and family health education services in the Bell cluster area.
$260,000	UCLA School of Dentistry, Wilson-Jennings-Bloomfield Venice Dental Center, Los Angeles. To expand dental diagnostic and treatment services for the low-income population in Venice.
$225,000	Valley Community Clinic, Los Angeles. To expand the agency's capability to provide primary health care for low-income population.
$139,000	Valley Organized In Community Efforts, Los Angeles. To develop a public education and awareness project promoting personal health and responsibility.
$124,740	Venice Family Clinic, Los Angeles. To expand the capacity to accommodate increased patient load.
$97,529	Maternal Outreach Management Systems (MOMS), Santa Ana. To provide assistance to indigent pregnant women and new mothers through health education, referral services, support groups, and case management using volunteers and community-based educators through a promoters model.
$60,375	Boys & Girls Club of West San Gabriel Valley, Monterey Park. To establish and maintain a citizen action coalition of community members and youth to reduce and prevent alcohol and drug problems in the San Gabriel Valley.
$98,979	Meet Each Need With Dignity (MEND), Pacoima, San Fernando Valley. To incrementally increase access to basic medical care from one day a week to five days a week over the next two years.

$43,000 REACH L.A., Los Angeles County. To support the HIV prevention program working with adolescent youth in Los Angeles County.

$58,366 Environmental Center of San Luis Obispo County, San Luis Obispo County. To support a planning initiative to promote collaboration and community building on environmental health issues affecting low-income populations in San Luis Obispo County.

$25,000 Ventura County Community AIDS Partnership, Ventura County. To provide matching grant funds for HIV/AIDS prevention programs targeting Latinas in Ventura County.

$35,000 Westside Neighborhood Medical Clinic, Santa Barbara County. To support a management assessment project to enhance technological and management capability for meeting managed care and privatization of county services.

$86,000 Community Action Board of Santa Cruz County, Inc., Santa Cruz County. To provide access to emergency shelter, case management, and voicemail services for homeless people to maintain contact with medical personnel.

$75,000 Santa Cruz Women's Health Center, Santa Cruz, San Benito, San Mateo, and Monterey Counties. To assist with the transition to managed care to accommodate Medi-Cal population; to support enhancement of clinical, administrative operations, staff education, and equipment upgrade.

$99,585 California Public Health Foundation, Stanislaus and Merced Counties. To support screening and educational programs related to cancer prevention and family planning to meet the needs of the underserved Among women and their spouses.

$25,000 Poverello House, Fresno County. To support transportation services for free clinic patients to hospital and specialty clinics.

$25,000 County Meals On Wheels, Alameda County. To provide funding to equip six Meals On Wheels kitchens in Alameda County and to maintain and expand services to home-bound seniors.

$37,500 New Conservatory Theater Center, Rural Northern Counties. To support the 1995-96 HIV Prevention touring season for school children and high-risk youth ages 5 to 19.

$95,000 Oakland Chinese Community Council, Inc., Oakland. To provide low-cost, linguistically and culturally appropriate home care services to low-income Asian elderly in Oakland.

$85,000 Community Medical Centers, Inc., dba San Andreas Family Practice, Calaveras County. To provide clinical and communications

Directors, Officers, Trustees:

Anderson, J. Kendall, Director
Atlas, Richard S., Director
Barnes, Leroy T., Jr., Director
Beacham, Hallie Ann, M.D., Director
Contreras-Sweet, Maria, Director
Coye, Molly Joel, M.D., Director
Crouch, James Alle, Director
Estrada, Leobardo Felipe, Director
Gallegos, Herman E., Director
Hamilton, Marilyn, Director
Hirota, Sherry M., Director
Kwoh, Stewart, Director
Ruis, Frederick R., Director
Stephens, Michael D., Director
Williams, Harold M., Director
Wiltz, Laura S., Director

California Wellness Foundation

c/o Gary L. Yates, Pres.
6320 Canoga Ave., Suite 1700
Woodland Hills, CA 91367-7111
(818) 593-6600
Internet: http://www.tcwf.org
EIN: 954292101
Source Date: 6/96

Geographic Restrictions:
Limited to CA.

Restrictions:
No grants for operating costs, annual fund drives, building campaigns, major equipment, or biomedical research.

To Whom:
Community Health Promotion: programs that achieve change in behaviors, risk factors, or social or physical environments relevant to improving the health of individuals and the community at large, integrate health promotion and prevention efforts into community systems to improve a community's health status.

Teenage Pregnancy Prevention: prevent teenage pregnancy and birth, promote sexual health, improve sexuality education and implement relevant local and state policies.

Work and Health Promotion: improve the health status of California workers and their families through health promotion, programs for smaller work sites and low-wage service, industrial and agricultural workers, improve the health status of the unemployed and underemployed through access to preventive services and/or work.

Violence Prevention Initiative: use a public health approach addressing agent, host, and environment, approaches that involve and empower youth and community residents, innovative programs that address changing local institutional policies and practices to prevent violence.

Population Health Promotion: development of collaborative partnerships and integrated systems of service among the public health system and the private health system that focus on prevention through health promoting policies and programs.

For What:
Conferences and seminars, publications, research, seed money, special projects.

Financial info:
Assets: $880,341,600.
Giving: $36,052,300 for 255 grants.

Application info:
Applications accepted. Submit letter of inquiry. No deadline. Board meets quarterly. Publishes annual report and application guidelines.

Recent Grants:

$57,000	Bay Area Health Ministries, San Francisco, CA. To support the production of a video that will provide an introduction and demonstration of Health Ministry Programs and how they are practiced in congregations.
$100,000	California Adolescent Nutrition and Fitness Program, Berkeley, CA. To support the Regional Training and Technical Assistance Project, a peer-to-peer, culturally sensitive model program for youth service providers and adolescents in five Bay Area counties that promotes healthier lifestyles among 10 to 14 year-olds.
$6,000	California Black Health Network, San Diego, CA. To support the Women's Wellness Weekend in San Diego in February

1997, aimed at increasing women's awareness of health status and risk.

$100,000	City of Inglewood, Inglewood, CA. To support the development of a Youth Master Plan that will involve participation by 1,000 youth in formulating local policy regarding services and programs that directly affect their health.
$40,000	Contra Costa County Community Wellness and Prevention Program, Martinez, CA. To support the Lead Poisoning Prevention Project to mobilize residents and resources to prevent lead poisoning and improve the health status and environment in two low-income neighborhoods in Contra Costa County.
$1,000,000	Education, Training, and Research Associates, Santa Cruz, CA. To support the Children and Youth Community Health Initiative, providing technical resources, communications networking, media conference logistics, and administrative services.
$10,000	Little Tokyo Service Center, Inc., Los Angeles, CA. To support the 1997 Tofu Festival in Los Angeles, to promote health education and nutrition counseling by encouraging low-fat diets.
$100,000	Urban Habitat Program, San Francisco, CA. To support the Community Environmental Health Project to educate community residents about negative impacts of environmental pollution, help residents identify sources of pollution, and make informed decisions toward resolving environmental health problems.
$3,500	California Association for Health, Physical Education, Recreation and Dance, Sacramento, CA. To support a three-hour intensive workshop on the adoption and diffusion of comprehensive school health education at the annual conference in March 1997 in Los Angeles.
$8,000	Drew Child Development Corporation, Los Angeles, CA. To equip adolescents with the skills and education necessary to become peer health educators.
$15,000	The Healthcare Forum Foundation, San Francisco, CA. To support the 1997 Healthier Communities Summit in San Francisco.
$7,000	Pacific Institute for Women's Health, Los Angeles, CA. To develop a "state-of-the-art" paper on key gender sensitive indicators of women's health and wellness in California.
$9,000	Pediatric & Family Medical Center, Los Angeles, CA. To provide health education on issues affecting families of children with asthma.

$6,400	University of La Verne, Center for Health Services Management Research, La Verne, CA. To support a health services symposium in February 1997 to help local hospitals respond to California Senate Bill 697 requiring hospitals to complete a community needs assessment, adopt a community benefits plan and reaffirm their mission statements.
$100,000	Reproductive Health Technologies Project, Washington, DC. To develop a public education campaign to promote understanding, acceptance, and wider access to emergency contraception by women, teens and health care providers in the San Francisco Bay Area.
$104,000	University of California, Los Angeles, CA. To develop and implement a comprehensive family life education program for disabled adolescents.
$100,000	Asian Pacific American Legal Center of Southern California, Los Angeles, CA. To pilot the development and implementation of a diversity training and conflict resolution curriculum to be offered to teachers and students in two Los Angeles public high schools.
$25,000	California Child, Youth and Family Coalition, Sacramento, CA. To support the Information and Education Program to inform policymakers, opinion leaders, program practitioners, and the general public about prevention-based public policies, program strategies, and services that shape the lives of youth.
$5,000	California State Coalition of Rape Crisis Centers, Los Angeles, CA. To support the 18th annual conference of the National Coalition Against Sexual Assault in San Francisco.
$100,000	California State University, Fresno Foundation, Fresno, CA. To conduct research that identifies risk and protective factors for youth gang involvement and assaultive behavior in a multi-ethnic, impoverished community.
$50,000	Center for Third Work Organizing, Oakland, CA. For Youth of Oakland United, a community-based youth organizing and advocacy project that will train a multi-ethnic team of youth to organize Oakland youth and adults to educate local policymakers about the need for youth violence prevention.
$10,000	Education Development Center, Inc., Oakland, CA. To convene a small interdisciplinary forum to initiate the development of an intergovernmental action plan for violence prevention activities in the State of California, on March 5 and 6, 1997.

$40,000	Legal Community Against Violence, San Francisco, CA. To support the Local Ordinance Project, which provides legal assistance to local governments to pass legally defensible firearms measures.
$100,000	The Marin Institute, San Rafael, CA. To continue a research study that supports community-based approaches to preventing alcohol-related youth violence.
$80,000	National Council on Crime and Delinquency, San Francisco, CA. To pilot a one-year project in San Diego County to design a continuum of health and support services for at-risk girls and young women of color based on a public health model of violence prevention.
$100,000	Prevention Research Center, Berkeley, CA. To support a study to qualitatively examine the link between alcohol outlet density and youth violence through assessment of predominantly Mexican-American communities.
$5,000	Santa Cruz Barrios Unidos, Santa Cruz, CA. To support the transportation of underserved, low-income families who have incarcerated family members in Santa Cruz County prisons and juvenile institutions to preserve positive family relations and promote family involvement in violence prevention.
$100,000	The Tomas Rivera Center/Policy Institute, Claremont, CA. To support a comprehensive, comparative study of the elements and "best practices" that determine exemplary community-based policing programs targeting youth in Latino and non-Latino communities.
$150,000	University of California, Davis, CA. To support a comprehensive study on firearm policy and prevention.
$100,000	University of California, Los Angeles, CA. To study youth violence in Asian-American communities in California.
$100,000	University of California, Riverside, CA. To conduct research that can be utilized to develop effective violence prevention programs that are client-outcome based and cost efficient.
$100,000	University of California, Santa Barbara, CA. To conduct research that can be utilized to develop effective prevention-based youth development and aggression reduction programs for ethnic minority boys and girls ages 8 to 12.
$70,000	Women Against Gun Violence, Los Angeles, CA. To support the Community Education and Outreach programs, to prevent violence in Los Angeles County.
$15,000	Bay Area Social Services Consortium, Berkeley, CA. To print and disseminate 5,000 copies of a booklet about welfare reform and its implications for the health of Californians.

$50,000	California Child Care Resource and Referral Network, San Francisco, CA. To conduct a family child care provider recruitment and training project in two Central Valley counties.
$60,000	California Institute for Mental Health, Sacramento, CA. To undertake research and development activities to create a package of behavioral health services that will be offered to welfare recipients to promote their health and facilitate their employment.
$75,000	College of San Mateo, San Mateo, CA. To provide support for the Workplace Wellness for Adult Disabled training program to better serve the disabled in San Mateo County who seek re-entry into the labor force.
$10,000	Hispanics in Philanthropy, Berkeley, CA. To plan and host a regional conference tentatively titled, "A Funders Dialogue on Technological Capacity Building Among Latino Nonprofits and Communities."
$75,000	University of California, Berkeley School of Public Health, Berkeley, CA. To develop a report on workplace health and safety issues facing rural youth, make strategic recommendations, and implement a community demonstration project in the Central Valley.
$10,000	Breast Cancer Action, San Francisco, CA. To support the production of "Rachel's Daughters," a documentary investigating the known and suspected causes of breast cancer.
$100,000	California Food Policy Advocates, San Francisco, CA. To support a multi-faceted project aimed at minimizing the harshest consequences of nutrition and income program changes; developing community capacity to initiate systems change; and reviewing the welfare reform bill for potential assistance for families.
$20,000	California Nonprofit Policy Council, Los Angeles, CA. To support the second annual California Nonprofits Week, April 21 - 25, 1997, in Sacramento and other sites.
$10,000	Centro del Pueblo, San Francisco, CA For general support.
$5,000	Children's Defense FundWashington, DC. To support the Los Angeles "Beat the Odds" Awards Program in April 1997 honoring Southern California high school students who have demonstrated excellence.
$25,000	Gifts to Share, Inc., Sacramento, CA. To support the 'Prime Time Team' Program, to mobilize and involve teens in the basics of early childhood development and to provide for teen participation in educational life skills workshops, community projects and work experience while attending school.

$72,000	Girls Incorporated, Los Angeles, CA. To provide girls with the skills necessary to enhance their self-esteem and overall sense of "wellness" through the use of Girls Incorporated research-based programming.
$58,000	Group Health Cooperative of Puget Sound, Seattle, WA. To conduct a statewide conference on community-based health programs.
$25,000	Health Care Council of Orange County, Santa Ana, CA. For general support to develop a viable health care system for all residents of Orange County; and to promote improved access to health care through research, coalition building, public and professional health education, and advocacy for better services.
$10,000	Living Well Project, San Francisco, CA. To support the merger between Living Well Project and the Asian AIDS Project.
$5,000	Manpower Demonstration Research Corporation, San Francisco, CA. To support a statewide conference, "Choices and Challenges: Welfare Reform in California," to provide a forum for dialogue on welfare reform.
$15,000	March of Dimes Birth Defects Foundation, Burbank, CA. To support a perinatal needs assessment describing the current needs and access to care of pregnant/parenting families in Southern California, for future planning of maternal-infant health care services.
$20,000	Mental Health Association of Alameda County, Oakland, CA. For general support with an emphasis on primary and secondary prevention programs that educate about mental illness and its effective treatment, provide screening services, and create access to appropriate care.
$10,000	Narcotic Educational Foundation of America, Santa Clarita, CA. To support the Office of National Drug Control Policy's conference on methamphetamine abuse in January 1997 in San Francisco.
$100,000	National Academy of Sciences, Washington, DC. To disseminate information about the health of California's immigrant children and families.
$100,000	National Advisory Board on Ethics in Reproduction, Washington, DC. To support development of an endowment to provide more stable long-term support for the organization's administration and programs.
$20,000	Pacific Institute for Women's Health, Los Angeles, CA. To support a Women's Health Summit in February 1997 and

related activities to address the health care delivery and policy issues facing women in Los Angeles County due to imminent implementation of the county's new managed care system.

$25,000 Paradigm Productions, Inc., San Francisco, CA. To support the production of "The Fight in the Fields: Cesar Chavez and the Farmworkers' Struggle," a two-hour film documenting the creation of the first successful union of farmworkers, to be aired nationally on PBS in April 1997.

$5,000 Pharmacists Planning Services, Inc., Sausalito, CA To help sponsor a two-day conference, "Overcoming Barriers to Condom Use," in February 1997 in Berkeley.

$25,000 Project Headway, Inc., Northridge, CA. For general support.

$140,000 Project on Community Capacity and Institution Building, San Francisco, CA. To involve low-income community leaders in the welfare reform system change efforts in the Greater Bay Area.

$25,000 Public Law Center, Santa Ana, CA. To support the Health Care Education and Assistance Project to help Orange County's indigent population in the transition and utilization of Cal-OPTIMA, the county's new managed care system.

$84,000 RAND Corporation, Santa Monica, CA. To objectively assess the health, financial and other benefits of early childhood interventions.

$10,000 Social Policy Corporation, New York, NY. To support a working seminar in New York in March 1997 on strategies to implement self-help groups in human service agencies and to disseminate policy recommendations to 150 organizations in California.

$10,000 State of California Department of Social Services, Sacramento, CA. To sponsor the first "Run for Their Lives" event, to raise money and to promote awareness for the child abuse and neglect prevention programs and services sponsored by the California State Children's Trust Fund.

$3,000 University of California, San Francisco, CA. To support the keynote presentation at the 30th annual post-graduate course, Advances and Controversies in Clinical Pediatrics, May 15-17, 1997, in San Francisco.

$150,000 Youth Advocates, Inc., San Francisco, CA. To support Cole Street Clinic's capacity to provide health promotion services to high-risk youth in San Francisco.

$5,000 Adolescent Pregnancy Child Watch of Los Angeles, CA. "Prevention Strategies for Teen Pregnancy: Unlocking the Public Policy Dilemma," Symposium designed to translate effective prevention strategies into coherent public policy in Pasadena.

$426,000	**North Bay Health Resources Center, CA. Evaluation of Teen Alcohol Prevention Project, program designed to reduce teen access and use of alcohol in 4 Noah Bay counties.**
$500	Valley Cultural Center. Improvements to new concert pavilion at Warner Park.
$500	Volunteer League of the San Fernando Valley. Centre Clothes Corner, providing low-income school children in San Fernando Valley with clothes and hygiene items.
$2,500	CA Consortium for the Prevention of Child Abuse. Participate in 8 day train-the-trainers program at Family Stress Center in Hawaii.
$288,000	**Sierra Kings District Hospital. Establish and evaluate CA Diabetes and Pregnancy Program for women in South Fresno County.**
$450,000	Senior Health and Peer Counseling. Provide screening, health promotion, and preventive care to senior women in 3 Samoan and Native American communities in Los Angeles County.
$1,551,000	California Public Health Foundation. Establishment of California Center for Health Improvement to provide public education; technical expertise concerning health policy improvements to policymakers and other key parties; research and policy analysis on key health: issues and development and implementation of groups and conferences on key issues with dissemination of results.
$230,000	**Southeast Asian Health Project. Implement and evaluate comprehensive home and school-base program to foster healthy lifestyles among Cambodian families.**

Directors, Officers, Trustees:

Abascal, Ralph Santiago, Director
Davidson, Ezra D., Jr., M.D., Director
Kizer, Kenneth W., M.D., Director
Lytle, Alice A., Director
Margen, Sheldon, M.D., Director
Mink, Earl G., Director
Yates, Gary L., Director, Officer

Compton Foundation, Inc.

c/o James R. Compton, Pres.
545 Middlefield Rd. Suite 178
Menlo Park, CA 94025
(415) 328-0101
EIN: 943142932
Source Date: 12/96

Geographic Restrictions:
International giving. U.S. giving for peace, population, and environment.

Restrictions:
No grants to individuals or capital or building funding.

To Whom:
Peace and World Order: prevent the proliferation of nuclear and other weapons of destruction, influence public policy to promote peaceful means of settling international disputes, support multilateral approaches to international issues, strengthen existing international institutions so that they may evolve into organizations that can improve law and order among peoples of the world, address the interrelationship between peace and world order, population growth, and environmental degradation, conflict resolution, national security and human rights, equitable distribution and management of technology, resources, energy, and food, economic interdependence and peace in developing countries, economic conversion.

Population: Education of the public, graduate training and fellowships, especially for students from developing countries, in the social sciences and demography, applied policy research, advocacy, family planning services, management assistance for family planning programs in developing countries, especially in Mexico, Central America, and sub-Saharan Africa, interrelationship between population, peace and world order, and environmental issues, U.S. population policy, **evaluation of family planning programs in developing countries**, problems of urban population growth, role and status of women in developing countries, problems of illegal immigration from Mexico to the U.S., teenage pregnancy prevention.

Environment: Land, river, and watershed protection and management for purposes of long term habitat and ecosystem preservation and restoration, graduate level training programs in environment and sustainable development for individuals from developing countries (this is Foundation initiated and not open to unsolicited proposals), energy conservation, incentives for energy efficiency, development of renewable resources and addressing the problem of overconsumption, both in U.S. and internationally, understand

and deal with adverse environmental consequences of population growth particularly in Mexico, Central America, and Sub-Saharan Africa.

24% of funding limited to higher education, community welfare and social justice, civil rights, health and mental health, services for children and youth, cultural programs, arts in the San Francisco Bay Area (San Francisco, Marin and Santa Clara Counties).

For What:
Endowment funds, fellowships, general purposes, matching funds, scholarship funds, operating budgets, continuing support, annual campaigns, seed money, special projects, consulting services.

Financial info:
Assets: $67,733,900 (from 1994 990PF).
Giving: $3,966,300 for 480 grants (high: $200,000; low: $100).

Application info:
Applications accepted. Submit proposal (4 page limit). Deadline is Mar. 1 and Oct. 1. Board meets in May and Dec. Publishes application guidelines.

Recent Grants:

$25,000	Albert Einstein Institution Civilian-Based Defense Initiative.
$53,575	Brown University Population Studies and Training Center Predoctoral Fellowships in Population.
$26,763	IPAS Safe Abortion Care in Nicaragua.
$33,000	Conservation International Wetlands Program: Sonora, Mexico.
$6,000	Junior Achievement of the Bay Area.
$40,000	Vassar College Minority Access Program.
$5,000	Second Harvest Food Bank.
$6,500	Joffrey Ballet National Tour to, San Francisco, CA.
$10,000	Library Foundation of San Francisco, CA.
$20,000	Global Fund for Women.

Directors, Officers, Trustees:
Compton, James R., Director, Officer
Compton, Randolph O., Director
Eddy, Edith T., Director
Luke, Mary M., Director
Powell, Lee Etta, Director
Stephens, Ann C., Director, Officer
Thompson, Kenneth W., Director
Wayburn, Laurie A., Director

Haigh-Scatena Foundation

c/o Ronald W. Clement, Exec. Dir.
P.O. Box 4399
Davis, CA 95617-4399
(916) 758-5327
EIN: 941753746
Source Date: 8/95

Geographic Restrictions:
Limited to northern CA.

Restrictions:
No grants to individuals, equipment, endowments, capital funds, general operating funds, projects limited to media production and distribution, projects limited solely to direct or treatment services.

To Whom:
At-risk children, youth and their families. Priority consideration for primary prevention projects targeting very young children. Prevent delinquency, child abuse, school failure, teen pregnancy, academic failure, homeless, welfare dependency, and alcohol and drug abuse.

For What:
Research, special projects, technical assistance, loans, seed money, conferences and seminars, emergency funds.

Financial info:
Assets: $3,985,400.
Giving: $234,600 for 20 grants (high: $35,000; low: $1,000).

Application info:
Applications accepted. Submit concept letter (3 page limit). No deadline. Board meets generally bi-monthly. Publishes application guidelines and grants list.

Recent Grants:

$36,000	California Consortium to prevent Child Abuse, Sacramento. "Healthy Families California". Fourth Year support of efforts to promote neonatal home visitation services for first time, high risk parents statewide
$30,000	Children's Research Institute of California, Sacramento. "The California Partnership for Children". Developmental underwriting of a multi-faceted organization committed to improving the status of children statewide

$30,600	San Francisco Study Center. Support over three years to research, write and publish monographs on the development of the "California Partnership for Children"
$30,000	**California Court Appointed Special Advocate Association, San Francisco. "Health end Education Passport Advocacy Project". Support of efforts to improve and evaluate services for dependent children in El Dorado, Humboldt and Lassen Counties**
$26,500	Indian Dispute Revolution Services, Sacramento. "Indian Youth Leadership Development Project". Support of efforts to identify end train young Indian leaders at several reservations and rancherias
$20,000	Sacramento Valley Organizing Community Second year support of a congregation based community organizing project in Solano County
$20,000	**The Mentoring Center, Oakland. Support over two years of data collection and evaluation activities**
$15,000	California Reinvestment Committee, San Francisco. "Community Access to Capital". Support of efforts to increase capital investment and access to financial services in poor communities statewide
$15,000	Commonweal, Bolinas. "Protect the Public, Protect the Children".Third year support of efforts to promote a rationale juvenile justice system statewide
$14,000	Western States Youth Services Network, Petaluma. To present the fourth annual Haigh-Scatena Foundation Grantee Retreat
$6,500	California Child, Youth and Family Coalition, Sacramento. "Youth Leadership Development". Second year support of efforts to promote the involvement of young people statewide in public policy matters impacting youth
$5,000	Parent Services Project, Fairfax. Fifth year support of training, technical assistance and resource development services for an affiliated group of low-income preschools throughout California and several other states
$2,500	Northern California Grantmakers, San Francisco. "Summer Youth Project". Continuing contribution to a pooled fund supporting summertime enrichment activities at hundreds of sites throughout the San Francisco Bay Area
$2,500	East Bay Community Foundation, Oakland. "East Bay Funders". Fifth year contribution to a collaborative effort of private funders to improve conditions in three East Bay neighborhoods

$2,000	Sonoma County Community Foundation, Santa Rosa. To assist West County Community Services, Guerneville, in recovering from flood damage
$1,000	Nonprofit Resource Center, Sacramento. Continuing support of services for nonprofit organizations

Directors, Officers, Trustees:

Bacigalupi, Jean, Director, Officer
Dunckel, Jeanette M.., Director
Eber, Andrew J., Director
Goldstein, Bruce D., Director, Officer
Haigh, Isabelle Simi (d), Donor
Haigh, Vivien (d), Donor
Hom, Gloria S., Director
Perkins, Arnold X. C., Director
Templin, Gary A., Director
Tower, Caroline, Director
Uribe de Mena, Joanna, Director, Officer

John Randolph Haynes & Dora Haynes Foundation

c/o F. Haynes Lindley, Jr., Pres.
888 W. Sixth St. Suite 1150
Los Angeles, CA 90017-2737
(213) 623-9151
E-mail: hfoundatio@aol.com
Internet: http://www.usc.edu/Library/Haynes/
EIN: 951644020
Source Date: 8/95

Geographic Restrictions:
Limited to the Los Angeles, CA, area [southern].

Restrictions:
No grants to individuals, building or endowment funding, or operating funds.

To Whom:
Study and research in the political science, economics, public policy, history, social psychology and sociology.

For What:
Fellowships, research, scholarship funds, internships.

Financial info:
Assets: $41,981,600.
Giving: $2,540,200 for 45 grants (high: $400,000; low: $500).

Application info:
Applications accepted. Submit 20 copies of proposal. No deadline. Board meets quarterly. Publishes application guidelines.

Recent Grants:

$67,275	California Institute of Technology, for the research and writing of a book, "A World to Gain: African Americans and the Making of Los Angeles, 1890-1940," Douglas Flamming, Principal Investigator.
$118,760	University of Southern California, Department of Religion, with a subcontract to University of California, Santa Barbara, Department of Religious Studies, for a study, "Religion and Multiethnicity in Los Angeles: Redefining Religion's Civic Role," Wade Clark Roof, Donald E. Miller, and John B. Orr, Co-Principal Investigators.
$82,000	**University of Southern California, School of Education, for an evaluation of "The Compton Project," Priscilla Wohlstetter and Donald W. Ingwerson, Co-Principal Investigators.**
$321,954	The Claremont Graduate School, Program in Politics and Policy, for "Solutions for Curtailing Gangs, Violence and Drugs in the Los Angeles County Schools," George T. Felkenes and Harold K. Becker, Co-Principal Investigators.
$180,281	University of California, Los Angeles, Lewis Center fair Regional Policy Studies, for "Manufacturing Matters: A Sectoral Approach to Combatting Low Wages in Los Angeles," Michael Storper, Principal Investigator, with Canal Zahin, Goetz Wolff, and Peter Clancy.
$288,936	Occidental College, for "Linking Regional and Community Development in a Changing Economy," Manuel Pastor, Jr., Peter Drier, Marta Lopez-Garza, and Eugene Grigsby, Co-Principal Investigators.
$269,281	University of California, Los Angeles, Graduate School of Education and Information Studies, for "Getting Along and Getting On: An Intervention to Increase Social Skills and Academic Motivation and Decrease Recidivism in Adolescent Offenders," Sandra Graham, Principal Investigator, with Bengt Muthen, Connie Kasari, and Michael Seltzer.

$79,603	The University of Southern California, School of Urban and Regional Planning, for "California Immigration and the American Dream: Integration of the New Arrivals," Dowell Myers, Principal Investigator.
$30,814	The Southwest Museum, for cataloging the Braun Research Library's collection of glass plate negatives of work by early Southern California photographers.
$73,803	The University of Southern California, School of Public Administration, for a study of "Options for Orange County's Government Reorganization in a Regional Context," Francine F. Rabinovitz, Principal Investigator.
$30,016	The Southern California Library for Social Studies and Research, for accessing twentieth century Los Angeles social history sources within the Library's collection.
$75,434	University of California, Santa Cruz, Environmental Studies Board, for research into "Community and Conservation in Southern California," Daniel Press, Principal Investigator.
$106,513	National Public Radio, toward The 1996 National Public Radio Election Project in Southern California.
$25,000	KCRW National Public Radio, toward the production of the public affairs program, Which Way, L.A.

Walter S. Johnson Foundation

c/o Kimberly Ford, Pgm. Off.
525 Middle field Rd., Suite 110
Menlo Park, CA 94025
(415) 326-0485
E-mail: info@wsjf.org
Internet: http://www.wsjf.org
EIN: 237003595
Source Date: 12/95

Geographic Restrictions:
Primarily in northern CA with emphasis on San Francisco Bay area, CA, and in Reno and surrounding Washoe County, NV.

Restrictions:
No grants for religious purposes, private schools, individuals, deficit financing, memorial funds, capital or endowment funding, general support, or equipment.

To Whom:
Education (47% of funding): professional development of educators, curriculum development, parental involvement in children's education.

Ensure the well-bring of children and youth (25% of funding): promote positive life-styles, respond to the complex academic, social, and emotional needs of children, prevent drug and alcohol abuse, teen pregnancy, and violence, community-based youth development and education support programs, provide technical assistance, curriculum development, networking, and professional development opportunities for community-based programs, families in crisis, such as homeless, divorce, violence, or institutionalization of a parent, provide children with stability and skills to cope, neighborhood development, early childhood education, early intervention for children at risk of failing in school.

Transition to adulthood (27% of funding): transition to work, youth as resources.

Families in Crisis (4% of funding): children in families facing transitions and crises such as homelessness, divorce, violence, or institutionalization of a parent for short-term assistance.

For What:
Operating budgets, seed money, special projects, research, technical assistance.

Financial info:
Assets: $69,894,700.
Giving: $2,372,500 for 80 grants (high: $20,000; low: $3,000).

Application info:
Applications accepted. Submit proposal. Deadline is Sept. 20, Jan. 13, Mar. 28, and June 20. Board meets in Apr. July, Jan., and Oct. with final notification in 2 to 4 months. Publishes annual report with application guidelines.

Recent Grants:

$70,000	Community Network for Youth Development (CNYD), Redwood City. over one year continued funding for CNYD, which, over the past the years, has provided high-quality professional development opportunities for youth workers through workshops, conferences, and individualized support. The grant supported the development of new workshops on such topics as technology, fostering resiliency, media access, and cultural and ethnic diversity.

$60,000 East Oakland Boxing Association (EOBA), Oakland. over two years continued to support EOBA's further development of Smart Moves, an after-school education program for youth. The new funding enabled EOBA to increase its outreach to students and parents as well as to deepen the content of its program.

$80,000 Girls Inc. of Alameda County, San Leandro. over two years continued support for the Eureka Teen Achievement Program, an intensive three-year summer program for low-income middle school girls that aims to enhance their self-confidence, decrease their likelihood of becoming pregnant, and facilitate their success in math, science, and computer courses in school. The new grant supports the ongoing summer programs and evaluation process, enables Girls Inc. to more than double the number of the school-year Saturday follow-up sessions it offers, and helps program alumni make the transition to high school-level programs.

$50,000 LarkinWorks, Inc., San Francisco. over two years for Larkin Business Ventures facilitated the research and development of several potential business opportunities that would allow former homeless youth to increase their job experience and work readiness. The recently opened Ben and Jerry's ice cream shop in the San Francisco marina district, which is staffed and operated by former homeless youth, is a prototype for this kind of opportunity. The funding supports feasibility studies and business development expenses.

$15,000 Polynesian Community Services (PCS), East Palo Alto. over one year funded PCS's educational assistance programs for Polynesian students on the San Francisco peninsula. PCS provides academic counseling, career counseling, and tutoring services for students as well as a support group for parents to help them better understand and participate in their children's education.

$90,000 East Bay Agency for Children, Oakland. for the Hawthorne Community Collaborative over two years enabled the Collaborative to hire a coordinator and a part-time assistant for the Family Resource Center at the Hawthorne-Whitton Year-Round School in order to be more responsive to the needs of the school families. In addition, the grant frees the principal to spend more time working with faculty on curriculum reform.

$90,000 Peninsula Community Foundation, San Mateo. for the Peninsula Partnership for Children, Youth and Families. over two years continued support for the Peninsula Partnership, which is governed by representatives of schools, cities, community-based organizations and businesses, high school students, foundation representatives, and county executives. The partnership works with six communities to design and implement approaches that support the healthy development of children, particularly those from low-income communities.

$15,000 Raphael House, San Francisco. for Children and Trauma Education Network (CTEN), Palo Alto. over one year strengthened community agencies' follow-up support services for former homeless children and families. Grant funds enabled CTEN to complete and disseminate a formal twelve-week curriculum for this use by support groups.

$50,000 San Francisco Foundation, San Francisco. for the Foundations Consortium for School-Linked Services, Sacramento. over one year continued to support a state-level partnership effort to provide, through school-linked, integrated services, more preventive and effective health, mental health, and social services for children and families from low-income communities. The funding also supported the development of interagency family support and preservation programs on the county level.

$50,000 San Francisco Foundation, San Francisco. for the Greater Bay Area Family Resource Network over two years to the Family Resource Network to expand and deepen its work with family resource centers through technical assistance and professional development activities. The network will work with Alameda and Contra Costa Counties to redesign service delivery to low-income families and with San Francisco City/County to develop family centers, offering youth development and family support activities. Washoe County School District, Reno, NE. $40,000 over one year established a Family Resource Center at Desert Heights Elementary School. This grant continued the previous year's work of creating a community center to improve the coordination and access to services for school families. Burlingame School District, Burlingame. $4,960 helped plan a New Teacher Training Program to institutionalize and expand on existing support mechanisms for teachers during their first years of teaching. A mentor teacher worked with new teachers and the district to create a curriculum for a multiple-year program of training and support for new teachers.

$200,000 Developmental Studies Center (DSC), Oakland. over two years provided professional development opportunities and support to elementary and middle schools that recognize the interdependence of children's social, intellectual, and ethical development. DSC is one of the few national school reform organizations to accompany its in-depth professional development with curriculum materials focused on improving actual instruction. The grant enables DSC to broaden its scope and serve a larger number of schools and districts.

$150,000 Early Childhood Resources (ECR), Carte Madera. over three years continued support for the Student-Centered Learning Project, based on constructivist teaching theory, in four to six Oakland schools. The funding provides professional development for teachers, as well as training for teacher-leaders, who will then train colleagues throughout the district. The grant allows ECR to expand its professional development efforts, previously offered in kindergarten through second grade in these schools, to teachers through the fifth grade.

$22,903 Petaluma Wildlife and Natural Science Museum, Petaluma. over two years continued support for a science education project in which high school students act as docents, helping to teach elementary students about the animals in the museum. The additional funding facilitates the expansion of the project to a new district, enabling the teacher-authors of the curriculum to revise lesson plans that prepare students to visit the museum.

$5,000 Sacramento County Office of Education, Sacramento. supported planning for school reform in rural Northern California. Rural school representatives participated in a series of meetings to assess the need, willingness, and readiness of rural schools and districts to form a rural schools league that would strive to create powerful learning situations for all its students.

$3,200 Salinas City School District, Salinas. supported planning for a summer pilot program, the initial step in implementing the "Vision of 2005" plan for districtwide reform through curriculum redesign. San Carlos School District, San Carlos. $130,000 over three years continued support for the San Carlos Charter Learning Center, which fosters project-based learning in multi-age, technology-rich classrooms. The charter makes wide use of community resources as a central part of teaching and learning. The grant funds will provide professional development opportunities for the charter staff, as well as for teachers from throughout the district' allowing them to work on joint research and development efforts.

$50,000 San Francisco Foundation, San Francisco. for the Bay Area School Reform Collaborative (BASRC). over one year enabled BASRC to help build the capacity of schools to pursue substantive reform. The grant funded intensive summer work with teachers and administrators from schools engaged in restructuring their curriculum and instruction, as well as initial research and development activities on issues identified as critical to the success of regional reform efforts.

$120,000 San Francisco State University, San Francisco. for the Bay Area School Development Program. over two years continued support for ten schools in their implementation of the School Development Program. The program has focused on parent involvement, mental health, and school governance as means to improve student outcomes. The additional funding enables educators in the participating schools to focus their efforts more directly and intensively on review and revision of curriculum and instruction.

$5,000 Santa Cruz City Schools, Santa Cruz. enabled planning for the next phase of the school restructuring process at Santa Cruz High School. Having established a block schedule that allows teachers to work with fewer students for longer periods of time, the faculty's next goal is to facilitate collaboration among faculty and to begin developing standards for graduation exhibitions. Santa Cruz County Office of Education, Capitola. $165,000 over two years enabled the New Teacher Project to intensify as well as expand its work with new teachers in the Santa Cruz area to include all teachers. The project will initiate partnerships with Bay Area school districts that are interested in designing similar beginning teacher support programs. The grant also supports in-depth work with a restructuring school to create an exemplary "professional development school," the completion and dissemination of a program assessment, and the production of a videotape to disseminate the project's work to a broader audience.

$37,505 Spreckels Union School District, Spreckels. for Under Construction. over one year gave more intensive support to, and increased the number of, Monterey County teachers implementing constructivist hands-on, student-centered teaching in their classrooms. The funds also facilitated planning for a model classroom to demonstrate constructivist teaching, working with California State University, Monterey Bay to develop a graduate program in education, and establishing a library of constructivist literature.

$75,000 Tides Foundation, San Francisco. for Bay Area Region Coalition of Essential Schools (BARGES). over one year to BARGES provided intensive professional development and ongoing support to six "lead" high schools and more generalized support to a network of more than forty other schools. Lead schools received on-site support from a trained coach, typically a master teacher, to encourage their progress toward schoolwide reform and restructuring

$101,736 Washoe County School District, Reno, Nevada. over one year trained teachers in Reading Recovery, a method for assisting first graders who are having difficulty learning to read. The grant paid a trained Reading Recovery teacher for one year to work halftime with twelve first-grade teachers. A district teacher concurrently took the one-year Reading Recovery program, enabling her to become a teacher/leader and train additional teachers in subsequent years.

$50,000 California Department of Education, Sacramento. for Partnership Academy Unit. over one year provided technical assistance and training for eight schools that are implementing school-to-work "partnership academies" without state support. The grant supported professional development for teams of teachers to begin to better integrate their curriculum through project-based learning and thematic instruction.

$88,000 Fremont Union High School District, Cupertino. over one year supported the redesign initiative at Homestead High School. The funding enabled further progress in the reorganization of the school into small houses with career foci, where students are taught by interdisciplinary teams using unifying themes and projects and are offered service learning, mentorship, and internship opportunities.

$57,700 Galt Joint Union High School District, Galt. over one year subsidized the cost of transforming a strong agricultural program into an Academy of Agriculture at Galt High School located in the central valley. Funding for the academy provided the teachers with preparation time to work on curriculum integration and thereby position the program for long-term funding from the state.

$100,000 Jobs for the Future (JFF), Boston, MA. over one year supported JFF's work with four Northern California communities in planning and implementing large-scale school-to-career initiatives. JFF provided technical assistance and professional development opportunities, tailored to the needs of each region, to develop employer understanding and commitment. It also helped high school and community college faculty integrate academic curriculum with vocational curriculum. Three of the regional collaboratives subsequently received multimillion dollar federal grants to implement their plans.

\$50,000	LEED-Sacramento, Sacramento. over two years developed and implemented thematic curriculum units, aligned with Banking Skills Standards, at eight high school banking programs in the Sacramento area. The grant also supports the development of an assessment and certification system to judge potential employees by the standards; the creation of a work-based learning model involving mentorships, internships, and apprenticeships; and the development of a regional industry collaboration.
\$5,000	Marcus A. Foster Educational Institute, Oakland. supported the Business-School Exchange Program's planning for a 1996 summer teachers institute and a student-run business venture. The institute includes workshops presented by local corporations, in addition to site visits and internships, through which career academy and other teachers become better informed of employer needs.
\$40,000	New Ways to Work (NWW), San Francisco. over one year provided technical assistance to community initiatives in four counties, bridging the gap between employers, schools, and job training organizations. In addition to creating more and better part-time employment opportunities for youth, NWW's goal is to ensure that placements are meaningful learning experiences. West Sonoma County Union High School District, Sebastopol. \$8,700 for a districtwide planning process culminating in a three-year Regional Education Plan for revitalizing the schools. The process involves a wide range of representatives from the community, business, and education and focuses on developing school-to-work, vocational training, and service learning programs for all students.
\$131,500	(Workforce Silicon Valley Corporation (WSV), Santa Clara. in three grants) over two years supported planning for industry-education partnerships in four model high school demonstration sites and, subsequently, the implementation of the Manufacturing Partnership. The grants support teacher release time to better integrate career-oriented coursework with academic subject areas. In addition to working at the site level to improve the quality of existing school-to-career programs, WSV works at the regional level to build employer commitment to creating work-based learning opportunities for large numbers of students and to employing qualified graduates in entry-level positions.
\$70,000	Youth Radio, Berkeley. over two years expanded a radio broadcasting training program, offering training in writing and editing, engineering, production, and presentation to a

diverse group of high school-age youth. Youth Radio is also working to develop further opportunities for its more advanced students through a formal industry internship program and to formalize its role in, and curriculum for, school-to-work partnerships with several high schools.

Directors, Officers, Trustees:

Bruckner, Sandra, Officer, Trustee
Eddie, Gloria, Officer, Trustee
Eddie, Gloria Jeneal, Trustee
Johnson, Christopher, Officer, Trustee
Johnson, Walter S. (d), Donor
Parmellee, Jean, Director, Officer
Shackelton, Scott, Officer, Trustee
Winston, Hathily J., Officer, Trustee

San Francisco Foundation

c/o Robert M. Fisher, Dir.
685 Market St. Suite 910
San Francisco, CA 94105-9716
(415) 495-3100
EIN: 941101547
Source Date: 6/95

Geographic Restrictions:

Limited to the Bay Area, CA [northern] counties of Alameda, Contra Costa, San Francisco, and San Mateo.

Restrictions:

No grants to individuals, annual campaigns, general fundraising campaigns, emergency or endowment funding, deficit financing, matching gifts, scholarships (except when so designated by donor), or fellowships.

To Whom:

Arts and Humanities (6% of funding): multicultural organizations, intermediary organizations (performing arts presenters, facilities, arts service organizations) that stimulate the development of audiences, visual arts, literary arts, and dance, cultural programs that inspire positive development for children and youth, building the capacity of elementary and secondary education to enhance the creative skills and critical reasoning abilities of youth.

Community Health (9% of funding): enhance the capacity of individuals with long-term and serious mental illness, especially the homeless, to live independently, women's health, to address the health needs of women and girls, prevent the spread of AIDS by targeting hard to reach and vulnerable populations, especially gay youth, create community-based systems of long-term care for seniors, increase access to health care either by providing public education and health care reform or by developing innovative models of health care delivery.

Education (4% of funding): schools and neighborhoods with significant proportions of low-income and ethnic minority students, systemic approaches to the problem of school failure, including institutional reform and integrated services, innovative or creative approaches that have the potential of being replicated and influencing public policy, collaborative and multidisciplinary strategies to address the needs of the whole child and family support, culturally sensitive approaches and those that promote cross-cultural understanding.

Environment (2% of funding): environmental education and career opportunities for children and youth of color, multicultural environmental leadership, sustainable patterns of resource use and stewardship, promote healthy condition for the San Francisco Bay/Delta ecosystem, public policy issues, preserve or restore land, water, air, and energy resources.

Neighborhood & Community Development (4% of funding): long-term revitalization for geographic areas impacted by physical deterioration, inadequate social infrastructure, and economic disinvestment, comprehensive, multidisciplinary, collaborative development activities, improve quality of life outcomes for children and youth, disabled, working poor, homeless, and immigrant populations, self-help solutions to effect community change, culturally sensitive approaches and those that promote cross-cultural understanding.

Social Services (3% of funding): engage newcomers and immigrants in the civic and social activities of the communities, building upon their talents and promoting respect and understanding across racial and cultural lines, support and strengthen families, engage youth as active participants in activities that develop leadership skills and promote civic involvement, inform communities of their civil rights, and encourage their active involvement in the exercise of these rights, legal services that advocate on behalf of the poor and other disenfranchised groups.

For What:
Operating budgets, seed money, loans, technical assistance, special projects.

Financial info:
Assets: $325,000,000.
Giving: $28,762,400 for 2,225 grants (high: $200,000; low: $50).

Application info:
Applications accepted. Submit letter of intent (2 page limit). Letters reviewed continuously; proposal deadline is Feb. 1, Apr. 1, July 1, and Nov. 1. Board meets in May, June, July, Sept., Oct., Feb. and Mar. Publishes annual report, newsletter, and application guidelines.

Recent Grants:

$5,000	Afro Solo, San Francisco. To enhance marketing for a performance festival featuring African-American artists.
$10,000	American Indian Contemporary Arts, San Francisco. To fund a financial plan to increase earned revenue, improve fundraising and secure institutional growth
$10,000	American Indian Contemporary Arts, San Francisco. To support a major gifts campaign for this Native American arts organization.
$15,000	American Indian Film Institute, San Francisco. To support a media mentorship project for Native American youth
$5,000	Artist In Exile Gallery, San Francisco. To present two exhibits featuring cross-cultural themes.
$800	**Technical Arts Education Professional Development Project, San Francisco. assistance for a consultant on the design of an evaluation.**
$20,000	Arts Education Funders Collaborative, San Francisco. To support a second year of arts education program development in San Francisco elementary schools. (co-funded with Education)
$5,000	Artsmart, San Francisco. To Implement A Computer Skills Workshop In Three San Francisco Schools. (Co-funded With Education)
$50,000	Asian Art Museum Foundation, San Francisco. To attract a larger base of Chinese-American audience and donors.
$10,000	Bay Area Dance Series, Oakland. To enhance marketing for a dance festival specializing in a diverse array of performances by soloists and small dance companies.
$5,000	Bay Area Intimate Theatre, San Francisco. To produce a five-day festival featuring Bay Area independent artists and small theater companies.
$50,000	Bay Area Video Coalition, San Francisco. Technical assistance for a capital campaign to acquire and upgrade a new facility.

$10,000	Bayview Opera House, San Francisco. To expand community programs and develop fundraising by hiring an executive director.
$150,000	Berkeley Repertory Theatre, Berkeley. To underwrite the costs of a capital campaign directed toward the construction of a second theater.
$20,000	Black Repertory Group, Berkeley. To support theater training programs for youth
$25,000	California Historical Society, San Francisco. To support the Society's relocation to downtown San Francisco through enhanced marketing and start-up of a museum store.
$50,000	Cal Performances, Berkeley. To partially underwrite the costs of an endowment campaign.
$15,000	Cartoon Art Museum, San Francisco. To support development of an interactive gallery using computer graphics.
$5,000	Chinese Cultural Production, San Francisco. To support a joint production by two dance companies, one Chinese-American and the other African-American.
$20,000	Center For Independent Living, Berkeley. To enable this agency serving the physically disabled in northern Alameda County to build its capacity to garner contributed income. Center For The Education Of The Infant Deaf, Berkeley. $10,000 Support to assist parents of deaf children to better communicate with and advocate on behalf of their children.
$20,000	Children's Hospital Oakland. For continued support of the Community Child Development Consultation and Training Program to enhance the capacity of community agencies to work with infants and children with developmental difficulties. (co-funded with Education)
$25,000	Clausen House, Oakland. To enable this agency serving developmentally disabled adults in the East Bay to add computer-related technology to its educational programs.
$20,000	Coalition For Alternatives In Mental Health, Berkeley. For continued support of this housing program run by and for people with mental disabilities.
$41,000	Coleman Advocates For Children & Youth, San Francisco. To support a parent advocacy and training team that would teach parents to become grassroots activists for children. (co-funded with Education and Social Services)
$20,000	Delta Community Services, Inc. Brentwood. To enable this agency to initiate an information and referral service for health and human service programs in eastern Contra Costa County. (co-funded with Education, Neighborhood & Community Development, and Social Services)

$105,000	East Bay Agency For Children, Oakland. To provide support to low income families in which a child or parent has cancer.
$25,000	Edgewood Children's Center, San Francisco. To initiate a therapeutic foster care program for severely disturbed children leaving residential treatment.
$25,000	Fred Finch Youth Center, Oakland. To initiate a therapeutic foster care program to provide family-based care for adolescents with emotional difficulties in the Bay Area.
$5,000	Fred Finch Youth Center, Oakland. Technical assistance to complete a merger with Youth Homes, a group home agency in Contra Costa County.
$8,000	Friendship House Association Of American Indians, San Francisco. Technical assistance to assist in space acquisition efforts for this multi-service center serving American Indians recovering from addiction.
$5,000	GAPA Community HIV Project, San Francisco. Support to hire a consultant to assist in the development of a long range plan for this agency serving the gay Asian and Pacific Islander community.
$31,500	Gilead House, Oakland. For support to develop a stronger fundraising capability in this agency serving homeless families in West Oakland.
$8,000	**Grandparents Who Care, San Francisco. To enable this organization providing support to grandparents raising their grandchildren in San Francisco to evaluate the effectiveness of its services.**
$25,000	Oakland Chinese Community Council, To develop an adult day health center and primary care clinic for low-income frail elders in Oakland's Chinatown.
$2,000	Over 60 Health Center, Berkeley. To support fundraising efforts to improve this agency's capacity to meet the health needs of Berkeley nd North Oakland's low-income elders.
$25,000	Parent Resource Network Program, San Francisco. 12 kilos. To implement a support program for parents of premature and critically ill babies at UCSF.
$40,000	Planned Parenthood of Alameda/San Francisco, San Francisco. To assist Planned Parenthood affiliates in shifting to a managed care service delivery system.
$40,000	Planned Parenthood of San Mateo. Support to improve this agency's management information system to better position itself among the network of managed care providers in San Mateo County.
$18,000	Protect Open Hand, San Francisco, Support to reorganize the hot meal and grocery delivery system in the Tenderloin for people with HIV/AIDS.

$100,000	Raphael House, San Francisco, Support for a new aftercare program aimed at breaking the cycle of recurring homelessness by providing comprehensive support to formerly homeless families with children in San Francisco. (co-funded with Education, Neighborhood & Community Development, and Social Services)
$5,000	Senior Action Network, San Francisco. For technical assistance to develop a strong base of contributed income for this organizing project focused on improving living conditions for San Francisco's elder population.
$12,000	Seton Medical Center, Daly City. Funding for the Teen/Young Adult Parenting Project which teaches young mothers and fathers in northern San Mateo County to become effective parents.
$8,000	San Francisco Alliance For The Mentally Ill. For continuing support of a project to develop a model of client and family-run long-term housing for people with mental disabilities in San Francisco.
$50,000,	San Francisco Community Clinic Consortium 24 most To build the capacity of this agency to develop contributed income to support its mission of strengthening San Francisco's clinics serving low income populations.
$70,000	San Francisco Council on Homelessness Support for bringing together public and private sectors to develop initiatives to alleviate homelessness. (co-funded with Neighborhood Community Development)
$4,000,	San Francisco Depressive And Manic Depressive Association 12 most To provide start-up funding for this self-help organization providing education and support to people with chronic mood disorders.
$10,000	San Francisco General Hospital Medical Center, Continued support for San Francisco General Hospital's Play Therapy Program for children and youth suffering from traumatic injuries or illness.
$20,000	San Francisco Network Of Mental Health Clients. For continued funding of this program by and for people with mental disabilities in San Francisco.
$3,000	San Francisco Suicide Prevention. For planning to develop a multi-agency program to address the growing problem of workplace violence in the Bay Area.
$25,000	Camp Fire Boys And Girls, San Francisco. To support City Kids program for at-risk, urban children.

Directors, Officers, Trustees:
Abrahamson, Lucille S., Trustee
Fisher, Robert M., Director
Hellman, F. Warren, Trustee
Hume, Leslie P., Trustee
Kingsley, Leonard E., Trustee
Lowe, Rolland C., Trustee
MacColl, Stephanie C., Trustee
Sanchez, David J., Jr., Trustee
Widener, Mary Lee, Trustee

Stuart Foundations

c/o Theordore E. Lobman, Pres.
177 Steuart St., Suite 420
San Francisco, CA 94105
(415) 495-1144
Source Date: 12/96

Geographic Restrictions:
Primarily in the states of CA and WA.

Restrictions:
No grants to individuals, endowments, building funds, annual campaigns, or political groups.

To Whom:
Strengthening Public Education: improve professional development strategies, leading to better teaching and improved student learning, strengthen infrastructure at district and school levels to support on-going professional development in teaching, more coherent public policies to promote excellence in the teaching profession, better methods and systems for assessing student learning, both to support teaching and learning and to promote better communication between schools and their surrounding communities about the purposes and outcomes of schooling.

Strengthening the Foster Care System: establish and strengthen Court-Appointed Special Advocate programs in CA, recruit and retain foster, adoptive, and kinship families, promote early permanent placement of children in their birth or adoptive families, improve data systems for public agencies.

Strengthening Systems that Serve Children, Youth, and Families: improve family functioning, prevent child abuse and neglect, improve social and academic performance, prevent first-time and repeat teen pregnancy, improve cross-sector coordination at the state, county, and local levels, technology development to support cross-agency communication and coordination, integrate family support, school reform, youth development and community social and economic development, develop consensus about best practices, **create useful evaluations.**

For What:
Operating budgets, seed money, special projects.

Financial info:
Giving: $8,631,000 for 115 grants (high: $200,000; low: $2,500).

Application info:
Applications accepted all year. First call for published guidelines. Call first to discuss project before submitting proposal.

Recent Grants:

$164,000	Galaxy Institute for Education. Develop long-distance staff development program in language arts for elementary teachers.
$100,000	Family Service Agency of San Francisco. Strengthen community-based family support center in Visitation Valley for low-income families and children by implementing community organizing and economic development program components.
$92,000	San Diego City Schools. New Beginnings County Collaboration, development of its management information system for elementary, middle, and high school-linked integrated services systems, and demonstration at Hamilton Elementary School.
$50,000	One Church, One Child of Washington State. Expand network of church congregations into communities of varied ethnicities to do advocacy, recruit and support foster and adoptive families and children.

Directors, Officers, Trustees:

Bank of America, Trustee
Lobman, Theodore E., Officer
Seafirst Bank, Trustee
Stuart, Dwight L., Advisor
Stuart, Dwight L., Jr., Advisor
Stuart, Elbridge A. (d), Donor
Stuart, E. Hadley, Jr., Advisor
Stuart, Elbridge H. (d), Donor
Stuart, Elbridge H., III, Advisor

Zellerbach Family Fund

c/o Katherine L. Armstrong, Exec. Dir.
120 Montgomery St., Suite 2125
San Francisco, CA 94104
(415) 421-2629
EIN: 946069482
Source Date: 12/95

Geographic Restrictions:
Primarily in the San Francisco Bay Area, CA [northern].

Restrictions:
No grants to individuals, capital or endowment funding, research, scholarships, or fellowships.

To Whom:
Encourage integrated services and community-strengthening activities in distressed neighborhoods, develop educational materials and activities to increase the mutual appreciation of people from different cultures, promote social services reforms and activities to help disadvantaged children and their parents, promote self-help services that are administered by and serve mental health clients and other activities that foster their independence, community arts grants to support local arts and their projects in dance, theater, visual arts, music, festivals, poetry, and publications.

For What
Continuing support, technical assistance, special projects.

Financial info:
Assets: $51,600,000.
Giving: $2,500,000 for 240 grants (high: $20,000; low: $1,000).

Application info:
Applications accepted. Foundation develops most of its own grant proposals. The foundation is currently committed to projects underway and does not expect to make grants to new programs over the next few years. Community arts groups can continue to seek funding. Submit letter or proposal (8 copies for arts proposals), 2 weeks prior to board meeting. Board meets quarterly. Publishes an annual report with application guidelines.

Recent Grants:

$65,000 — Bay Area Social Services Consortium. To support and participate in an organization composed of Social Services department directors from Alameda, Contra Costa, Marin, San

Mateo, Santa Clara, Santa Cruz, Solano, Sonoma and Napa counties, and deans of Schools of Social Welfare at San Jose State, San Francisco State and the University of California, Berkeley. The purpose of the Consortium is to engage in regional program planning.

$15,000	Bay Point Family Resource Center. For organizational consultation and community events designed to help establish a Community Council that will represent the community served by Bay Point's Service Integration Team.
$75,000	Center for Integrated Services for Families and Neighborhoods. To promote the development of financially stable neighborhoods in Sacramento, Oakland and other urban areas, and to develop the integration of services in those neighborhoods.
$30,000	Contra Costa County. Consultant to work toward integrated services and community governance in North Richmond and Bay Point.
$25,000	East Bay Community Foundation. To support and participate with the East Bay Funders, a consortium of foundations, in developing and implementing a comprehensive, collaborative program for at-risk families in selected Oakland neighborhoods.
$10,000	Foundation Consortium for School-Linked Services. To support development of collaborative models of school-linked services for children and families.
$10,000	CARECEN. To provide services to El Salvadorans and other Central American refugees who seek asylum in the United States. Coalition for Immigrant and Refugee
$60,000	Rights and Services. To support coordination of services and community advocacy efforts on behalf of refugees and immigrants.
$15,000	Korean Community Center. To enable Korean and African American leaders in the East Bay to convene a roundtable discussion and retreat to promote mutual understanding and alleviate racial tensions.
$129,235	New Faces of Liberty. To develop interactive, multicultural curriculum materials for educators, with an emphasis on immigrants and refugees.
$1,500	San Francisco Study Center. To provide funds for a candid examination of efforts to improve failing San Francisco schools.
$11,000	School of Social Welfare, U.C. Berkeley. To support the research and publication interests of Zellerbach Family Fund's Chairholder, Professor Lewelle Taylor Gibbs.

$5,000	Third Baptist Church. To support a summer music program that helps at-risk, inner-city, African American youth appreciate their cultural heritage and motivates them toward academic achievement.
$100,000	Zellerbach Family Fund Chair, School of Social Welfare, U C. Berkeley. Final payment of a $400,000 grant to establish the Zellerbach Family Fund Chair in Social Welfare Policy, Community Organization and Practice.
$5,000	Action Alliance for Children. For planning a 1996 conference entitled Beyond Broken Promises: Helping Children and Families in Troubled Times.
$35,000	Alameda County Social Services Agency. For planning Shared Family Care programs and Contra Costa counties.
$11,000	California Family Action. To create a statewide multicultural, multiethnic family organization to ensure that government programs address families' basic needs.
$10,000	California Social Work Education Center. To improve the quality of the education of social workers by reorganizing child welfare and mental health curriculum and field experience.
$25,000	Children's Research Institute. To improve services to foster children and youth.
$10,000	Mandela House. The Solid Foundation. To support family maintenance and reunification, healthy child development and community outreach programs for drug-addicted mothers and their infants. In collaboration with Alameda County Drug and Alcohol Services.
$54,000	**National Abandoned Infants Assistance Resource Center. Family Welfare Research Group For development and evaluation of the Shared Family Care model for family preservation or reunification.**
$10,000	AIDS Task Force. Northern California Grantmakers. To educate hard-to-reach, at-risk minority populations about AIDS.
$10,213	Bay Area Network of Mental Health Clients. Support of regional network of Mental Health Client Self-Help organizations.
$42,500	Center for Independent Living (CIL). General support and development of an Oakland Center for Independent Living office to serve Asian and Latino clients and incorporate the Asian and Latino outreach efforts into core services.
$15,000	Family Health/Mental Health Advisory Committee. To promote supported employment for mentally ill adults.
$49,500	Mental Health Client Self-Help Projects. A cooperative effort to enable mental health client groups in four Bay Area counties to operate self-help programs In collaboration with the

	Marin Community Foundation, the Peninsula Community Foundation and The San Francisco Foundation.
$25,000	California Parks and Recreation Society, Inc. For the Ann Arge Nathan Spirit Award Fund that provides scholarships to further the education of therapeutic recreation majors who have outstanding records as volunteers and also need financial assistance. The grant honors Ed Nathan's retirement as Zellerbach Family Fund executive director.
$15,400	Consultants Reserve. San Francisco Study Center. To provide for consultants' time and other assistance to Zellerbach Family Fund grantees.
$2,500	Council on Foundations. Zellerbach Family Fund contribution to the activities and events connected with the Council on Foundations' annual conference that was held in San Francisco in 1995.
$2,000	Foundation Center, New York. Continued support for information services.
$3,500	Foundation Center, San Francisco. Continued support for information services.
$5,000	Glide Foundation. To support art programs for homeless children at Glide Memorial Methodist Church in San Francisco's Tenderloin.
$5,000	Judes L. Magnes Museum. To enable the museum's Western Jewish History Center to host the 103rd annual conference of the American Jewish Historical Society in San Francisco.
$15,000	New Ways To Work. To study how the growing use of involuntary part-time workers, who receive no benefits and have no job security, negatively affects families, and to suggest remedies for this situation.
$12,500	Center for the Arts/Yerba Buena Gardens. Support for performing arts programming at the Yerba Buena Gardens Center.
$12,500	Fine Art Museums of San Francisco. General support.
$20,000	Jewish Welfare Federation. General support.
$25,000	San Francisco Art Institute. Support for the Graduate Center and to increase the capacity of the Institute.
$12,500	San Francisco Ballet Association. General support.
$12,500	San Francisco Opera Association. General support.
$12,500	San Francisco Symphony Association. General support.
$25,000	Temple Emanu-El. Maintenance and refurbishment of Temple Emanu-El.
$20,000	United Way of the Bay Area. For support of United Way Information and Referral Service.
$75,000	Zellerbach Hall-Cal Performances. For improvements to the Playhouse.

$5,000	**Special one-time renewal grant to expand and evaluate Effective Black Parenting classes.Marin County**
$10,500	To develop Life Books (health, education and personal histories) for children in foster care. (Project to be administered by Marin CASA).
$5,000	To establish supportive, educational groups for parents of children served by Community Mental Health Services.
$5,000	To carry out a job shadowing and internship program pairing county employees with teen parents. To produce interactive workbooks and hold seminars, conducted by women in a prison treatment program, for adolescent girls in a juvenile facility.
$5,000	To develop a computer bulletin board service for students
$5,000	in five therapeutic day schools. San Francisco Study Center

Connecticut

Charles E. Culpeper Foundation, Inc.

c/o Mary Ellen Bucci, Pgm. Off.
Financial Centre
695 E. Main St., Suite 300
Stamford, CT 06901-2155
(203) 975-1240
Internet: http://www.culpeper.org/
EIN: 131956297
Source Date: 12/96

Geographic Restrictions:
Limited to organizations in the U.S.

Restrictions:
No grants to individuals, conferences, conduit organizations, operating funds, travel, endowment or building funding.

To Whom:
Health: basic biomedical research, research in health care delivery, study of social, ethical, and other issues in human health and disease, **evaluation advancement and reform of American medical education**, clinical services, including ambulatory and hospital program.

Education: undergraduate education in the liberal arts and sciences at private higher education institutions, foreign language teaching programs, particularly those using new technologies, environmental studies, increase the use of technology in teaching and research.

Arts and Culture: educational outreach.

Administration of Justice: programs evaluating the state of education of criminal justice professionals and recommending improvements with the objective of ascertaining how best to prepare them for the challenges they fact, programs heightening public understanding of the workings and complexities of the criminal justice system in the conviction that an informed citizenry is the most efficient engine for needed change, programs considering how best to target scarce resources to achieve maximum results in the area of prevention and reduction of violent crime.

For What
Research, general purposes, special projects, seed money.

Financial info:
Assets: $179,680,000.
Giving: $7,509,000 for 190 grants (high: $500,000; low: $500).

Application info:
Applications accepted. Submit letter. No deadline. Board meets quarterly. Publishes annual report and application guidelines.

Recent Grants:

$132,631	Dana-Farber, Inc., Boston, MA. Toward the research of Ezekiel Emanuel, MD, PhD, on the methods of allocating health care resources and the development of a model, "The Impartial Community Allocator Method"
$125,210	National Academy of Sciences, Washington, DC. Toward a study by the Institute of Medicine on decisionmaking about care at the end of life
$45,872	University of Washington School of Medicine, Seattle, WA. Toward the research of Albert R. Jonsen, PhD, on a comprehensive cultural and intellectual history of bioethics in the United States
$180,763	Acadia Institute, Bar Harbor, ME. Toward a study of the merger of the Hahnemann University and Medical College of Pennsylvania Schools of Medicine and its impact on medical education and health care delivery
$75,000	Beth Israel Medical Center, New York, NY. Toward the development of institutional policies on medical ethics issues; the expansion of ethics education programs for physicians, nurses and other health care providers; and the establish-

ment of an ethics resource center for patients and their families

$105,006 Medical College of Pennsylvania and Hahnemann University, Philadelphia, PA. Toward the development and assessment of a model program of structured medical ethics training exercises for the improvement of future physicians' clinical competency

$156,005 Northwestern University, Evanston, IL. Toward a new computer technician position and multimedia equipment to enhance the Medical School's program in student clinical skills evaluation

$300,000 University of California, Los Angeles, Los Angeles, CA. Toward the development and the implementation of an interdisciplinary generalist doctoring curriculum over the third and fourth years of medical school

$132,000 University of Missouri, Kansas City, MO. Toward the design of a core curriculum in Medical Humanities

$60,000 Washington University, St. Louis, MO. Toward research by Kenneth Ludmerer, MD, entitled, "American Medical Education in the Twentieth Century"

$90,552 South End Medical Center, Inc., Stamford, CT. Toward improved medical care for the underserved, including a full-time registered nurse position and the prescription emergency fund

$324,000 University of New Mexico, Albuquerque, NM. Clifford R. Lyons, MD, PhD, for research on mechanisms of host defense against Mycobacterium tuberculosis

$324,000 University of Pennsylvania, Philadelphia, PA. Lewis A. Chodosh, MD, PhD, for research on the role of BRCA1 in differentiation pathways

$324,000 Washington University, St. Louis, MO. Dwight A. Towler, MD, PhD, for research on the molecular genetics of osteoblast-specific gene expression

$150,000 Gustavus Adolphus College, St. Peter, MN. Toward multimedia equipment for the teaching of foreign languages, the new position of Language Laboratory Coordinator, faculty development and foreign language assistants

$121,000 Hamilton College, Clinton, NY. Toward upgrading the language laboratory and faculty training in the uses of multimedia technology

$87,850 Kalamazoo College, Kalamazoo, MI. Toward the establishment of a joint faculty position in Chinese language and history

$150,762 Pacific Lutheran University, Tacoma, WA. Toward equipping a Multicultural Language Learning Center to serve language

	programs, international studies programs across the curriculum and special needs of Asian, Hispanic and hearing-impaired students
$153,508	Swarthmore College, Swarthmore, PA. Toward the establishment of a multimedia Language Learning Center including hardware/software and faculty training in the use of technologies
$42,000	Association of Governing Boards of Universities and Colleges, Washington, DC. Toward the publication of a special issue of Trusteeship magazine dedicated to technology and its impact on higher education
$115,840	Bennington College, Bennington, VT. Toward training faculty, students and local public school teachers in the use of multimedia and Internet technologies
$165,500	Hartwick College, Oneonta, NY. Toward information technology hardware and software for applications throughout the curriculum, faculty training and dissemination of project results
$174,000	Illinois Wesleyan University, Bloomington, IL. Toward the establishment of a faculty development and training program in the uses of instructional technologies
$100,000	Marymount College, Tarrytown, NY. Toward the establishment of a multimedia teaching and resource center, including hardware/software and related faculty training
$97,440	New England Board of Higher Education, Boston, MA. Toward a telecommunications initiative to help institutions develop distance learning strategies
$100,000	Scripps College, Claremont, CA. Toward software for the application of state-of-the-art technologies to teaching and learning toward the end of increasing the use of computing technology throughout the curriculum
$203,208	Trinity College, Hartford, CT. Toward the new position of Director of the Center for Technology-Assisted Learning, the establishment of a Center Associates Program to promote the objectives of the center and to foster faculty development
$156,500	Washington College, Chestertown, MD. Toward multimedia hardware/software, the establishment of a multimedia Instructional Technologist position and faculty training
$142,555	William Marsh Rice University, Houston, TX. Toward the establishment of the positions of Reference Librarian and Educational Specialist to help train faculty in adopting multimedia technology for their courses
$126,000	Carleton College, Northfield, MN. Toward the interdisciplinary environmental studies program, including program

administration, faculty and curricular development, the establishment of a visiting professorship and student internships

$75,000	American Craft Museum, New York, NY. Toward an outreach initiative to increase the museums visibility and audience by promoting an understanding of craft
$25,000	American Symphony Orchestra League, Washington, DC. Toward the Music Assistance Fund, a national scholarship program for talented, young, minority musicians
$25,000	Asia Society, New York, NY. Toward a multidisciplinary exhibition-based educational program for New York City youth, including teacher workshops, artist-teachers and educational materials
$100,000	Carnegie Hall Society, Inc., New York, NY. Toward Link Up!, an educational outreach program for New York City public elementary school students, including artist training, teacher training and classroom workshops
$25,000	Chamber Music Society of Lincoln Center, Inc., New York, NY. Toward expansion of an educational concert series for New York City school children, ages 10-14, including teacher workshops and preparatory in-school artist visits
$25,000	Civil War Trust, Washington, DC. Toward the creation of the Civil War Discovery System, an interactive, multimedia program for grades 6-12 that explores the life and times of the Civil War era
$75,000	Connecticut Grand Opera and Orchestra, Stamford, CT. Toward the establishment of the position of Director of Education and Outreach to work toward the institutionalization of outreach efforts
$67,570	Dallas Theater Center, Dallas, TX. Toward the establishment of the Dallas Theater Center Institute to prepare public school teachers to lead in the study of the arts using teaching artists and experiential methods
$70,000	The Folger Shakespeare Library-Amherst College, Washington, DC. Toward the creation of the Shakespeare Gallery, an interactive multimedia information center for the library's general public visitors
$300,000	Metropolitan Opera Association, New York, NY. Toward the expansion of the Metropolitan Opera Presents telecast series, the Met's national and international outreach programming on PBS.
$158,534	Museum of Fine Arts, Houston, Houston, TX. Toward a Place for all People, a program designed to increase the accessibility of the permanent collection and to cultivate a diverse audience
$50,000	National Actors Theatre, New York, NY. Toward the expansion of the High School Outreach Program for New York City stu-

	dents, including enhancement of classic theatre production-based educational activities and curriculum materials
$150,000	National Building Museum, Washington, DC. Toward the expansion of outreach/audience diversification initiatives, school programs K-6, programs for secondary students and programs for adults and families
$138,313	The National Museum of Women in the Arts, Washington, DC. Toward a pilot program in Texas and Arkansas, in collaboration with Girl Scouts of the U.S.A., to promote an awareness of women in the arts and to foster individual creativity
$25,000	The New Museum, New York, NY. Toward art programs for New York City high school students to encourage understanding of diverse cultures through contemporary art
$100,000	New York City Ballet, New York, NY. Toward City Ballet Bridges, a pilot program to reach new, diverse audiences in Brooklyn, Queens and the Bronx
$150,000	New York City Opera, New York, NY. Toward the expansion of education and community service staff and the institutionalization of the High School Partnership and the Opera is Elementary programs
$49,900	New York Landmarks Conservancy, New York, NY. Toward an expanded edition of the Restoration Directory and an historic building workshop related to maintenance, repair, rehabilitation and restoration of landmark-quality structures
$190,000	Old State House Association, Hartford, CT. Toward the establishment of an education department and the development of educational programs to foster citizen participation in and recognition of the democratic process as basic to American culture
$50,000	Roundabout Theatre Company, New York, NY. Toward the expansion of outreach programs for New York City schools: From Page to Stage, a classroom-based theatre education program, and Teacher's Outreach Program, a seminar series for teachers
$60,000	Spanish Theatre Repertory Company, Ltd., New York, NY. Toward the establishment of the position of Education Outreach and Development Director to advance outreach initiatives and relationships with area schools
$25,000	The Stamford Symphony Society, Inc., Stamford, CT. Toward the establishment of an arts-based curriculum in partnership with Stamford public schools, including teacher and artist training
$50,000	Vivian Beaumont Theater at Lincoln Center, New York, NY. Toward the Membership Expansion/Diversification Project, a subscription program targeting nontraditional audiences

$147,000	Wadsworth Atheneum, Hartford, CT. Toward the development and implementation of a K-12 teacher training program and the establishment of a minority, education fellowship program
$383,520	The Governance Institute, Washington, DC. Toward a study of how law enforcement can be better organized to meet the challenges of violent crime
$100,000	The Governance Institute, Washington, DC. Toward research entitled, "Citizen Involvement in State Court Understanding and Support"
$100,000	American Inns of Court Foundation, Alexandria, VA. Expansion of Inn affiliations with law schools to enhance law school programming in practical lawyering, legal ethics and professional responsibility.
$100,000	Arena Stage, Washington, DC. Theater as Discovery, production-based program for high school students, including in-school play writing, workshops, teacher education and related humanities seminars.
$25,000	Ballet Theatre Foundation, Inc. New York, NY. Expansion of educational outreach initiatives for New York City school children and their families including lectures, demonstrations, workshops and performances.
$150,000	Haverford College, Haverford, PA. New position of Director of the Language Center and acquisition of multimedia equipment.
$186,802	Fairfield University, Fairfield, CT. Establishment of multimedia language resource center.
$89,929	Harvard University, Boston, MA. Research of Linda Emanuel, MD, PhD, entitled, "A Process Theory of Death: Medical Policy Implications".
$60,000	Case Western Reserve University. Cleveland, OH. Preservation of 60 collections of records on New Medical Curriculum for purposes of scholarly use.

Directors, Officers, Trustees:

Campbell, Colin G., Director
Culpeper, Charles E. (d), Donor
Drake, Philip M., Director, Officer
Fahey, Joseph F., Jr., Director
Jacobs, Linda E., Officer
Lynch, Ronald P., Director
McNamara, Francis J., Jr., Director, Officer
Morning, John, Director
Rose, John C., M.D. Director

District of Columbia

Paul & Annetta Himmelfarb Foundation, Inc.

c/o Lillian Kronstadt, Exec. Dir.
4545 42nd St., Suite 203
Washington, DC 20016
(202) 966-3795
EIN: 520784206
Source Date: 12/95

Geographic Restrictions
Primarily in the Washington, DC, area and Israel.

Restrictions:
No grants to individuals.

To Whom:
Jewish welfare, Israel, early childhood and other education, seniors, disabled, homeless, health, medical research, AIDS, educational research, environment, cancer research.

Financial info:
Assets: $7,565,400.
Giving: $198,300 for 100 grants (high: $20,000, low: $50).

Application info:
Applications accepted. Submit letter. No deadline. Board meets monthly.

Recent Grants:

$200,000	Forward in the Fifth, Berea, KY. Support to design and pilot the Student Leadership Initiative Project (SLIP), a leadership, entrepreneurship, and workforce skills development curriculum to be implemented throughout eastern Kentucky through the involvement of teachers, students, local businesses, and community agencies.
$49,550	Kids Working/Peterstown Library, Peterstown, WV. Support to promote the incubution of social and economic entrepreneurship among youth through mentoring activities, apprenticeships, the establishment of the youth-run Job and Service Center, youth enterprise developmental, and youth leadership activities.
$199,968	South Bronx Community Coalition, New York, NY. Support to implement the Hunts Point Multi-Media Education/Leadership Initiative — a community economic development project for youth.

$200,000	Southend Community Services, Hartford, CT. Support to develop and implement Our Piece of thc Pie (O.P.P.), a program to provide young people with concrete work experiences and career enhancement activities and to assist teams of youth in starting and operating their own businesses in Hartford and Greater Hartford.
$201,905	Chugachmiut, Anchorage, AK. Support for the implementation of the Chugachmiut Career Development Project, which provides the youth of the Chugach region education and training including initial assessment, career exploration and planning, job shadowing and mentoring, and education or job placement assistance.
$200,000	Detroit One to One, Detroit, MI. Support to design and implement career awareness and mentoring "prototypes" to be piloted at Spain Elementary (beginning with talc eighth grade) and Central High (beginning with tenth grade) schools.
$187,500	Greater Washington Urban League, Washington, DC. Support to establish an intergenerational mentoring program linking middle school/junior high students and working or retired seniors, to help students increase academic and employment abilities, gain confidence, and increase awareness of employment options and how to pursue them.
$188,700	One to One Philadelphia, Philadelphia, PA. Support to enhance, expand, and link three programs - Shadowing Day, Business Education Goes Into Neighborhoods (BEGIN), and Work-Based Learning (WBL) - and to integrate and institutionalize them in schools and businesses.
$271,152	Impact Services Corp., Philadelphia, PA. Support for the implementation of the Community Blockbuilders Program, a community development training program that enhances the academic achievement and economic self-suffiiciency of disadvantaged youth in the Kensington area.
$294,340	Cornerstone Community Partnerships, Santa Fe, NM. Support to strengthen and coordinate the academic component of a job training program that builds job skills through historic and cultural preservation projects in Zuni Pueblo, Dona Ana, and two other sites.
$298,150	**Girls, Inc. of Alameda County, San Leandro, CA. Support to enhance the workforce preparation component of the Eureka! Program by reconstructing, strengthening, and extending its summer internship and training component, performing an evaluation, and building long-term sustainability.**

$275,062 Association of Science-Technology Centers, Washington, DC. Support to enhance the existing YouthAlive! Program with activities to help middle and high school students become aware of and develop the skill competencies they need and to create a workplace network that endorses those skills. Project work will involve ten museums as pilot sites.

Directors, Officers, Trustees:

Kronstadt, Annette, Director
Kronstadt, Lillian N., Director, Officer
Naiman, Ada, Director, Officer
Naiman, Norma Lee, Director
Parker, Carol Himmelfarb, Director, Officer
Preston, Carole, Director, Officer

Hitachi Foundation

c/o Laurie Regelbrugge, Dir. of Pgms.
1509 22nd St., NW
Washington, DC 20037-1073
(202) 457-0588
Fax on Demand Information System: (202) 457-0588, ext. 551
EIN: 521429292
Source Date: 3/97

Restrictions:

No grants for sectarian or denominational religious organizations, health programs, individuals, fundraising events, building funding, publications, conferences and seminars, preservice teacher education, comparative education studies, fellowship and exchange programs, endowments, advertising, capital funds, underwrite exhibitions or performances, arts-in-the-schools programs, medical research, political activities, purchase of equipment, or research and assessment.

To Whom:

Community development: develop and engage community leadership, bring a variety of community actors to the table, facilitate the building of strong and accountable community institutions, build community capacity, particularly at the local level, in an integrative way, make more effective use of existing resources, while mobilizing new financial, material, and human resources for community development.

Education [preschool, elementary, and secondary, higher]: reflect the necessity of preparing individuals to participate more fully as citizens and productive members of society, recognize that schools can play a significant role in building and stabilizing communities, develop and improve the connection between schools, parents and communities, recognize the diversity of learning styles and therefore the variety of pedagogical approaches needed to educate all America's students, incorporate the arts or museums as educators and providers of increased opportunities for creativity and problem solving, link education to economic opportunity, utilize community resources, such as arts organizations, corporations, churches, and synagogues, and community service organizations.

Global Citizenship: promote an understanding of the complex nature of international communication, rapidly changing technology, and environmental degradation, related causes and consequences to community, U.S., and international problem-solving, develop guidelines for the institutional and individual to practice global citizenship, identify the international infrastructure needed for an effective global system, promote strategic planning and action responsive to new mandates for participation, focus, responsibility, accountability, effectiveness, and commitment, based on new global imperatives, promote greater knowledge of global experience, particularly identifying successful approaches to community problem-solving developed around the world and exploring their broader application and replication.

For What
General purposes, program-related investments, seed money, special projects, technical assistance, employee matching gifts.

Financial info:
Assets: $35,591,700 (from 1996 990PF).
Giving: $2,417,600 for 30 grants (high: $300,000; low: $500).

Application info:
Applications not accepted. Accept proposals submitted in response to public requests for proposals.

Recent Grants:

$25,000	Action Against Crime and Violence, Washington, DC.
$65,000	The Aspen Institute, Washington, DC.
$170,410	ASPIRA Association, Inc., Washington, DC.
$275,062	Association of Science-Technology Center, Washington, DC.
$100,000	Chesapeake Bay Foundation, Annapolis, MD.
$2,000	The Children's Museum, Boston, MA.
$2,000	City of Westminster, Westminster, CA.
$294,610	Cornerstones Community Partnerships, Santa Fe, NM.

$17,170	First Nationsl Development Institute, Fredericksburg, VA.
$35,000	Georgia Environmental Organization, Inc., Atlanta, GA.
$298,150	Girls Inc., of Alameda County, San Leandro, CA.
$174,398	Greater DC Cares, Inc., Washington, DC.
$40,000	The Heartwood Institute, Pittsburgh, PA.
$271,152	Impace Services Corp., Philadelphia, PA.
$14,661	Montana Indian Manufacturers Network, Billings, MT.
$100,000	The New Press, New York, NY.
$22,500	The Reach Center, Seattle, WA.
$169,000	Salish Kootenai College, Pablo, MT.
$274,000	University of Virginia, Charlottesville, VA.
$149,994	The Volunteer Center of San Francisco, CA.
$16,200	World Resources Institute, Washington, DC.
$10,000	American Association of Museums, Washington, DC.
$25,000	Arab Community Center for Economic and Social Services, Dearborn, MI.
$59,467	Campus Outreach Opportunity League (COOL), Washington, DC.
$250,000	CIVICUS, Washington, DC.
$150,000	Conflice Management Group, Cambridge, MA.
$141,050	East-West Center Foundation, Honolulu, HI.
$175,000	Futures for Children, Albuquerque, NM.
$165,251	The Hopi Foundation Hotevilla, AZ.
$159,500	Illinois Mathematics and Science Academy, Aurora, IL.
$62,830	Institute for Local Self-Reliance, Washington, DC.
$25,000	International Center for Not-for-Profit Law, Farmington, CT.
$109,500	International Studies Education Project of San Diego, CA.
$275,160	Jobs for the Future, Cambridge, MA.
$160,000	Leadership Development in Interethnic Relations Program, Los Angeles, CA.
$182,050	Maryland Student Service Alliance, Baltimore, MD.
$80,000	Migizi Communications, Minneapolis, MN.
$150,000	The Ms. Foundation for Women, New York, NY.
$140,000	The National Society for Experiential Education, Raleigh, NC.
$148,000	North Carolina Center for Nonprofits, Raleigh, NC.
$40,000	Penn Center, St. Helena Island, SC.
$212,491	Points of Light Foundation, Washington, DC.
$120,000	Puente Project, Oakland, CA.
$35,000	The Asia Foundation. San Francisco, CA. Launching of Asia Pacific Philanthropy Consortium. Consortium will establish networks and exchanges to support leadership development, as well as international collaboration, research, and database services on region's not-for-profit-sector. The Consortium will provide technical assistance. Overall goal is

to promote role of philanthropy in addressing critical issues in Asia Pacific region.

$110,000 **Coalition of Neighborhood Developers. Los Angeles, CA. Collaboration among neighborhood clusters of organizations and assist Coalition of Neighborhood Developers (CND) in working with these organizations to design and conduct topical and management training programs. These steps are necessary to implement locally-defined development strategies devised through Neighborhood Planning Project. Funds will support CND's strategic planning and evaluation exercises.**

$150,000 Conflict Management Group. Cambridge, MA. Establishment of Youth Community Conflict Resolution and Violence Prevention Center. Center will offer training in conflict resolution to youth, parents, and community leaders in 3 disadvantaged, violence-ridden Boston communities. Training will help establish effective channels of communication, create a stable environment, and build cooperation and sense of community.

$10,000 The Ellington Fund. Washington, DC. Programs and facilities associated with contribution of sound recording equipment from another donor. Joint grant with Hitachi, Ltd.'s Washington office, which is contributing $30,000.

$3,600 Foreign Policy Association. New York, NY. Convening of master teachers involved in Foreign Policy Association's secondary education initiative, Civic Competence Through Global Studies. Funds support involvement of teachers in training institute to test curriculum materials developed within initiative. Foreign Policy Association has three-year program to develop new secondary curriculum materials linking civic participation to study of global issues.

Directors, Officers, Trustees:

Apodaca, Clara R., Director
Black, Sherry Salway, Director
Graham, Patricia Albjerg, Director
Green, Carl J., Director
Hitachi, Ltd., Donor
Kasputys, Joseph E., Director
Pierre, Percy A., Director
Richardson, Elliot Lee, Director, Officer
Ripley, S. Dillon, Director
Roy, Delwin A., Director, Officer
Stanley, Peter W., Director

National Environmental Education & Training Foundation, Inc.

c/o Kevin J. Coyle, Pres.
734 15th Street, N.W., Suite 420
Washington, DC 20005
(202) 628-8200
Source Date: 12/95

To Whom:
Education and training to further environmental protection and sustainable development. Provide U.S. and international [global] focal point for information about, access to, and support for environmental education, bring national and international recognition to the actions of individuals and institutions working for environmental protection and sustainable development, expand the read of environmental education programs and projects, increase the qualifications of environmental management professionals, increase the quantity and quality of environmental education programs, recognize, involve and support traditionally under-represented or disenfranchised populations, including Native American, African American, Asian, Hispanic, seniors, and physically and mentally challenged, in environmental protection and sustainability, education and training programs focused on environmental health of urban and rural populations, scholarships and fellowships to students pursuing research projects or careers in environment related areas.

For What:
Matching funds.

Financial info:
Assets: $1,875,800.
Giving: $1,247,000 for grants.

Application info:
Applications accepted. Submit preposal letter (2 page limit, 4 copies). Application form required. Deadline is Jan. 16 and July 15. Board meets in May and Dec.

Recent Grants:

$25,000	Environmental Health Sciences Summer Institute for Educators, Environmental and Occupational Health Sciences Institute, Piscataway, NJ. Support for an in-service teacher training institute for 130 K-12 teachers on environmental health issues including toxicology, ecology, hazardous products, lead poisoning prevention, water pollution and air pollution.

$24,000	Great Lakes Pollution Prevention Project, Ecology Center of Ann Arbor, Ann Arbor, MI. Conduct education and training for students, educators, parents, employees, and community leaders in ten Michigan communities, testing models that address pollution problems affecting human health.
$25,000	Recruitment of Minorities into Environmental Training, American Industrial Hygiene Association, Foundation, Fairfax, VA. Educate minority youth about environmental health and promote the recruitment of minorities into the field of Industrial Hygiene through a mentor program, summer camp, and community outreach.
$17,750	Urban Site Remediation Project, Isles, Inc., Trenton, NJ. Develop a model for teaching communities about the environmental health hazards of toxic industrial sites— "brownfields" — and issues associated with cleanup and redevelopment.
$12,500	Who's Minding the Stack, Tellus Institute, Boston, MA. Conduct a series of workshops in Northeast Boston communities that have incinerators to teach policy makers and citizens how to monitor and analyze incineration emissions and potential health affects.
$7,436	Well Safety Demonstrations, SAIF Water Committee of Lancaster/Northumberland Interfaith Service Council, Lively, VA. Support 17 community demonstrations of rural homes with contaminated water wells, educating over 160 residents on drinking water hazards and teaching them how to safeguard their wells from contamination.
$25,000	Leap Into Lakes, Wisconsin Childrens Center/Madison Children's Museum, Madison, WI. Support an environmental educational exhibit about lakes, fresh water, and water quality, designed to give children ages 6-12 an in-depth look at how Madison's lakes, the Great lakes, and lakes of the world function.
$30,000	Thinking Like a Watershed: The Lake Superior Community Education Project, Lake Superior Center, Duluth, MN. Students, teachers and service club members from 18 communities in the Lake Superior watershed will engage in a lake study to increase their knowledge of the environmental and health issues which effect Lake Superior.
$12,000	Water Chemistry Manual River Watch Network, Inc., Montpelier, VT. Complete and disseminate a manual for schools and community groups on monitoring chemical indicators of water quality, providing information on concepts underlying water quality and clear procedures for laboratory and field analysis.

$9,000	Theatrical Performance about Water Issues Gaia Theater, Chicago, IL. Produce an interactive educational play and follow-up activities for more than 2,400 Chicago elementary students about water issues and how individuals affect local water sources.
$10,000	After School Adventure Program, Lime Hollow Nature Center, Cortland, NY. Develop and implement an environmental education after-school program for elementary students using a natural playground focusing on water issues.
$5,196	North Dakota Wetlands and Water Demonstration Day, North Dakota Wetlands Institute, Bismarck, ND. Hands-on wetlands and water management educational program for North Dakota policy makers featuring cooperative resolution of wetlands issues through education.
$75,000	**Using Interactive Television to Provide Teacher In-service Education Environmental and Occupational Health Sciences Institute, Piscataway, NJ. Develop and evaluate a new model for in-service training on environmental health issues using the interactive television network (ITV), and comparing the effectiveness of this model with face-to-face trainings.**
$37,255	**The Indiana Dunes National Lakeshore Parks as Classrooms Evaluation, Indiana University, Bloomington, IND. Measure and assess the effectiveness of teacher training to 130 4th-6th grade teachers and specific field trip experiences of 3,000 urban 4th-6th grade students using National Parks as teaching grounds. Serve as a model for the U.S. Park System.**
$35,000	Creating Model Links: EE and Educational Reform WA Office of Superintendent of Public Instruction, Olympia, WA. Create ten school prototypes demonstrating that environmental education is a powerful tool for schools to implement Washington State House Bill 1209, "Essential Student Learnings" in reading, writing, communication, and math.
$28,000	Living Labs, Columbus Center, Baltimore, MD. Recruit and train scientists to participate in research activities with young people to demonstrate how science is used to solve environmental problems.
$15,000	Resource Apprenticeship Program for Students, BLM-RAPS, Anchorage, AK. Support for 50 Alaska Native students to learn about natural resource career opportunities in Alaska through apprenticeships with the Bureau of Land Management, U.S. Park Service, U.S. Fish and Wildlife Service, the Environmental Protection Agency, or the Alaska Department of Natural Resources.

$18,830	Urban Rangers, School District No. 1, Multnomah County, Portland, OR. Support a school-to-work partnership providing sixteen high school students the opportunity to work on summer conservation projects in the Portland area.
$10,000	Project Re-Seed, Operation Greenthumb, NYC Department of General Services, New York, NY. Provide a 10-session summer workshop series plus monthly school-year workshops to assist 15 schools in transforming school gardens into Urban Environmental Study Sites.
$7,000	Sand Canyon Environmental Education Program, Eastern Kern County Resource Conservation District, Inyokern, CA. Develop a 6th grade hands-on environmental education program to meet state mandates and empower students to make environmentally conscious decisions about living within a sustainable arid ecosystem.
$7,000	Waste Prevention Environmental Education, The ReStore, Montpelier, VT. Bring real waste management problems from the community into the classroom, for students to assess their own material consumption patterns and those of area businesses.
$25,000	Earth Education Partnership Program, Education Development Center, Inc., Newton, MA. Provide classroom goals, school standards and resource support to strengthen the quality of high school environmental education and develop an international network to further students' understanding of the global connection of environmental problems.
$25,000	The Main Street Project (Phase One), The Watercourse, Bozeman, MT. Analyze major civic, service, and conservation organizations to determine interests in, and barriers to, increasing involvement in community-based environmental education and service projects.
$10,000	LEAP Fifth Grade Environmental Education Project, Learning Through an Expanded Arts Program, Inc., New York, NY. Develop and field test a training model and environmental education curriculum guide to support federal, state, and local reform efforts. Sixty-plus fifth grade teachers and 1,800 students will participate in the project.
$50,000	Richmond Enterprise Zone Environmental Training Partnership, J. Sergeant Reynolds Community College, Richmond, VA. Educate and train small business owners in minority and low-income neighborhoods in a designated Enterprise Zone on government requirements and opportunities to use environmentally safe procedures and technologies in their businesses.

$40,000	University-Community Partnerships for Environmental Quality, Management Institute for Environment and Business, Washington, DC. Engage MBA students and faculty at the University of Massachusetts, Vanderbilt University, Southern University, and the University of Houston in environmental problem solving in their communities.
$27,750	Project Learning Tree Secondary Curriculum Materials on Risk And Cost-Benefit Analysis, American Forest Foundation, Washington, DC. Develop a supplementary curriculum module on risk and cost-benefit analysis to help high school students understand the environmental costs of doing business.
$24,970	Clay Street Community Projects, Alliance for Community Education, Bowie, MD. Develop ecological micro-businesses that incorporate environmental business opportunities into environmental benefits for the community.
$20,000	Green Schools Program, Youth for Environmental Sanity, Santa Cruz, CA. Provide 195 schools with educational materials and support to audit energy use and implement retrofits for lighting, heating, ventilation, and air condition systems in schools, homes and businesses.
$8,500	Green Procurement Guide, Green Seal, Washington, DC. Develop and disseminate a "Green Procurement Guide" to help large-volume consumers, including corporations and governmental agencies, choose energy-efficient and environmentally preferable products and services.
$7,851	Rural Innovations Program, Nature Conservancy: Wyoming Chapter, Lander, WY. Support for landowner education seminars in the most economically threatened rural communities of Wyoming; ranchers, landowners, county commissioners and others will learn options for balancing growth with the open space needs of ranching.
$5,000	The Bitterroot Ecological Awareness Resource Co-op, Bitterroot Down Home, Hamilton, MT. Expand the use of a network of local professionals with diverse skills and often opposing viewpoints for panel presentations to over 5,000 students, providing information and perspectives on the ecosystem that sustains that region.
$12,500	Integrating Environmental Learning into the Community and Curriculum, Vermont institute of Natural Science, Woodstock, VT. Integrate Environmental Learning for the Future Program (ELF) into two schools with ethnically and economically diverse student populations. ELF is a partnership that trains parents and community volunteers to teach elementary students about the environment.

$8,500 Reforestation Education Program, WA State Society of American Foresters, Yakima, WA. Develop a program, using video and written materials developed by foresters and educators to foster in-depth educational discussions and participation in reforestation efforts, targeting regional middle school students.

$35,000 Sharing Approaches that Work, Mega-Cities Project, New York, NY. Adapt four successful community-based environmental education initiatives in the most environmentally damaged and at risk areas of New York and Los Angeles to promote cross-community training and dissemination of information.

$10,000 Pennsylvania Forest Stewardship Volunteer Initiative, Pennsylvania State University, University Park, PA. Train Pennsylvania forest landowners in the principles of forest stewardship to help them manage their own forest lands and expand peer outreach of natural resource professionals to other landowners.

$30,000 Project WET: Leadership Training and Network Building Initiative, Project Water Education for Teachers, Bozeman, MT. Conduct 20 state leadership training workshops for over 600 educators nationwide, strengthening their knowledge of and capacity to teach activities that address people's relationship to watersheds.

$25,000 Manufacturing Employees Environmental and Education Training System, Calumet Project for Industrial Jobs, East Chicago, IND. Develop and organize a program to address the lack of environmental training for manufacturing employees in the heavily industrialized Northwest Indiana region.

$20,000 Creating an Environmentally Aware Workforce in a Long-Term Care Organization, Loretto, Syracuse, NY. Create an environmentally aware workforce in the field of longterm care through the development and implementation of environmental standards, employee and resident education, and environmental training programs. A training manual and video will facilitate replication nationwide.

$17,500 Environmental Education Leadership Training, World Wildlife Fund, Washington, DC. Develop and test a teacher workshop model to increase environmental literacy on biodiversity for 36 urban middle school teachers.

$12,000 Water Chemistry Manual River Watch Network, Inc., Montpelier, VT. Complete and disseminate a manual for schools and community groups on monitoring chemical indicators of water quality, providing information on con-

	cepts underlying water quality and clear procedures for laboratory and field analysis.
$9,000	Theatrical Performance about Water Issues Gaia Theater, Chicago, IL. Produce an interactive educational play and follow-up activities for more than 2,400 Chicago elementary students about water issues and how individuals affect local water sources.
$10,000	After School Adventure Program, Lime Hollow Nature Center, Cortland, NY. Develop and implement an environmental education after-school program for elementary students using a natural playground focusing on water issues.
$5,196	North Dakota Wetlands and Water Demonstration Day, North Dakota Wetlands Institute, Bismarck, ND. A hands-on wetlands and water management educational program for North Dakota policy makers featuring cooperative resolution of wetlands issues through education.
$75,000	**Using Interactive Television to Provide Teacher Inservice Education Environmental and Occupational Health Sciences Institute, Piscataway, NJ. Develop and evaluate a new model for in-service training on environmental health issues using the interactive television network (ITV), and comparing the effectiveness of this model with face-to-face trainings.**
$37,255	**The Indiana Dunes National Lakeshore Parks as Classrooms Evaluation, Indiana University, Bloomington, IND. Measure and assess the effectiveness of teacher training to 130 4th-6th grade teachers and specific field trip experiences of 3,000 urban 4th-6th grade students using National Parks as teaching grounds. Serve as a model for the U.S. Park System.**
$35,000	Creating Model Links: EE and Educational Reform, WA. Office of Superintendent of Public instruction, Olympia, WA. Create ten school prototypes demonstrating that environmental education is a powerful tool for schools to implement Washington State House Bill 1209, "Essential Student Learnings" in reading, writing, communication, and math.

John S. & James L. Knight Foundation

Attn: Grant Request
2 S. Biscayne Blvd., Suite 3800
Miami, FL 33131-1803
(305) 539-0009
EIN: 650464177
Source Date: 12/96

Geographic Restrictions:
Limited to areas where Knight-Ridder newspapers are published: Long Beach and San Jose, CA, Boulder, CO, Boca Raton, Tallahassee, Miami, and Bradenton, FL, Columbus, Milledgeville, and Macon, GA, Fort Wayne and Gary, IND, Wichita, KS, Lexington, KY, Detroit, MI, St. Paul and Duluth, MN, Biloxi, MS, Charlotte, NC, Grand Forks, ND, Akron, OH, State College and Philadelphia, PA, Columbia and Myrtle Beach, SC, and Aberdeen, SD.

Restrictions:
No grants for organizations whose mission is to prevent, eradicate and/or alleviate the effects of a specific disease, religious purposes, political activities, individuals, fundraising campaigns, general operating support, deficit financing, trips or uniforms for bands, films, videos, or television programs, conferences, honoraria, scholarly research leading to a book, group travel, memorials, or medical research.

To Whom:
Community Initiatives: limited to areas of company operations: arts and culture, education, child welfare, social services, citizenship, community development, homeless, literacy.

Journalism: limited to U.S. organizations. Advance the quality and effectiveness of the free press, journalism education, defense of first amendment rights and support of a free press at home and internationally.

Arts and Culture: significant arts and cultural institutions with demonstrated U.S. impact with emphasis on art museums and galleries, other museums such as historical, natural history, science and children's museums, historic preservation, music, specifically symphony orchestras and opera companies, theater, dance and ballet.

Education: private and public higher education, community colleges, improve elementary and secondary education.

Education (26% of funding), Social Services (27% of funding), Culture (24% of funding), Journalism (23% of funding).

For What:
Special projects, building, funds, capital campaigns, endowment funds, fellowships, general purposes, matching funds, scholarship funds, seed money, renovation projects.

Financial info:
Assets: $957,500,000.
Giving: $37,509,400 for 295 grants (high: $1,000,000; low: $5,000).

Application info:
Applications accepted. Submit Cover Sheet (original and 1 copy) and support material (2 copies). No deadline. Board meets in Mar., June, Sept., and Dec. Publishes annual report with application guidelines.

Recent Grants:

$250,000	Akron Community Foundation, Akron, OH. To supplement an existing donor-advised fund
$250,000	Community Foundation for Southeastern Michigan, Detroit, MI. To supplement an existing donor-advised fund
$250,000	Community Foundation of Santa Clara County, San Jose, CA. To supplement an existing donor-advised fund
$250,000	Dade Community Foundation, Miami, FL. To supplement an existing donor-advised fund
$250,000	The Denver Foundation, Denver, CO. To establish a donor-advised fund for the Boulder area
$250,000	The Fargo-Moorhead Area Foundation, Fargo, ND. To establish a donor-advised fund for the Grand Forks area
$250,000	Foundation for the Carolinas, Charlotte, NC. To supplement an existing donor-advised fund
$250,000	The Philadelphia Foundation, Philadelphia, PA. To supplement an existing donor-advised fund
$54,000	Accountants for the Public Interest, Washington, DC. To distribute copies of an accounting guide for nonprofits, a guide to the nonprofit audit and to conduct workshops for community-based nonprofits in 22 Knight Foundation communities
$1,000,000	American Youth Work Center, Washington, DC. For general support to promote self-sufficiency of the (over 3 years) publication Youth Today and expand news coverage and circulation in Knight Foundation communities
$600,000	(over 3 years) Community Anti-Drug Coalitions of America, Alexandria, VA. For core support to expand activities and

	build new coalitions and strengthen existing groups in Knight Foundation communities
$850,000	(over 2 years) Kids Voting USA, Tempe, AZ. For a partial challenge grant for continuing support to enable this citizenship education program to expand into all regions of the country for the 1996 elections
$750,000	(over 3 years) National Urban League, New York, NY. For a youth development policy mobilization campaign in three Knight Foundation communities and for general operating support
$25,000	Twin Cities Public Television, St. Paul, MN. Educational outreach to middle and high school students for Hoop Dreams, much-acclaimed documentary that details the lives of two young basketball players
$20,000	Abstinence the Better Choice, Cuyahoga Falls, OH. For general operating support for an organization providing educational programs to schoolchildren to promote sexual abstinence
$20,000	Angela Hospice Home Care, Livonia, MI.For My Nest is Best, a pediatric hospice program
$5,000	Arc Duluth, Duluth, MN. For a community education project that promotes awareness of the dangers of alcohol use during pregnancy
$25,000	Bay Area Community Resources, Larkspur, CA. To add a mentoring tutoring component to agency services provided at two middle schools in East Palo Alto
$12,500	Boy Scouts of America, Calumet Council, Munster, IND. For a challenge grant for a pilot project providing scouting programs in three public housing developments in Gary
$25,000	Boy Scouts of America, Great Trail Council, Akron, OH. For the second year of the special needs pilot program for children with disabilities
$50,000	(over 3 years) Boy Scouts of America, Indian Waters Council, Columbia, SC. For a capital campaign to build a new camp to be used for scouting and other community activities
$35,000	Boys and Girls Club of Baldwin County, Milledgeville, GA. For construction costs of a new gymnasium
$35,000	Boys and Girls Clubs of Broward County, Fort Lauderdale, FL. For building renovations for the creative arts program
$50,000	Akron Summit Community Action Agency, Akron, OH. For expansion of the Self-Help and Resource Exchange (SHARE) program in Summit and surrounding counties
$25,000	American Red Cross, Capital Area Chapter, Tallahassee, FL. For an emergency grant for disaster relief and recovery

	efforts related to Hurricane Opal in designated counties around Tallahassee
$50,000	American Red Cross, Greater Miami Chapter, Miami, FL. To renovate a new facility
$20,000	Appalshop, Whitesburg, KY. To expand the reach of its community radio station to rural communities in central Appalachia
$20,000	Associated Services for the Blind, Philadelphia, PA. To renovate a fire escape tower and install talking fire alarms, as part of a larger building renovation project
$30,000	Daily Bread Food Bank, Miami, FL. To purchase and implement a new computer system, which will eliminate duplication of efforts, facilitate strategic planning and expedite warehouse operations
$15,000	(over 3 years) Donors Forum of Miami, Miami, FL. For general operating support
$20,000	Goodwill Industries of Akron, Ohio, Akron, Ohio. For an updated telecommunications system
$10,500	Goodwill Industries of Kentucky, Lexington, KY. For a new truck to support expansion of vocational and rehabilitation services in southeastern Kentucky
$25,000	Hope Center, Miami, FL. For a challenge grant to renovate the main client residence and administration building to improve accessibility and upgrade plumbing and electrical wiring
$5,000	Manatee County Volunteer Services, Bradenton, FL. For the Community Partners Assistance Program, a pilot project for individuals who have unexpected financial problems and are willing to perform volunteer community service in exchange for financial assistance on a one-time basis
$9,000	Northwest Wisconsin Community Services Agency, Superior, WI. To acquire computer hardware and software to automate the agency's operation
$50,000	American Society of Newspaper Editors, Reston, VA. To increase newsroom diversity
$1,500,000	Arizona State University, Tempe, AZ. To establish a Knight Chair in Journalism for computer-assisted journalism
$150,000	The Center for Foreign Journalists, Reston, VA. For a challenge grant for general support
$27,500	First Amendment Congress, Denver, CO. To reprint the Education for Freedom curriculum and update selected lessons for the next phase of a national training and distribution program
$175,000	(over 5 years) Harvard College, Cambridge, MA. To continue support for the Knight Latin American Fellowship in the

	Nieman Fellowship program for journalists
$125,000	The Independent Journalism Foundation, New York, NY. For the centers in Prague, Bratislava, Bucharest and a new center in Budapest
$1,500,000	(over 5 years) Indiana University, Bloomington, IND. For a project to reshape journalism education by developing a new curriculum, retraining faculty and educating a new generation of teachers and scholars
$484,280	(over 2 years) Inter American Press Association, Miami, FL. To investigate the causes and consequences of unpunished crimes against journalists in Colombia, Guatemala and Mexico and to produce a remedial action plan, including a hemispheric conference
$20,000	International Press Institute, Allentown, PA. For general support
$50,000	Investigative Reporters and Editors, New York, NY. For minority journalists to attend IRE-sponsored seminars
$16,000	Alleghany County Schools, Sparta, NC. For special projects at Sparta School
$100,000	American Association for Higher Education, Washington, DC. To support the Sixth National Conference on School/College Collaboration, including special programming for Excellence in Education representatives and for continued work on issues related to school-to-college transitions
$250,000	**Cities In Schools, Alexandria, VA. For detailed planning for expansion, evaluation and a national capital campaign**
$20,000	Cornell University, Ithaca, NY. To plan outreach activities to share successful elements of the John S. Knight Writing Program with other colleges and universities
$50,000	Developmental Studies Center, Oakland, CA. For dissemination of At Home in Our Schools: A Guide to Schoolwide Activities that Build Community, which documents lessons drawn from the Child Development Project

Georgia

Lettie Pate Evans Foundation, Inc.

c/o Charles H. McTier, Pres.
50 Hurt Plaza, Suite 1200
Atlanta, GA 30303
(404) 522-6755
E-mail: fdns@woodruff.org
Source Date: 12/96

Geographic Restrictions:
Primarily in GA.

Restrictions:
No grants to individuals, operating expenses, research, scholarships, fellowships, or matching gifts.

To Whom:
Higher and other education, museums, libraries, performing arts, cultural programs, educational associations, health, youth, civic affairs, child welfare, family services, social services.

For What:
Building funds, equipment, land acquisition, seed money, renovation projects, capital campaigns.

Financial info:
Assets: $227,983,100.
Giving: $25,374,000 for 25 grants (high: $2,500,000; low: $10,000).

Application info:
Applications accepted. Submit letter of inquiry. Deadline for proposals is Feb. 1 and Sept. 1. Board meets in Apr. and Nov. Publishes application guidelines.

Recent Grants:

$100,000	Seven Stages, Inc., Atlanta, GA. Completion of renovation of existing building with expanded public areas and more efficient building systems.
$50,000	Horatio Alger Association of Distinguished Americans, Alexandria, VA. Three-year support for the Horatio Alger National Scholars Program in Georgia.
$325,000	American Humane Education Society, Boston, MA. Introduction of new reading curriculum in elementary schools in Atlanta.

$200,000	Brewton-Parker College, Mount Vernon, GA. Construction of the Herbert Saliba Chapel and Auditorium
$500,000	Episcopal High School, Alexandria, VA. Endowment of the Lettie Pate Whitehead Evans Faculty Enrichment Program.
$200,000	University of Georgia, Athens, GA. Grant of $600,000 for expansion of statewide school improvement program linking public school teachers and administrators with University faculty.
$500,000	Interdenominational Theological Center, Atlanta, GA. $2.5 million campaign for program support and campus improvements.
$250,000	National Science Center Foundation, Inc., Augusta, GA. Development of the Learning Logic curriculum for use in Georgia schools.
$2,500,000	Oglethorpe University, Atlanta, GA. Final payment on grant of $3.5 million for construction of a new performing arts center and other capital needs included in $35 million capital campaign.
$200,000	Southern Center for International Studies, Atlanta, GA. Four-year grant of **$700,000 for production, distribution and evaluation of social science educational materials for use in secondary schools.**
$300,000	Trinity School, Atlanta, GA. $1.5 million capital campaign.
$250,000	The Walker School, Marietta, GA. $2.5 million capital campaign to construct a new lower school and athletic center, and renovate the middle school, upper school and library.
$200,000	Young Harris College, Young Harris, GA. Expansion and improvement of computer resources.
$25,000	The Foundation for Hospital Art, Roswell, GA. Support for organization which organizes volunteers to produce murals and other art works for hospitals.
$200,000	Atlanta Community Food Bank, Atlanta, GA. Two-year grant of $400,000 to establish working capital, expand volunteer program and improve computer system.
$100,000	Housing Starts, Inc., Atlanta, GA. Costs to be incurred for a project to convert surplus railroad cars into housing for the homeless.
$10,000	Westminster-Canterbury Foundation, Richmond, VA. Maintenance of the Whitehead mausoleum and annual observance of Lettie Pate Day.
$150,000	The Nature Conservancy, Atlanta, GA. Three-year grant of $450,000 for continuation of Altamaha River Bioreserve program.
$500,000	Zoo Atlanta, Atlanta, GA. Payment on grant of $3 million toward $8.5 million campaign to improve the Zoo.

Directors, Officers, Trustees:

Evans, Lettie Pate (d), Donor
Goizueta, Roberto C., Trustee
Hardin, P. Russell, Officer
Jones, Joseph W., Officer, Trustee
McTier, Charles H., Officer
Sibley, James M., Trustee
Spalding, Hughes, Jr., Officer, Trustee
Tribble, J. Lee, Officer
Williams, James B, Trustee
Woodruff, Robert W. (d), Donor

Hawaii

Samuel N. & Mary Castle Foundation

c/o Hawaii Community Foundation
900 Fort Street Mall, Suite 1300
Honolulu, HI 96813
(808) 537-6333
EIN: 996003321
Source Date: 12/95

Geographic Restrictions:
Limited to HI, with emphasis on Oahu.

Restrictions:
No grants to individuals, continuing support, endowments, or scholarships.

To Whom:
Private education (45% of funding): preschool, elementary, secondary and higher education.

Arts and culture (31% of funding): museums, public broadcasting, theatre, music, dance.

Humanities and Protestant and Christian religion (1% of funding).

Social services (6% of funding): hunger, youth, AIDS.

Health (1% of funding): medical support.

Environment (15% of funding): environmental education, energy conservation.

For What

Special projects, building funds, operating budgets, equipment, seed money, land acquisition, renovation projects, general purposes, capital campaigns.

Financial info:

Assets: $27,742,500.
Giving: $1,386,600 for 60 grants (high: $200,000; low: $1,000).

Application info:

Applications accepted. Submit 1 copy of proposal and support material; two copies of executive summary (1-2 page limit) and budget. Deadline is Jan. 2, Apr. 1, July 1, and Oct. 1. Board meets in Mar., June, Sept., and Dec. Capital proposals are due Oct. 1. Publishes annual report with application guidelines.

Recent Grants:

$30,000	Damien Memorial High School - Renovation and modernization project
$50,000	Hawaii Preparatory Academy - Capital campaign
$10,000	Ho'ala School - Equipment and supplies to establish ninth grade
$20,000	Island School - Repair and renovation of classroom for upper division
$5,000	Kona Christian Academy Incorporated - Playground equipment
$8,500	The Lokahi School, Inc. - Purchase of office equipment
$2,500	Makua Lani Christian School - Facility upgrade, classroom furniture and computer equipment
$5,910	Malamalama School - Library expansion
$25,000	Maryknoll Schools - Capital campaign
$10,000	Mohala Pua Schools - Capital campaign
$10,000	Montessori Community School-Computer equipment and software
$205,000	Montessori School of Maui-Phase II-Classroom construction
$10,000	Parent Participation Nursery School - Purchase of property
$30,000	Saint Andrew's Priory School for Girls - Capital campaign
$6,000	Saint Joseph School - Hilo - Macintosh computers for learning center
$5,000	**Aloha Special Technology Access Center - Development and purchase of evaluation tool kit**
$5,000	The English-Speaking Union of the United States - 1995-96 Excellence in English Awards and the Shakespeare competition

$10,000	Hawaii Association of Independent Schools - Second year support for statewide professional development
$4,500	Hawaii Branch the Orton Dyslexia Society - Teacher and parent training on children with learning disabilities or dyslexia
$5,000	Hoover Presidential Library - W R. Castle, Jr Fellowship Program
$4,000	The Hualalai Academy, Inc. - Start-up costs for independent school
$10,000	Maui Special Learning Center - Expansion of program
$5,000	Sacred Hearts Academy - Elementary math and science program
$25,000	Diamond Head Theatre - Capital improvements
$100,000	The Hawaii Children's Museum - Capital campaign
$6,000	Alliance for Drama Education - Production of RUMORS: I Heard it thru the Grapevine
$20,000	Hawaii Community Foundation - Development of publication of Hawaiian National Bibliography - Volume 1
$7,500	Hawaii Opera Theatre - Second year support for HOT's mini-residency program
$5,000	Honolulu Theatre for Youth - Second year support for story-telling and creative drama in libraries
$5,000	Kaua'i Children's Discovery Museum - Traveling exhibit
$10,000	Maui Community Arts and Cultural Center Project support for "Partnering for arts and Education"
$5,000	Ma'alaea Community Garden, Inc., - Youth educational outreach program
$13,000	The Nature Conservancy of Hawaii - Environmental education project
$2,500	Council on Foundations -Project to enhance the effectiveness of family foundations
$10,000	Hawaii Community Foundation - 1997 Council on Foundations conference
$12,000	Saint Timothy's Children's Centers, Inc. - Construction of administration facility
$12,000	The Salvation Army - Improvement for playground and purchase of equipment - The Ohana Keiki Day Center in Kailua-Kona
$5,000	California State University-San Marcos Foundation - Literature review by Lillian Vega Castenada
$25,000	Hawaii Association for the Education of Young Children - Public awareness campaign on early childhood education and care
$12,000	Hawaii Literacy, Inc. - Toy and book lending library
$9,025	Camp Mokuleia Inc. - Repair seawall
$50,000	Child and Family Services - Capital campaign

$5,000	Ka Lima O Maui - Plant nursery teaching program for young children conducted by people with developmental disabilities
$20,000	Kama Aina Care, Inc. - Teacher apprentice program
$25,000	KCAA Pre-Schools of Hawaii - A model comprehensive system for delivery of early childhood education and care
$3,200	The Koloa Early School-Teacher and parent education project
$180,000	Hawaii Nature Center - Capital campaign
$10,000	Honolulu Armed Services YMCA of the USA - Expansion of PlayMorning program
$9,000	Wai'anae Coast Day Care Centers, Inc. Learning materials and curriculum development
$10,000	Parents and Children Together - Parent training classes

Directors, Officers, Trustees:

Baldwin, John C., Trustee
Castle, Alfred L., Officer, Trustee
Castle, Donald, Officer, Trustee
Castle, Mary Tenney(d), Donor
Castle, W. Donald, Officer, Trustee
McIntosh, James C., Trustee
Quisenberry, Cynthia, Trustee

Illinois

Chicago Community Trust

c/o Bruce L. Newman, Exec. Dir.
222 N. LaSalle St., Suite 1400
Chicago, IL 60601-1009
(312) 372-3356
EIN: 362167000
Source Date: 12/95

Geographic Restrictions

Primarily in Cook County, IL.

Restrictions:

No grants for religious purposes, individuals (except for the Community Service Fellowship Program), annual campaigns, deficit financing, endowments, publications, conferences or scholarships, purchase of computer hardware.

To Whom:

Health, social services, AIDS, immigrants and refugees, urban affairs, women, employment training, youth, higher, secondary, and elementary education, cultural programs, civic affairs, seniors, environment, hospitals, homeless, hunger, minorities, libraries, fellowships to individuals in leadership positions in local community service organizations.

Health (17% of funding), Social Services (19% of funding), Arts and Humanities (40% of funding), Education (7% of funding), Civic Affairs (18% of funding).

For What

Operating budgets, continuing support, emergency funds, building funds, equipment, land acquisition, loans, research, special projects, renovation projects, capital campaigns, general purposes, technical assistance, matching funds, program-related investments, seed money.

Financial info:

Assets: $362,529,500

Giving: $30,962,700 for grants (high: $500,000; low: $100) and $267,200 for loans.

Application info:

Applications accepted. Submit proposal (2 copies). No deadline. Application form required for various special programs. Board meets in Jan., Mar., June, and Sept. Publishes annual report and application guidelines.

Recent Grants:

$250,000	Alivio Health Center to support its capital campaign for purchase of the site of its proposed new facility
$25,000	Austin People's Action Center to partially support renovating its building at 5931 West Corcoran
$100,000	Howard Brown Health Center to support its campaign to raise $1,000,000 toward the costs of its new facility
$5,000	Cancer Wellness Center for general operating support made in recognition of Robert F. Reusche's service to the Trust
$100,000	Chicago Clergy Association to support expansion of services in the Dr. James West Clinic of its Haymarket House
$500,000	Core Foundation a one-time, two-year grant to support its capital campaign to build, equip, and operate the Cook County/Rush Health Center
$25,000	El Rincon Supportive Services Organization to support its Phase III facility rehabilitation program to provide a medically safe treatment environment
$20,000	Health Works Theatre for general operating support

$54,000	Illinois Caucus For Adolescent Health for salary support of a senior health policy staff person and associated program support
$15,000	Metropolitan Chicago Information Center a one-time grant to partially support the cost of a statewide survey of health status and insurance coverage
$100,000	Misericordia Heart Of Mercy to support its capital campaign for acquiring off-campus residences
$45,000	Oak/Leyden Developmental Services a one-time, two-year grant for salary support of a new part-time staff person to help implement the marketing and community awareness segment of its strategic action plan
$10,000	St. James Catholic Church to partially support "Making the Right Connections" program for violence prevention and gang diversion
$25,000	South East Alcohol And Drug Abuse Center to support its Intensive Outpatient program
$30,000	Special Leisure Services Foundation to support the purchase of an accessible vehicle to transport mentally or physically challenged individuals
$53,325	University of Illinois Foundation for salary support of a coordinator of community development for the Chicago Project for Violence Prevention
$25,000	Uptown Community Learning Center to support its "100% Campaign for Basic Health Care" program
$12,000	**Chapin Hall Center For Children to support the inclusion of Chicago Youth Centers' project in the process evaluation of the Trust's Children, Youth, and Families Initiative**
$11,250	**Chapin Hall Center For Children a two-year grant to support the inclusion of Chinese Mutual Aid Association/Uptown-Edgewater Multicultural Youth Project's program in the process evaluation of the Trust's Children, Youth, and Families Initiative**
$11,450	**Chapin Hall Center For Children to support the inclusion of YMCA of Metropolitan Chicago's project in the process evaluation of the Trust's Children, Youth, and Families Initiative**
$240,000	Chicago Youth Centers to support its Community Arts Initiative
$225,000	Chinese Mutual Aid Association as fiscal agent for the Uptown-Edgewater Multicultural Youth Project a two-year grant for general operating support
$15,000	for general operating support
$100,000	The Night Ministry for general operating support

$20,000	Oak Park Y.M.C.A. for salary support of a development director
$35,000	Olive Branch Mission for salary support of a program director for its Residential Recover Program
$15,000	Pilsen Homeless Services Clinic for salary support of a part-time clinic coordinator and case manager
$5,000	St. Fidelis Social Service Agency for salary support of a meal/food coordinator
$20,000	Shelter, Inc. to support a data base computer system
$100,000	The Port for general operating support
$20,000	The Living Room Cafe to support renovations to bring its site up to code
$10,000	Arab-american Action Network for general operating support
$15,000	Chicago Bar Foundation to partially support planning activities of the 1999 Juvenile Court Centenary
$54,000	Chicago Coalition For The Homeless for salary support of a senior youth policy analyst
$50,000	Child Abuse Prevention Services for support of its "From Day One" program
$38,000	Chicago Lighthouse For The Blind a one-time grant for salary support of a marketing sales representative in its manufacturing program
$30,000	Chicago Mutual Housing Network a two-year grant to support its Tenant Organizing Project
$25,000	Horizons Community Services, Inc. for salary support of two youth service workers
$50,000	Illinois Hunger Coalition for general operating support
$15,000	Inspired Partnership to support its demonstration phase of "Celebrating Chicago's Black Churches: Reclaiming a Legacy"
$12,000	Lakeview Shelter, Inc. for salary support of its coordinator of supplies
$10,000	La Vivienda Housing Development Corporation for general operating support
$5,000	A Safe Place for general operating support made in recognition of Robert F. Reusche's service to the Trust
$20,000	Windows Of Opportunity, Inc. to support the Cook County Information Initiative
$50,000	Horizons Community Services, Inc. for general operating support
$23,000	Housing Options For The Mentally Ill In Evanston for partial salary support of an assistant director
$20,000	Family Service Centers to support its Nueva Vista program
$25,000	Civitas Initiative to partially support the judicial internship program at the Cook County Juvenile Court

$15,000	Council For A Parliament Of The World's Religions to support the Metropolitan Chicago Inter-religious Initiative
$60,000	Mary Crane League for salary support of a financial manager

Harris Bank Foundation

c/o Donna Streibich Curtis, Secretary/Treasurer
111 W. Monroe St.
P.O. Box 755
Chicago, IL 60603
(312) 461-5834
EIN: 366033888
Source Date: 12/95

Geographic Restrictions:
Limited to the Chicago, IL, area, except for matching gifts program.

Restrictions:
No grants for sectarian or religious organizations, fraternal organizations, political activities, individuals (except for employee-related scholarships), research, publications, conferences, testimonials, or advertisements.

To Whom:
Arts and Culture: major cultural and fine arts organizations.

Higher Education: private higher education in Cook County.

Education: Chicago Public School reform movement by providing advocacy, training and/or evaluation of the ongoing effort to strengthen and serve the Local School Councils and Professional Personnel Advisory Committees, promote urban education and advance educational opportunities.

Civic: affordable housing, urban affairs, crime prevention, youth, environment, legal services, minorities, voluntarism.

Community Revitalization.

Health: provide access to primary health care, teen health, hospitals, mental health.

Social Services: minorities, low-income urban development, family services, hunger, leadership development, job training, drug and alcohol abuse.

For What:
Operating budgets, continuing support, annual campaigns, seed money, building funds, equipment, matching funds, technical assistance, scholarship funds, special projects, employee-related scholarships, employee matching gifts, renovation projects.

Financial info:
Assets: $1,011,500.
Giving: $1,089,700 for 95 grants (high: $100,000; low: $500).

Application info:
Applications accepted. Submit proposal (5 page limit). Deadline is Dec. 1., Feb. 1, May 1, July 1, Sept. 1, and Nov. 1. Board meets in Jan., Mar., June, Aug., Oct., and Dec. Publishes annual report with application guidelines.

Recent Grants:

$14,000	The Art Institute of Chicago. General operating support
$50,000	Chicago Symphony/Lyric Opera. Facilities Fund Pledge for capital campaign
$15,000	The Chicago Theatre Company. Youth Outreach Program
$10,000	Museum of Contemporary Art. Pledge to Chicago Contemporary Campaign
$14,750	Museum of Science and Industry. Campaign 2000 and general operating support
$15,000	The People's Music School. Capital campaign
$5,000	The DuSable Museum. General operating support
$5,000	Mexican Fine Arts Center Museum. Pledge to Capital Endowment Campaign
$3,500	ETA Creative Arts Foundation Inc. General operating support.
$5,000	Field Museum of Natural History. Community Outreach Program
$10,000	Chicago United, Inc.. Hire the Future and Job Readiness Programs
$25,000	Civic Committee of the Commercial Club of Chicago. General operating support
$10,000	Bickerdike Redevelopment Corporation. General operating support
$10,000	Lakefront SRO. Housing Development Program
$10,000	Local Initiatives Support Corporation. General operating support
$10,000	YMCA of Metropolitan Chicago. Duncan YMCA renovation and expansion
$10,000	St. Joseph's Carondelet Child Center. General operating support

$10,000	Chicago Youth Centers. Pledge for the renovation of 14 centers
$10,000	Chicago Panel on School Policy. General operating support
$10,000	Chicago Zoological Society. General operating support
$10,000	Designs for Change. General operating support
$12,500	Chicago Association of Neighborhood Development Organizations. General operating support
$10,000	Chicago Community Loan Fund. General operating support
$10,000	Chicago Rehab Network. Urban Developers Program
$5,000	ACORN Housing Corporation of Illinois. General operating support
$5,000	Association of Rehabilitation Contractors. General operating support
$3,000	Chicago Mutual Housing Network. General operating support
$15,000	City Year. General operating support
$10,000	Covenant Development Corporation. General operating support
$3,000	Habitat for Humanity Uptown Chicago. General operating support
$5,000	Jane Addams Resource Corporation. Targeted Development Project
$5,000	Jobs for Youth/Chicago, Inc. General operating support
$5,000	Center for Neighborhood Technology. General operating support
$6,000	Centers for New Horizons, Inc. General operating support
$8,400	Chicago Urban League. General operating support
$5,000	The Chicago Academy of Sciences. Pledge to expansion and renovation capital campaign
$5,000	Chicago Cities in Schools. General operating support
$2,500	Chicago Public Schools Student. Science Fair, Inc. General operating support
$5,000	ChildServ. Home Instruction Program for Preschool Youngsters
$5,000	Latino Institute. Bilingual Education Project
$3,000	Youth Guidance. Rites of Passage Program
$3,000	The Newberry Library. General operating support
$5,000	Project Education Plus. General operating support
$2,500	Sherwood Conservatory of Music. ACCESS MUSIC! Tuition Assistance Program
$4,000	South-East Asia Center. Youth Delinquency Prevention Program
$5,000	Chicago Crime Commission. General operating support
$3,000	Gamaliel Foundation. Leadership Training Program
$5,000	Teen Living Programs. Belfort House, a transitional shelter
$2,500	United Methodist Homes and Services. General operating support
$3,000	Westside Holistic Family Services. Health care delivery equipment

Directors, Officers, Trustees:

Coffey, Robin S., Director
Curtis, Donna Streibich, Officer
Davis, Trevor L., Director
Harris Trust & Savings Bank, Trustee
Hunt, Donald S., Director
Jackson, Darrell B., Director
Kato, Robert Y., Director
Neal, Joan F., Officer
Thorsen, Jamie K., Officer, Director
Williams, Edward J., Director, Officer
Wilner, Alvin G., Director

Massachusetts

Bruner Foundation, Inc.

c/o Simeon Bruner, Treasurer
130 Prospect St.
Cambridge, MA 02139
(617) 492-8404
EIN: 136180803
Source Date: 12/94

Geographic Restrictions:
Limited to U.S.

Restrictions:
No grants to individuals, general support, building or endowment funds, scholarships, or fellowships.

To Whom:
Urban excellence through the Rudy Bruner Award for Excellence in the Urban Environment: **evaluation of public school reform.**

For What
Research, special projects.

Financial info:
Giving: $435,300 for grants (high: $100,000; low: $1,000).

Application info:
Applications accepted. Application form required. Deadline is Dec. 30. Publishes application guidelines.

Directors, Officers, Trustees:

Bruner, Joshua E., Officer, Trustee
Bruner, Martha (d), Donor
Bruner, R. Simeon, Officer, Trustee
Bruner, Rudy (d), Donor
Herson, Richard J. L., Officer

Michigan

Community Foundation of Greater Flint

c/o David K. Swenson, VP for Program
502 Church St.
Flint, MI 48502-1206
(810) 767-8270
Internet: http://www.flint.lib.mi.us/cfflint/
Source Date: 12/94

Geographic Restrictions:
Limited to Genesee County, MI.

Restrictions:
No grants to individuals, endowments, capital funds drives, operating budgets, fundraising events, religious purposes, scholarships, fellowships, deficit financing, or equipment.

To Whom:
Persistent and Pervasive Poverty: families in poverty with children under the age of 10, teenage female heads of households, African-American at-risk males ages 13-14, community and individual self-image, build individual self-image by provide racial and/or ethnic pride through cultural and/or artistic experiences, build community and peer support systems to improve the self-image of low income female heads of households and at-risk inner city youth, leadership training to inner city youth and adults, provide role models and mentors for inner city youth, bring together suburban and inner city residents around common goals or to resolve common problems, improve neighborhood involvement in developing and implementing community development strategies designed to benefit low and moderate income residents, identify neighborhood leaders and avail them of the skills necessary to realize

that potential, training and technical assistance to organize neighborhood residents so as to increase their capacity to define and resolve pressing local issues, support involvement of low income residents in organizations which address neighborhood problems or interact with other communities to address common concerns, support inter-generational activities at the neighborhood level, alleviate the debilitating personal and environmental health problems, such as inadequate prenatal nutrition, or exposure to lead paint, improve the access to poor people to family planning, pre- and postnatal, early childhood and the preventive health services, improve service delivery systems and agencies through data collection, **training, and improving access so that local nonprofit agencies and systems learn to use information to plan and evaluate services**, support programs which restructure health and social services, assure appropriate educational opportunities for all low income children, improve accessibility to both popular and traditional arts experiences to low income individuals.

Children Under the Age of 10: improve prenatal and neonatal health care and education, parent education, particularly among young teenaged, predominantly female parents;

Advancing Philanthropy: involve youth decision making processes to access community needs and consider asset allocation to meet those needs, provide youth opportunities to learn the dynamics and benefits of philanthropy and community services;

Arts and Humanities: increase the availability of participatory arts experiences for Genesee County children, facilitate the ability of young children to be exposed to and understand a wide variety of the arts, increase awareness and appreciation of children for the artistic values and expressions of a wide range of ethnic groups and cultures;

Conservation and the Environment: increase awareness of the young children of Flint and Genesee County of the importance of protecting the environment, encourage efforts to education youth about protecting and improving the Saginaw Valley watershed.

Community Affairs.

Education: increase the number of young (0-4) children who participate in quality early childhood education programs, promote the use of educational institutions as sites of early and appropriate family interventions so that the health and welfare of families is enhanced, promote and nurture the involvement of parents in educational experiences of their grade school children, support educational programs, both traditional and nontraditional education settings, which instill in young children an understanding of the workings of a democratic society.

Health: improve pre- and postnatal health care to children, regardless of the ability of their parents to pay, improve the exposure to and practice of sound mental and physical health care practices on the part of area young children and their families, improve understanding and support by the general population of the importance of providing appropriate maternal and child health care services, support innovative strategies for delivering mental and physical health care services to children and their families, including nontraditional settings and services provided by paramedical personnel, support programs conducive to involving health care professionals in volunteer activities.

For What:
Annual campaigns, continuing support, general purposes, special projects, endowment funds, matching funds.

Financial info:
Assets: $41,576,000.
Giving: $1,787,100 for 125 grants (high: $50,000; low: $200).

Application info:
Applications accepted. Application form required. Deadline is Feb. 1, June 1, Aug. 1, and Dec. 1. Board meets quarterly. Publishes annual report with application guidelines.

Recent Grants:

$8,000	Flint Institute of Arts. General Operations.
$1,000	City of Flint. 4th of July Homecoming Festival.
$3,502	Association for Child Development. Baker College Flint Child Care Science Center.
$16,103	Genesee Parks and Recreation. Capital Improvements.
$2,750	Detroit Children's Hospital Burn Unit. General Operations.
$5,000	City of Linden. Loose Senior Citizens Project.

Steelcase Foundation

c/o Susan Broman, Exec. Dir.
Location CH-5C
P.O. Box 1967
Grand Rapids, MI 49501-1967
(616) 246-4695
EIN: 386050470
Source Date: 11/96

Geographic Restrictions:
Limited to areas of company operations, including Kent and Ottawa Counties, MI (89% of funding), Orange County, CA [southern] (3% of funding), Ashville, NC (4% of funding), Athens, AL (3% of funding).

Restrictions:
No grants for religious purposes, conferences, or individuals.

To Whom:
Social services, community funds, AIDS, health, higher, secondary, and other education, arts, environment, disadvantaged, disabled, youth, seniors, women.

Arts and Culture (8% of funding), Community and Economic Development (18% of funding), Education (24% of funding), Environment (6% of funding), Health (4% of funding), Social Services (41% of funding).

For What:
Building funds, general purposes, capital campaigns, special projects, employee-related scholarships.

Financial info:
Assets: $65,281,200.
Giving: $5,115,500 for 100 grants (high: $300,000; low: $2,000).

Application info:
Applications accepted. Submit letter of inquiry. No deadline. Board meets quarterly. Publishes annual report with application guidelines.

Recent Grants:

$60,000	Grand Rapids Art Museum. General operations.
$20,000	Opera Grand Rapids. General operating support.
$500,000	Grand Action Foundation. New downtown arena project.
$15,000	Home Repair Services of Kent County. Start up funding for volunteer/client education coordinator.

$125,000	Calvin College. Library additionnual Fund challenge.
$100,000	Hope College. Expansion of DeWitt Theatre Scene Shop.
$250,000	West Michigan Horticultural Society, Inc. Develop "Michigan Botanic Garden."
$21,985	Laguna Beach Community Clinic. Purchase essential medical equipment.
$79,595	**Planned Parenthood Centers of West Michigan. Prevention, education and public awareness programs with evaluation.**
$2,000	Camp Blodgett. Camperships for disadvantaged youth.
$100,000	Children's Assessment Center. Startup funding for Center for sexually abused children.

Directors, Officers, Trustees:

Hackett, James P., Trustee
Hunting, David D., Jr., Trustee
Hunting, David D., Jr., Trustee
Martin, Roger L., Trustee
Merlotti, Frank H., Trustee
Old Kent Bank & Trust Company, Trustee
Pew, Robert C., Trustee
Steelcase, Inc., Donor
Wege, Peter M., Trustee

New Hampshire

New Hampshire Charitable Foundation

c/o Deborah Cowan, Assc. Dir.
37 Pleasant St.
Concord, NH 03301-4005
(603) 225-6641
EIN: 026005625
Source Date: 12/95

Geographic Restrictions

Limited to NH.

Restrictions:

No grants to individuals (except for student aid), building funding, land acquisition, equipment, endowments, operating support, or deficit financing.

To Whom:
Structural innovation and reform: support reform, new approaches and partnerships involving both the public and voluntary sector to improve the quality of life.

Economic development and opportunity: promote economic opportunity, benefit people who are unemployed or underemployed.

Funding transitions and planning for adversity: aid in dealing with financial adversity by examining current programs, prioritize services, reduce expenditures and actively collaborate with others to preserve or enhance key programs.

Nonprofit management, financial condition and governance: improve their financial condition through development initiatives with clear goals or substantially increase voluntary or other resources, develop more effective boards of directors/trustees and improve organizational assessment, goal setting and planning, improve efficiency of operation or focus on improvements in management.

Demonstrations, public education and advocacy: lead the public agenda, educate about needs and the impact of public policy choices and serve as a laboratory for more effective approaches to social problems, particularly in providing health and social services and in job training, retraining the workforce and community development.

Startup funding-service expansion.

Diversity, participation and self-help: address racial, socio-economic and other issues of diversity, advocacy and service programs which are consumer led and community based self-help organizations.

Arts & Humanities (10% of funding), Education (10% of funding), Environment (11% of funding), Health (5% of funding), Social Services (17% of funding), Civic Affairs (25% of funding).

For What:
Seed money, loans, student aid, scholarship funds, general purposes, special projects, student loans, consulting services, technical assistance.

Financial info:
Assets: $113,175,700.
Giving: $4,926,400 for grants (high: $50,000; low: $100), $1,487,500 for grants to individuals (high: $3,000; low: $500), $118,000 for loans to organizations and $284,700 for loans to individuals.

Application info:
Applications accepted. Application form required. Deadline is Dec. 1, Apr. 1, and Sept. 1. Board meets in Feb., June, and Nov. Publishes application guidelines.

Recent Grants:

$15,000	Tri-County Community Action, Berlin to support expansion of substance abuse outpatient and prevention services in conjunction with the Grafton County Correctional Facility
$10,000	University of New Hampshire, Durham continued funding of the Program on Consensus and Negotiation
$15,000	Bancroft Products, Concord to support further development of Project Star, a welfare-to-work demonstration program
$11,000	Moultonboro Area Community Development to support the Institute for Enterprise Development
$12,000	New Hampshire College/Portsmouth to expand the Papoutsy Seminar for Women Entrepreneurs and to support the Women's Business Center
$2,300	New Hampshire Commercial Fishermen's Association to develop an educational display about the NH fishing industry
$8,474	Northeast Lakes Region Task Force, West Ossipee startup funding for the Whittier Farmers' Market
$20,000	Northern Forest Heritage Park, Berlin to support development of the Heritage Park as a community and economic development project
$3,000	Southwestern Community Services, Claremont to implement a peer lending program for women interested in starting a small business
$14,250	STA-NORTH, Groveton Fishermen's Association for part-time staff support, publication of a local newsletter and other operating costs of a community and business development organization
$3,000	Wakefield Economic Resource Committee, Sanbornville to provide information from the NH Works program through a computer station at the local library
$12,500	Women's Rural Economic Network, Twin Mountain continued general funding for enterprise training and support
$40,000	Working Capital, Cambridge MA continued general funding for micro-enterprise lending and technical assistance program
$15,000	Central NH Community Mental Health Center, Concord interim general support for the Parent-Child Centers in two communities

$9,000	NH State Council on the Arts, Concord to study attitudes and perceptions of key leaders on public support for the arts
$4,250	Grafton County Senior Citizen's Council, Lebanon Interim funding to supplement local fundraising to continue volunteer home repair program initiated with a federal grant
$5,535	New Hampshire Legal Assistance, Concord to provide facilitation services on corporate and service restructuring
$6,000	Northeast Resource Recovery Association, Concord interim general support for core services to municipalities and businesses
$19,000	Children's Alliance of New Hampshire, Concord for organizing and information services to communities on changes in Federal funding programs
$5,000	League of Women Voter's Education Fund, Hanover continued funding to support Upper Valley 2001 and Beyond, community forums and the development of regional quality of life indicators
$15,000	New Hampshire Citizen Action, Concord to support research on New Hampshire's health safety net as provided through hospital charity care
$6,000	New Hampshire Hospice Organization, Peterborough for expanded staffing to support legislative work on health policy and reform
$20,000	New Hampshire Comparative Risk Project, Concord to support a ranking of environmental risks by a public advisory group with business, government, environmental and citizen representation and to develop priorities for action
$6,400	**Appalachian Mt. Teen Project, Wolfeboro for a consultation with Harvard Graduate School of Education to develop a program evaluation component**
$6,500	Apple Hill Center for Chamber Music, East Sullivan for board development and team building to strengthen strategic planning
$5,668	Fellowship House/Riverbend Mental Health Center, Concord for organizational restructuring to reduce overhead costs and improve productivity
$3,500	Monadnock Area Pastoral Counseling Services, Keene to support participation in a national assessment of quality and effectiveness of counseling services
$6,645	Seacoast Mental Health Center, Portsmouth for a survey by consumers to support quality improvements to increase consumer satisfaction
$15,000	Concord Area Trust for Community Housing to support current programs and for development of affordable housing in communities beyond Concord

$7,250	Good Neighbor Health Clinic, White River Junction, VT to support planning and development of a free dental clinic
$5,000	Project Second Start, Lebanon to support addition of a math component and training of additional volunteers for the Adult Tutorial Program
$7,000	Stratford County Community Action, Dover startup funding for a volunteer outreach program to assist elderly residents of the Rochester area
$10,000	Valley Regional Healthcare, Claremont to implement a sexual assault Nurse Examiners Program in the emergency room and outpatient clinic
$5,900	Children's Health Center, North Conway continued funding for early intervention services to families with young children
$5,040	Community Child Care Center, Portsmouth to support "Through the Cracks" program offering behavior intervention to families and children
$5,000	Exeter Area High School, Exeter for a project addressing violence within the family, academic and social world of youth
$8,000	Families Matter in Carroll County, Ossipee for a support and education program for teen parents
$6,000	Good Beginnings of Sullivan County, Claremont for expansion of the home visitor program
$4,000	Hannah House, Lebanon for parenting support groups for young parents with infants and young children
$6,000	North Country Education Foundation, Gorham to provide training on behavior disorders for parents and teachers of young children
$3,500	Rockingham County Community Action, Portsmouth to support a home-based family literacy program in the Seabrook area
$3,600	Betty's Dream, Portsmouth to recruit students with disabilities to participate in a horticultural therapy program
$10,000	New Hampshire Community Loan Fund, Concord for development and management of the NH Home of Your Own Program, an initiative to provide home ownership opportunities to citizens with developmental disabilities
$5,000	Nite Owl Consumers Association, Franklin toward purchase of a vehicle for transporting program participants
$2,150	North Hampton Elementary School, North Hampton for development of a program that promotes global awareness and ethnic tolerance
$7,000	Twin Rivers Community Corporation, Tilton for the Transitional Housing Program to assist individuals and families in developing self-reliance

Directors, Officers, Trustees:
Barba, Stephen P., Director
Crosier, John D., Director
Eades, Juliana, Director
Feldstein, Lewis M., Officer, Trustee
Gross, Martin L., Director
O'Donnell, Kendra Stearns, Director
Smith, Stuart V., Jr., Director
Weeks, John F., Jr., Director
Wright, Elizabeth Story, Director
Zachos, Anne C., Director, Officer

New Jersey

Robert Wood Johnson Foundation

c/o Edward H. Robbins, Proposal Mgr.
P.O. Box 2316
Princeton, NJ 08543-2316
(609) 452-8701
Internet: http://www.rwjf.org
EIN: 223048720
Source Date: 12/96

Geographic Restrictions:
Limited to the U.S.

Restrictions:
No grants for basic biomedical research, individuals, operating expenses, deficit financing, endowment or capital funds, construction, renovation, equipment, conferences or symposia, publications or media projects, research on unapproved drug therapies or devices, or international programs and institutions.

To Whom:
Access: assure that Americans of all ages have access to basic health care, explore options for expanded coverage for the uninsured and underinsured, **develop and evaluate new payment incentives to promote primary care services**, stimulate the U.S. debate on restructuring health care financing, influence the supply and distribution of generalist physicians and other primary care providers, address the underrepresentation of minorities in health care professions, strengthen primary care infrastructure and the public health safety net, increase understanding of the contribution of race, socioeconomic status, and culture in health and health care, work with communities to iden-

tify and address their health problems, help providers become more responsive to needs of diverse patient populations.

Drug and Alcohol Abuse: encourage service demonstration models that connect substance abuse services to organizations that reach significant populations of individuals, such as juvenile justice system, education system, business community, religion community, and neighborhood centers, models that connect substance abuse services with larger health care system, understand the causes of substance abuse and its prevention and treatment, including identification, **evaluation, and dissemination of promising new approaches that are appropriate for persons with varied environmental and risk factors**, comprehensive community-wide communications projects and efforts to change societal norms regarding the use of substances, improve the effectiveness of substance abuse services, the organization, delivery, and financing, policy research, promote changes in community and social environments that will reduce substance abuse.

Chronic Health Conditions: development and testing of exemplary models for reorganization and delivery of needed services to those with chronic health conditions, research projects and policy analysis, promote better clinical practice in chronic care, alter the focus of medical practice to include the effective management of services for people with chronic illness, communications projects that illuminate the complexity of the problem.

Cost Containment: policy analysis, health services research and demonstration projects that explore the feasibility of new cost control strategies, **evaluate the impact of different cost control strategies on costs, access and quality, as well as on different sectors of the economy**, educate the public about the tradeoffs inherent in different cost control strategies, bring together the major actors in health policy to promote better understanding of the long-term problems facing the health care system and the need for more systemic approach to controlling health care expenditures.

For What:
Seed money, research, special projects, fellowships, program-related investments.

Financial info:
Assets: $5,257,995,500 (from 1995 990PF).
Giving: $255,193,500 for 945 grants.

Application info:
Applications accepted. Submit letter of inquiry (4 page limit). No deadline. Board meets quarterly. Publishes newsletter and application guidelines.

Recent Grants:

$1,600,000	Memorial Hospital, Pawtucket, RI. For the Volunteer Physician Technical Resource Program.
$2,500,000	University of California, CA. For improving access to care by restructuring provider payments.
$50,000	Children's Hospital Foundation of Austin, TX. For planning for the privatization of a school-based health services program.
$450,000	The Greater Kansas City Community Foundation, Kansas City, MO. For a campaign to mobilize the community to address the needs of children.
$200,000	Marshall Heights Community Development Organization, Washington, DC. For planning a primary care delivery network.
$349,199	National Academy of Sciences Institute of Medicine, Washington, DC. For a study of children, health insurance and access to care.
$100,000	Public Health Foundation Enterprises, City of Industry, CA. For wellness care at work sites in Central Los Angeles.
$250,000	The Urban Institute, Washington, DC. For assessing the new federalism in New Jersey.
$220,679	Greater Cleveland Hospital Association. Linking Supply to Demand: A Long-Range Nursing Workforce Project.
$1,500,000	American Medical Association, Chicago, IL. For a program to train physicians in end-of-life care.
$773,644	George Washington University, Washington, DC. For assessing the implementation of health-related provisions of the Welfare Reform Act.
$188,804	the Alliance for Health Reform, Washington, DC. For issue briefings on managed care and vulnerable populations for Washington-based policymakers and the media.
$489,307	Family Voices, Algodones, NM. For resources for families with special-needs children.
$197,045	Group Health Cooperative of Puget Sound, Seattle, WA. For planning for a program of chronic disease management in organized health systems.
$180,000	**University of Maryland Center on Aging, College Park. MD. For focus groups and surveys for RWJF Cash and Counseling Demonstration and Evaluation Program.**
$498,640	Medical Pathfinders, Anchorage, AK. For development of a computerized patient support network for people with chronic illnesses.
$203,018	National Conference of State Legislatures, Denver. CO. For education for state policymakers on workers' compensation health reform issues.

$113,280	National Hospice Organization, Arlington, VA. For a project to train residents in end-of-life care.
$355,703	National Multiple Sclerosis Society, New York. NY. For a syndicated radio program on chronic health conditions.
$184,998	New Jersey Institute of Technology Foundation, Newark, NJ. For a manual to assist parents of children with physical disabilities in creating a supportive home environment.
$100,000	University of North Carolina at Chapel Hill School of Nursing, NC. For a project to update a nursing text on death and dying.
$379,954	University of Southern Mississippi Institute for Disability Studies, Hattiesburg, MS. For improving systems of care for chronically ill Mississippians.
$110,068	University of Virginia Health Sciences Center, Charlottesville, VA. For a national survey of hospice volunteers and staff.
$810,223	**University of Minnesota School of Public Health, Minneapolis, MN. For evaluation of RWJF's Reducing Underage Drinking Through Community and State Coalitions.**
$482,219	American Bar Association Fund for Justice and Education, Washington, DC. For development of unified family courts to assist families with substance abuse problems.
$138,404	Boston University School of Public Health, MA. For coordinating community coalition participation in Home Box Office outreach activities.
$2,200,000	University of California, Los Angeles, CA, Center for Health Sciences. For a household survey on substance abuse and mental health care.
$95,050	The National Center on Addiction and Substance Abuse at Columbia University, New York, NY. For a survey of Californians' understanding of Proposition 215: Medical Use of Marijuana.
$451,185	National Foundation for the Centers for Disease Control and Prevention, Atlanta, GA. For research on racial and gender differences in teen smoking.
$96,991	Treatment Research Institute, Philadelphia. PA. For research on the effects on employers of covering substance abuse services.
$853,446	East Bay Community Recovery Project, Oakland, CA. Fighting Back: Community Initiatives to Reduce Demand for Illegal Drugs and Alcohol.
$500,000	American Cancer Society, Georgia Division, Atlanta, GA. SmokeLess States: Statewide Tobacco Prevention and Control Initiatives.

$899,375	The Carter Center, Atlanta, GA. For developing community responses to youth firearm violence.
$237,533	Aspira of Puerto Rico, San Juan. Emergency assistance for the victims of Hurricane Hortense in Puerto Rico.
$200,000	Association of Academic Health Centers, Washington, DC. For a study of the organizational structures of academic health centers.
$230,000	Harvard Law School, Cambridge, MA. For research to develop policy models aimed at assuring that children grow up in nurturing homes.
$351,228	Institute for the Arts of Democracy, Brattleboro, VT. For expansion of a news service on civic engagement.
$425,000	National Academy of Sciences & Institute of Medicine. For a study of injuries in the US and the response of public and private agencies.
$450,000	National Academy of Sciences & Institute of Medicine. For a research study on health and behavior.
$499,944	The New York Academy of Medicine, New York, NY. For defining and measuring community benefit in managed health care.
$440,011	University of Pennsylvania, The Annenberg School for Communication, Philadelphia, PA. For improving educational television opportunities for children.
$350,000	The United Way of Central Jersey, Milltown, NJ. Support for the 1996-97 campaign.
$1,100,000	New Jersey Health Initiatives, awards to six sites.
$50,000	Assessment of sexuality research opportunities Social Science Research Council, New York, NY
$287,642	Design and implement a system for monitoring quality of care and beneficiary and provider satisfaction Commonwealth of Puerto Rico, Puerto Rico Health Insurance Administration, San Juan, PR
$594,385	Improving Service Systems for People with Disabilities, Stavros Center for Independent Living, Inc. Amherst, MA
$100,000	Partners in Caregiving: The Dementia Services Program, Central Adult Daycare Services, Inc. Warwick, RI
$50,000	Using graphic displays of medication history to improve psychiatric care. State of Vermont, Department of Mental Health, Waterbury, VT
$572,827	Expansion of model needle exchange program. City of New Haven, Department of Health, New Haven, CT
$495,206	Managed care model for high-risk families, The Center for Mental Health, Inc. Washington, DC
$977,728	Improving the Quality of Hospital Care. Public Hospital Institute, San Mateo, CA

$149,829	Healthy Nations:Reducing Substance Abuse Among Native Americans. Confederated Tribes of the Colville Reservation, Nespelem, WA
$968,895	SmokeLess States Program - Implementation. Alaska Native Health Board, Anchorage, AK
$150,000	Healthy Nations:Reducing Substance Abuse Among Native Americans. White Mountain Apache Tribe of the Fort Apache Indian Reservation, Whiterriver, AZ

Victoria Foundation, Inc.

c/o Catherine M. McFarland, Exec. Off.
40 S. Fullerton Ave.
Montclair, NJ 07042
(201) 783-4450
EIN: 221554541
Source Date: 12/95

Geographic Restrictions:
Limited to Newark, NJ area. Environmental grants limited to NJ.

Restrictions:
No grants for organizations dealing with specific diseases, afflictions, or geriatric needs, individuals.

To Whom:
Improve opportunities for poor and disadvantaged families, encourage leadership development, improve the quality of education, further sensible and wise use of land, water, air and energy, major community institutions, performing arts.

Education (48% of funding): teacher training and recruitment, academic enrichment, arts education, inner-city schools, literacy, policy research/school reform, elementary and secondary education.

Environment (12% of funding): preservation and protection of natural resources, public policy education and advocacy, environmental action and leadership training.

Neighborhood Development and Urban Revitalization, (20% of funding): job training and placement, neighborhood development, affordable housing, human needs, cultural, museums, leadership development.

Youth and Families (22% of funding): leadership development, at-risk youth and families, camp programs, after-school programs, family planning.

For What:
Operating budgets, continuing support, seed money, emergency funds, deficit financing, building funds, matching funds, scholarship funds, special projects, research, consulting services, technical assistance, general purposes, renovation projects.

Financial info:
Assets: $165,473,400.
Giving: $6,693,000 for 155 grants (high: $100,000; low: $10,000).

Application info:
Applications accepted. Submit proposal. Deadline is Feb. 1 and Aug. 1. Elementary and Secondary education deadline is Mar. 1. Board meets in June and Nov. Publishes annual report and application guidelines.

Recent Grants:

$30,000	A Better Chance, Inc. Now in its fourth year, ABC's "Pathways to College" program provides about 90 minority students from Newark, Irvington and Hillside with guidance and support in their quest to attend college. Victoria provided operating support.
$40,000	Kids In Business. Kids in Business helps elementary school students in several Newark public schools to improve their basic skills by running their own business. Victoria provided general operating support for the program.
$35,000	New Jersey Cities In Schools, Inc. Cities in Schools is the nation's leading drop-out prevention program and has been operating in Newark for five years. Victoria again supported CIS activities at Newark Central High School.
$50,000	New Jersey Institute Of Technology. The Center provides an array of enrichment programs in math, science and technology to students and their teachers. Victoria funded two of these programs for students and teachers from Newark schools.
$46,300	New Jersey Seeds. This is an intensive three-phase, 14-month program designed to prepare academically talented 7th graders with financial need, for success in New Jersey independent schools. The grant underwrote Phases I and II of the New Jersey SEEDS program at Montclair Kimberly Academy for the period of May 1995 through April 1996.
$1,000	Rutgers, Department Of Organization Management. This department of the State University places management

interns in community agencies. Victoria provided equipment for the intern resource room.

$60,000 Student/Partner Alliance. S/PA provides improved educational opportunities to minority youth from Newark, East Orange and Jersey City. Currently serving 80 students, S/PA provides scholarships to private high schools for individuals who also agree to act as mentors to scholarship recipients. Victoria provided general operating support.

$50,000 Urban Education Project Of The Oranges, Inc. UEP is a model of job training and youth education, directing New Jersey Youth Corps members in building and operating the Jersey Explorers Children's Museum in East Orange. Victoria provided general operating support to the Museum.

$20,000 After School/Summer Programs Bessie Green Community, Inc. Bessie Green provides a variety of social services for needy residents of Newark. Victoria supported job readiness programs for homeless citizens, as well as after-school and summer programs for 100 children, most of whom live in Baxter Terrace Housing and attend the Burner Street School.

$3,000 New Jersey Network. To support the television production of the Newark Boys Chorus cross-cultural trip to New Zealand and Australia.

$60,000 Newark Community School Of The Arts. NCSA is committed to providing instruction in the creative, performing and vocational arts to over 800 young people, regardless of their ability to pay. Victoria supported the financial aid program.

$2,500 Carolyn Dorfman Dance Company. To underwrite the creation of a new collaborative work of dance, music and storytelling, DANCE/STORIES, for presentation at the Newark residency program.

$35,000 Project Thistle. THISTLE, which stands for Thinking Skills in Teaching and Learning, consists of graduate level course work for Newark teachers to strengthen their ability to impart critical thinking skills to students. Victoria's grant covered partial costs of program operation.

$3,000 Rutgers, Consortium For Educational Equity. To support four Newark teachers in Science Teams Programs.

$1,170 Seton Hall University. Victoria provided scholarship assistance for a Newark school teacher to attend the University.

$40,000 The Hudson School. This independent school in Hoboken provides talented students with a challenging college preparatory program. Victoria provided scholarships for students from Newark.

$30,000 Link Community School. This private, non-denominational, alternative junior high school in Newark offers young people at risk of leaving school a quality education, a "link" between elementary and high school. Victoria's grant provided scholarships.

$50,000	New Jersey Audubon Society. Victoria funded the project, Linking Our Natural Treasures: Children and the Environment in Newark and the Highlands, at two Newark elementary schools, Clinton Avenue School and Brown Academy. The program provides environmental education activities for children, their teachers and parents, focusing on water resources and Newark's Pequannock Watershed while developing creativity, critical thinking skills and pride in Newark's stewardship of its internationally significant watershed.
$8,000	Urban League Of Essex County. The Urban League is the lead organization in the Parent Education Network of Newark which offers programming to maximize the educational and life chances for students and families, and to promote reform in Newark schools. Victoria provided support for the Parent Education Network.
$60,000	St. Benedict's Preparatory School. St. Benedict's Prep provides a rigorous pre-college education to young men from Newark and nearby communities. Victoria provided $35,000 for general faculty support and $25,000 for student financial aid.
$300,000	Saint Vincent Academy. The Academy is dedicated to empowering teenage girls through a program emphasizing rigorous academic and community service. Victoria awarded $100,000 for general operating expenses and $200,000 for the capital campaign.
$200,000	The Chad School Foundation. Victoria provided $75,000 in general operating support and $125,000 in scholarship funds for this independent elementary school and Science Academy High School in Newark
$700,000	New Jersey Performing Arts Center. The New Jersey Performing Arts Center, under construction in Newark, will provide the state with a world-class, multi-purpose hall and small theater. Victoria made the final $500,000 payment of a $2.5 million commitment, which supports the strategic planning aspect of NJPAC's development, emphasizing attention to job creation, audience development and community outreach. We also gave $100,000 to underwrite the pilot On School Time theater series and approved a two-year, $200,000 grant to support the Arts Education Program, paying the first installment of $100,000.

$100,000 New Jersey Symphony Orchestra. To support and strengthen the activities and collaborations the Orchestra has planned and implemented to ensure and nurture a culturally-educated and appreciative audience for the move into the New Jersey Performing Arts Center in 1997.

$235,000 The Newark Museum. Since 1909, the Museum has provided open access to a broad range of collections in art, culture, science and technology and has a particular strength in programming for families. Victoria's grant funded evaluation and strategic planning efforts for the Education Department, an evaluation of the lending collection, and installation of a Management Information System to strengthen financial planning, reporting and budgetary analysis.

$20,000 Natural Resources Defense Council. NRDC is dedicated to protecting and preserving the nation's resources and public health through constant and vigorous defense against damage from pollution and over exploitation. Victoria supported efforts to protect the New Jersey coast, focusing on alleviating damage from sewage, coastal development and oil spills.

$250,000 The Nature Conservancy. The Nature Conservancy is an international non-profit organization devoted to preserving global biodiversity. Victoria provided funds to the New Jersey Chapter, earmarked for the purchase of land within the Johnsonburg Swamp, an ecologically important natural area in Northwestern New Jersey.

$50,000 Regional Plan Association/New Jersey. Victoria's grant to the RPA helped complete a computer-aided design and visioning project in the Newark Watershed involving the Township of West Milford and the Newark Watershed Conservation and Development

$40,000 Association Of New Jersey Environmental Commissions. ANJEC serves as a resource for members for New Jersey's 350 environmental commissions, other local and state officials and citizens interested in protecting natural resources. The grant underwrote the production of Environmental Tools for Municipal Officials, a handbook of specific techniques to protect and conserve environmentally significant lands.

$50,000 The Student Conservation Association. Our grant to SCA funded year-round academic and career training to students involved in the Newark Conservation Career Development Program

$40,000	Pinelands Preservation Alliance. PPA is dedicated to the preservation of the New Jersey Pinelands through monitoring, advocacy and the promotion of an increased public awareness. Victoria supported a large scale public information campaign to broaden public support for preserving the Pinelands National Reserve.
$40,000	Trust For Public Land New Jersey Field Office. TPL creates, enlarges and preserves parks, urban gardens and natural areas throughout the United States; protects the integrity of environmentally sensitive urban and rural lands from incompatible land uses; and insures public access to these areas for educational and recreational purposes. Victoria provided $40,000 to support the general operations of the New Jersey Field Office.
$60,000	Inform, Inc. INFORM is a national environmental organization that uses case study research to identify ways of preventing the creation of industrial and municipal waste. Victoria supported continued research and promotion of cost-effective waste prevention strategies in New Jersey
$50,000	New Jersey Future. NJF's mission is to promote a productive economy, a viable natural environment and a just society for ourselves and for future generations. Victoria provided $25,000 in general operating support for public policy research, analysis and advocacy related to New Jersey's State Plan. Another $25,000 went to honor a challenge grant in support of the project "One New Jersey"
$10,000	Montclair Grass Roots, Inc. Victoria provided general operating support for this day camp which provides a summer experience for Montclair area youth and leadership training for adults.
$5,000	Episcopal Diocese Of Newark. Victoria provided scholarship assistance for children of incarcerated parents to attend summer camp.
$20,000	Ad House, Inc.. AD House supports abandoned, neglected and abused adolescents through an intensive peer leadership and counseling program. Victoria provided general operating support.
$30,000	American Friends Service Committee. AFSC is a Quaker organization which includes people of various faiths who are committed to social justice, peace and humanitarian service. Its New Jersey Criminal Justice Program offers a variety of support services for incarcerated individuals and their families. Victoria funded the New Directions for Youth project, which provides intensive mentoring for first time offenders ages 13-16.

$20,000	Hospice, Inc.. The Hospice provides a comprehensive system of care for the terminally ill and their families and has developed a training program on grief and loss to address the needs of Newark youth. Victoria provided support for the training of counselors in the Newark Public Schools.
$49,000	Young Fathers' Program. This program employs social and support group activities to enhance young fathers' ability to be responsible parents. Our grant funded general operations and employment skills training.
$50,000	Independence: A Family Of Services, Inc. Independence provides emotionally disturbed, economically and socially disadvantaged youth with comprehensive educational, mental health and social services, reaching 250 young people each year. Victoria provided a $50,000 grant for operating support and issued a $10,000 challenge grant to encourage a broader base of funders.
$25,000	Ready Foundation. READY works to improve the lives of Newark children and their families by providing academic and social support. Victoria partially underwrote the salary and associated costs of one READY coordinator.
$25,000	The Princeton-Blairstown Center, Inc. The Center provides challenging adventure-based activities and services to urban youth, their families, and their agency sponsors. Victoria underwrote the participation of Newark agencies in the Center's programs.
$30,000	Project U.S.E. Using the outdoors as a vehicle, this program is designed to help young people build self-confidence and appreciation for the environment. Victoria supported year-round adventure education activities and special projects of Project U.S.E.'s Newark Wilderness Coalition.
$50,000	Aspira, Inc. Of New Jersey. The oldest Latino organization in New Jersey, Aspira has identified the development of a better educated and more community-conscious youth as its primary mission. Victoria provided $25,000 in operating support and $25,000 as a challenge grant to encourage a broader base of support.
$30,000	Habitat For Humanity Newark, Inc.. Offering low-income families the opportunity to build and own their own homes, Habitat uses the energies of volunteers who work side-by-side with the prospective home owners to build their homes. Victoria provided operating support.
$50,000	Local Initiatives Support Corporation. LISC is a national organization providing grants, loans and technical assistance to local community development corporations nationwide.

Our grant helped fund Newark LISC's Capacity Building Program for Newark CDC's.

$40,000 Renaissance Newark Foundation (For The Regional Business Partnership). Victoria's grant to the Regional Business Partnership helped underwrite planning for a marketing campaign to retain, expand and attract businesses to the northeastern part of New Jersey

$50,000 Focus Hispanic Center For Community Development. FOCUS sponsors educational and developmental programs which advance the quest of Hispanics in Newark toward self-sufficiency, empowerment and a better quality of life. Victoria supported the Job Development and Allied Health Careers Programs.

$20,000 Partnership In Philanthropy. PIP raises a pool of funds from foundations and corporations to pay fund-raising consultants and match them with small non-profit organizations. The consultants have worked with 32 agencies around New Jersey over the past three years to upgrade fund-raising skills and commitment. Victoria supported consultants for Newark agencies.

Directors, Officers, Trustees:

Chapin, Charles M., III, Trustee
Chubb, Corinne A., Trustee
Chubb, Hendon (d), Donor
Chubb, Percy, III, Officer, Trustee
Chubb, Sally, Trustee
Coggeshall, Mary, Trustee
Curvin, Robert, Trustee
McFarland, Catherine M., Officer
Millspaugh, Gordon A., Jr., Officer, Trustee
Parker, Margaret H., Officer, Trustee
Shanley, Kevin, Officer, Trustee
Thompson, Gail L., Trustee
Turnbull, William, Trustee
Yamba, A. Zachary, Trustee

New York

Robert Bowne Foundation, Inc.

c/o Dianne Kangisser, VP
345 Hudson St.
New York, NY 10014
(212) 924-5500
EIN: 132620393
Source Date: 12/95

Geographic Restrictions:
Limited to New York, NY, only. Requests from providers in Bronx, Brooklyn, Queens and Staten Island are especially welcome.

Restrictions:
No grants for religious organizations, primary or secondary schools, colleges, or universities, except when some aspect of their work is an integral part of a program supported by the foundation, individuals, capital expenses or endowments.

To Whom:
Literacy programs for New York City youth living in poverty, after school particularly. Programs that integrate literacy instruction with on-going activities that attract young people. Focus on programs which demonstrate the value of reading and writing to youth, build on natural interests of youth, bring an awareness of literacy into environments where it is lacking, and provide young people with a variety of reading and writing experiences. **Funding available for advocacy, feasibility studies, technical assistance, staff development, and evaluation related to youth literacy issues.**

For What:
Operating budgets, seed money, special projects, technical assistance, consulting services, continuing support, general purposes, matching funds, research.

Financial info:
Assets: $11,986,500.
Giving: $687,000 for 35 grants (high: $25,000; low: $500).

Application info:
Applications accepted. Submit letter. No deadline. Publishes application guidelines.

Recent Grants:

$20,000	Hudson Guild. Enhance the educational context of their afterschool program.

$15,000	Ice Hockey in Harlem. Hire a part-time education professional who will develop an integrated hockey/literacy curriculum and train and support volunteer teachers to use the curriculum.
$5,000	Coalition for the Homeless. Develop the reading program at Camp Homeward Bound (a summer camp for homeless children) that integrates literacy activities into ongoing camp activities.
$10,000	Creative Arts Workshops for Kids. General operating support for their afterschool program for homeless and relocated formerly homeless children.
$15,000	Union Settlement Association. Salary of a professional educator who will facilitate the integration of computers into all learning activities at the Comprehensive Adolescent Resource Center.

Directors, Officers, Trustees:

Bauer, Douglas F., Officer, Trustee
Bowne & Company, Inc., Donor
Carothers, Suzanne, Trustee
Kangisser, Dianne, Officer, Trustee
Koontz, Richard H., Trustee
Stanley, Edmund A., Jr., Donor, Officer, Trustee
Stanley, Jennifer, Officer, Trustee
von Ziegesar, Franz, Officer, Trustee

Carnegie Corporation of New York

c/o Dorothy W. Knapp, Secretary
437 Madison Ave.
New York, NY 10022
(212) 207-6289
Internet: http://www.carnegie.org
EIN: 131628151
Source Date: 10/96

Geographic Restrictions:
Primarily in the U.S. International giving in Africa, South Africa, and the Caribbean.

Restrictions:
No grants for the arts, operating expenses of educational institutions or day care centers, or general support for social service agencies, annual cam-

paigns, deficit financing, capital, building, or endowment funding, scholarships, or matching gifts.

To Whom:
Education and Healthy Development of Children and Youth: focuses on children to age 15.

Strengthening Human Resource in Developing Countries: Expanding indigenous scientific capacity to identify and solve social and economic problems as an essential element for societies to achieve and sustain development, healthy development of adolescent girls and women, in South Africa-women's health and development, in U.S.-improve understanding among the public, practitioners and policymakers.

Preventing Deadly Conflict: prevent mass intergroup violence, strengthen democratic institutions in the former Soviet Union and Eastern Europe, cooperative security and nonproliferation.

For What:
Operating budgets, continuing support, seed money, program-related investments, special projects, research, publications, conferences and seminars, exchange programs, general purposes, fellowships.

Financial info:
Assets: $1,300,000,000.
Giving: $60,452,700 for 275 grants.

Application info:
Applications accepted. Submit letter. No deadline. Publishes annual report and application guidelines.

Recent Grants:

$253,000	Child Welfare League of America, toward a project to prevent pregnancy in adolescents in out-of-home care, conducted in collaboration with the Council of State Governments
$376,000	Children's Aid Society, as a final grant toward information and technical assistance on developing community schools
$23,300	**University of Colorado, toward an evaluation of test construction and validity for students with experience in innovative and tradition al advanced mathematics curricula**
$418,000	Teachers College, Columbia University, toward implementation of recommendations from a commission on teacher development.
$300,000	Teachers College, Columbia University, toward the Fred M. Hechinger Institute on Education and the Media

$300,000	**Community Television of Southern California, toward evaluation and educational out reach for a television series on inter group understanding and prosocial behavior for preschool children**
$135,000	Educational Broadcasting Corporation, for production and educational outreach for two In the Mix special programs
$120,000	Finance Project, toward research and planning on the financing of programs for young children and their families
$25,000	University of Florida, toward enhancing science curriculum materials on CD-ROM for elementary school students
$1,000,000	Harvard University, toward the creation of a children's studies program
$10,000	Johns Hopkins University, toward an international conference on school effectiveness and improvement
$300,000	**Judge Baker Children's Center, toward an evaluation of a social skills and literacy development program**
$800,000	National Academy of Sciences, toward support of the Forum on Adolescence
$1,000,000	National Board for Professional Teaching Standards, toward support
$250,000	**National Committee to Prevent Child Abuse, toward a research network to evaluate an early childhood intervention and family support program**
$400,000	National Governors' Association Center for Best Practices, toward assistance to states in implementing national goals for education in the 1990s
$25,000	National Head Start Association, toward a project to promote excellence in Head Start programs for disadvantaged preschool children
$25,000	New York Academy of Sciences, toward an inventory of science education resources, programs, and reform efforts in New York City
$10,000	North Carolina School of Science and Mathematics, toward revision of a precalculus textbook
$25,000	Philadelphia Education Fund, toward a study of eighth-grade students' transition to high school
$350,000	Puerto Rico Community Foundation, toward a project to improve middle grade schools in Puerto Rico
$449,000	University of Rhode Island, for research on the impact of adopting middle grade reforms
$25,000	Rutgers University, toward a videoconference and documentary on media literacy
$137,000	Laura Sessions Stepp, for research and writing on parents and young adolescents in the United States

$150,000	WGBH Educational Foundation, toward production of a television program on scientific discovery and related outreach activities
$300,000	University of Wisconsin, Madison, for technical assistance to school districts designing new teacher compensation plans and research documenting the process
$300,000	Yale University, toward dissemination of the final report of the Quality 2000 Initiative for the Advancement of Early Care and Education
$518,000	The Aspen Institute, for discussions between U.S. and Russian policymakers conducted by the Aspen Strategy Group
$1,000,000	The Brookings Institution, toward research on the transformation of international relationships and its implications for international security
$3,400,000	Carnegie Corporation of New York, for the Carnegie Commission on Preventing Deadly Conflict
$25,000	Center for Strategic and International Studies, as a final grant toward a project on U.S. policies toward Europe
$25,000	Coalition for International Justice, toward support
$200,000	Columbia University, toward research on evaluating the strategies of nongovernmental organizations to promote democracy and prevent conflict in the former Soviet Union
$250,000	Conflict Management Group, toward a project on managing ethnic conflict within the former Soviet Union
$25,000	Council on Foreign Relations, toward a task force on U.S.-Russian arms control, a joint project with the Nixon Center for Peace and Freedom
$150,000	Council on Foreign Relations, toward a study of political, economic, and social change and international relations in the post-Cold War era
$20,000	Donetsk Scientific-Applied Association Psychological Center, toward support of conflict resolution in Ukraine and development of a network of conflict resolution organizations and practitioners
$25,000	Fund for Peace, for dissemination of a conference report on aid to the newly independent states of the former Soviet Union
$25,000	Georgetown University, toward a conference on Russian science policy
$25,000	Harvard University, for a workshop on post-Soviet security for younger scholars
$75,000	Harvard University, toward a project to strengthen democratic leadership in Eastern and Central Europe

$850,000	Harvard University, toward a project on strengthening democratic institutions in the former Soviet Union
$25,000	Harvard University, toward a study of the effect of Track II discussions in conflict resolution
$150,000	Institute for Defense and Disarmament Studies, as a final grant toward an international survey of cooperative policy on conventional arms control
$25,000	Institute for EastWest Studies, toward an alliance with the Association for the Study of Nationalities
$75,000	Institute for Multi-Track Diplomacy, as a final grant toward a series of conflict resolution meetings for public policy leaders in Cyprus
$25,000	Institute for Technology Assessment, for completing a study of the uses of technology to support international peace operations
$15,000	International Research and Exchanges Board, for technical assistance in computer telecommunications for projects between the United States and former Soviet Union
$105,000	International Research and Exchanges Board, as a final grant for technical assistance in computer telecommunications for projects between the United States and former Soviet Union
$250,000	National Academy of Sciences, toward support of activities of the Committee on International Security and Arms Control with China and Ukraine

Commonwealth Fund

Harkness House
1 East 75th St.
New York, NY 10021-2692
(212) 535-0400
Internet: http://www.cmwf.org
Source Date: 12/96

Restrictions:
No grants to individuals (except for Harkness Fellowships), building funds, general support, capital funds, renovation of facilities, equipment.

To Whom:
Picker/Commonwealth Patient-Centered Care Program: helping hospital executives and medical professionals identify and quantify crucial patient observations and develop better systems to provide patient-responsive care.

Youth Opportunities Program: developing the capabilities of youth people, complementing the continuing work of the Career Beginnings Program which helps build respect and opportunity for skilled work training within the educational system and to help non-college-bound youth shape a vision of themselves in careers as skilled workers. Seeking to develop new working relationships among high schools, junior colleges, and business and industry so that young people can gain workplace experience simultaneously with academic instruction.

For What:
Research, special projects, fellowships.

Financial info:
Giving: $12,954,300 for 155 grants (high: $500,000; low $1,000) and $887,400 for 35 grants to individuals (high: $50,000; low: $500).

Application info:
Applications accepted. Submit letter or proposal (3 copies). No deadline. Board meets in Apr. July, and Nov.

Recent Grants:

$150,000 The Commonwealth Fund. Health Insurance Coverage for Families, Cathy Schoen. For many heads of families who work at jobs that provide minimal or no insurance, and for many more who are temporarily unemployed, obtaining and keeping health insurance coverage pose financial hardships and impede access to needed care. This series of papers will provide background information on the uninsured and the problem of affordability of health insurance, as well as analyze costs and administrative issues related to various incremental coverage options. These reports, to be released over the course of the next year, will supply sequential information on a topic that deserves renewed attention from policymakers.

$175,000 United Hospital Fund of New York. Evaluation of Medicaid Managed Care in New York City, Phase Two, David Gould, Ph.D. The expansion of Medicaid managed care in New York City is an experiment whose outcome has yet to be determined. In the past year, the New York Consortium for Health Services Research—which includes analysts at the United Hospital Fund of New York, New York University, and Columbia University—has tracked the evolution of Medicaid managed care in New York City and developed a baseline to understand its impact on low income residents, the providers who tradi-

tionally serve them, and the managed care plans involved. With Medicaid managed care expected to grow even more in the year ahead, the consortium's goal is to provide timely and accurate information to national, state, and local policymakers, health care providers, managed care organizations, and consumer organizations. Cofunders of the project include the New York Community Trust, the Engelberg Foundation, Pfizer, Inc., J. P. Morgan, and the United Hospital Fund of New York.

$115,118 National Committee for Quality AssuranceDeveloping a Report Card to Enhance Consumer Choice of Health Plans, Phase Four, Margaret E. O'Kane and Phyllis Torda. Managed care is evolving under a number of different structures, making it difficult for consumers to easily compare quality and cost. This Picker Program Grant will support the final phase of the Consumer Information Project of the National Committee for Quality Assurance (NCQA), which has developed a report card on health plan quality for consumers. Field testing of the report card will occur in late 1996 with employees in Denver and St. Louis. Work under phase four will expand and strengthen preliminary evaluation of the report card through a series of employee surveys. NCQA will disseminate the project's findings through publications for purchasers of health insurance and health plans and through presentations to the media.

$149,920 Rand Corporation. Analysis of Managed Care Quality Indicators, Elizabeth A. McGlynn, Ph.D. The new Quality Compass database of the National Committee for Quality Assurance (NCQA), developed in part with a loan from the Fund, will be analyzed by Rand researchers to determine how plan performance varies by health plan characteristics. This Picker Program Grant will also provide analytic support to NCQA in developing improved performance measures for the Health Plan Employer Data and Information Set (HEDIS), the leading source of information on the quality of managed care plans, and in preparing a technical assistance manual.

$165,000 Institute of Medicine, National Academy of Sciences. National Roundtable on Health Care Quality, Year Two, Kenneth I. Shine, M.D. Ensuring health care quality is the goal of a three-year Institute of Medicine initiative. The National Roundtable on Health Care Quality and a liaison panel on managed care, which include leading experts on health care quality from the public and private sectors, will continue to research issues of quality during the second year of this Picker Program Grant. First-year activities will result in a formal statement on quality and managed care at the end of 1996. Work in the year ahead will include additional workshops, commissioned papers for scholarly publication, and press briefings. Cofunding is expected from the Agency for Health Care Policy and Research of the U.S. Department of Health and Human Services and from private sources.

$202,649 American Association of Health Plans Foundation. Improving Health Services for Women Enrolled in Managed Care Plans, Carmella Bocchino, R.N., M.B.A., and E. Liza Greenberg, R.N., M.P.H. This work will capitalize on the potential of managed care to improve services to women by identifying and disseminating information on the practices that best enhance their health. The in-depth analysis of the most effective current strategies will assist health plans in improving the services they offer. Work also will focus on encouraging managed care plans to make women's health a priority.

$206,428 University of Connecticut Health Center. A Domestic Violence Initiative in Community Health Centers, Phase Three, Anne H. Flitcraft, M.D. The Connecticut Community Health Center's Domestic Violence Initiative was established in 1994 to enhance the safety and well-being of battered women in medically underserved communities. The project's first two phases focused on incorporating domestic violence screening into routine clinical practice in Connecticut's 10 community health centers and on developing and implementing a training and education program to improve providers' skills in identifying victims of domestic violence. The health centers' quality assurance program was expanded to include domestic violence risk assessment as an indicator of quality of care. The project's third and final phase will include an assessment of the training and intervention programs. Work will also involve the dissemination of results to the broader health and social service communities.

$15,800 United Hospital Fund of New York State Options for Financing Graduate Medical Education, Kathryn Haslanger. Medical education is at the crossroads of a fiscal dilemma sparked by the nation's changing health care environment. This grant is supporting the development of a policy paper based upon a one-day invitational meeting, held by the United Hospital Fund of New York, for representatives of state governments and national researchers and analysts, to enhance understanding of how funding for medical education contributes to the financial viability of institutions with major teaching commitments. The paper will be disseminated to managers of teaching institutions and to state and national policymakers, researchers, and analysts.

$25,000 Northwestern University, Institute for Health Services Research and Policy Studies. Health Policy Options for the Future, Peter P. Budetti, M.D. Health care policy options for the next five years are likely to be determined by developments in three broad areas: economic and social trends, the political setting, and the health care system. From these categories, five major health care policy issues are emerging as candidates to dominate the debate: Medicare Part A solvency, state flexibility regarding Medicaid, safety-net issues and the uninsured, tax policy, and consumer health care quality issues. This research will examine each of these factors in relation to the others and produce an analytical framework for predictions of the system's future as a whole. Results will be published in the Journal of the American Medical Association in early 1997.

$15,000 Policy Resource Center, Inc. Managed Mental Health Care, Gail Robinson, Ph.D. Managed care is rapidly transforming the organization and delivery of mental health care to low income women. With more and more low income women moving into Medicaid managed care, a critical analysis of women's experiences with the public systems of managed care is needed. This research describes both public and private sector managed health care and examines its impact on utilization and outcomes. The paper raises a series of questions on low income women's access to mental health services, the quality of those services under different managed care arrangements, and the cost and burden on these women. The report was presented as background material for the Commission on Women's Health Symposium on Mental Health, held in Atlanta in October 1996.

$25,000 Northwestern University. Physician Organizations in a Restructured Health Care System, Stephen Shortell, Ph.D. The way in which medical care is delivered is changing not only for patients, but for physicians as well. A profession once viewed as consisting of small, independent practices is now increasingly populated by health maintenance organizations with staff physicians and networks or alliances of more loosely constructed groups. More and more physicians are joining these practices, but little is known about the impact of these groups on decision making, costs, quality, or outcome of health care. This project will examine various group models and their methods of accountability, payment, and patient care management. The results will be peer-reviewed, published, and disseminated to professional audiences and policymakers.

$250,320 George Washington University. Review of Urban Hospital and Health System Strategies, Thomas W. Chapman. Access to health care continues to be a major problem in many low income minority communities. Detailed case studies will examine current approaches to assuring access to health care in major metropolitan areas for minority residents. Taking into account the challenges presented by expansions in managed care and reductions in public funding, the studies will detail the strategies inner city hospital systems are employing to meet the challenge and assess the strengths and weaknesses of each option. Findings will be disseminated to urban hospital leaders, county and city health officers, elected officials, and state and federal policymakers.

$646,871 Harvard Medical School. The Commonwealth Fund/Harvard University Fellowship in Minority Health Policy, Support for Program Direction and Fellowships, 1997-98, Joan Reede, M.D., M.P.H., M.S. The Commonwealth Fund/Harvard University Fellowship in Minority Health Policy was established in November 1995 to prepare U.S. physicians, particularly those from racial and ethnic minority groups, for leadership positions in minority health and public policy. Up to five fellowships will be awarded each year for five years to enable fellows to pursue a one-year enriched course of study at the Harvard University School of Public Health. Each fellow will receive a master's degree in public health at the completion of the fellowship year. During the past year, the program office recruited and selected the first group of three fellows, who began the fellowship in July 1996. Staff also developed a program of forums, seminars, and site visits, which complement the fellows' regular academic course of study. The second class of fellows will be recruited and selected by early 1997. Activities for the 1997-98 year will include administering the fellowships of the second class of fellows, recruiting the third class, and beginning an evaluation of the program. The program's first annual symposium will be held in May 1998.

$549,185 Urban Institute, Support for Program Direction and Policy Analysis, 1996-97, Marilyn Moon, Ph.D. The debate over the structure and financing of Medicare is likely to resume in 1997 because of concern over the short-term solvency of the Part A Trust Fund and continuing pressure to reduce the federal budget deficit. The Program on Medicare's Future has already analyzed major proposals to reshape Medicare, reviewed options for filling existing gaps in Medicare coverage, and begun research and analysis on managed care and other key issues likely to arise in policy discussion. In its second year, the program will focus on disseminating the results of this work and on providing rapid and authoritative analysis of new proposals, with a continued emphasis on the impact of proposed changes to the Medicare program on low income or chronically ill beneficiaries. New research will move beyond the short-range budget debate and stress options for improving Medicare over the long term.

$288,730 Georgetown University, Picker/Commonwealth Program on Frail Elders. In its fourth year, the Picker/Commonwealth Program on Frail Elders will continue to analyze proposed changes to the Medicaid and Medicare programs and other developments likely to affect access to long-term care or the quality of care for frail elderly Americans. Work will include examining specific policy proposals, identifying options for managing home health and personal care, and assessing issues in the integration of acute and long-term care.

$206,861 Urban Institute. Assessment of the New York Long-Term Care Capitation Project, Korbin Liu, Sc.D. New York State, with support from the Fund, has designed and is now implementing a demonstration project under which Medicaid long-term care services will be provided under capitated payment arrangements at six sites, including three in the New York metropolitan area. Under this Picker Program Grant, detailed case studies will evaluate the implementation process at each site, focusing on strategies to coordinate acute and long-term care service use, payment methods, and client enrollment and satisfaction. The feasibility and value of conducting a more comprehensive evaluation of the project will also be assessed.

$25,000 Medicare Rights Center, Inc. Medicare HMO Counseling Tips, Diane Archer. Elderly, sick patients are often confused and frightened when confronted with options in choosing their medical care. The Medicare Rights Center will compile Medicare HMO counseling tips and develop and disseminate guides for Medicare counselors to help beneficiaries make informed choices in selecting an HMO, and to help Medicare counselors in advising them. The center will promote the availability of these materials through the media.

$482,197 **ICF Incorporated. Support for Program Direction and Operations, 1996-97, Michael C. Barth, Ph.D. The Healthy Steps for Young Children Program, based on a partnership of local providers, community foundations, and The Commonwealth Fund, represents a new approach to health care for children from birth to age three. It is committed to fostering babies' healthy physical, emotional, and intellectual growth and development through promoting a closer relationship between health care professionals and parents. In the year ahead, the Healthy Steps program will formalize partnership agreements with local funders and health care providers that have organized Healthy Steps local initiative sites and monitor operations at 15 sites that are participating in a national evaluation. The program will then provide technical assistance to sites, including an Internet-based Healthy Steps information and communications system, conduct program research and analysis, and disseminate information about the program and its research efforts through newsletters and a background paper series.**

$554,733 **Johns Hopkins University School of Hygiene and Public Health. National Evaluation of Local Initiatives of the Healthy Steps for Young Children Program, 1996-97, Bernard Guyer, M.D., M.P.H. Careful documentation and evaluation of the Healthy Steps for Young Children Program by independent health services researchers is crucial to the widespread and permanent adoption of the Healthy Steps approach to pediatric care. The goals of the evaluation are to assess the program's success in reorienting pediatric practice to emphasize child development, to increase parents' knowledge about child development and earlynurturing of infants, to promote parental practices that improve the health and safety of children and their use of health care services, and to assess the cost-effectiveness of Healthy Steps to health care providers. This work will cover the first year of a five-year process, outcome, and economic evaluation of 15 Healthy Steps sites. Work in year one will focus on site start-up activities and the collection of baseline data.**

$10,000 The Children's Village. Replication of the Work Appreciation for Youth Scholarship Program, Geraldine Alpert, Ph.D. The Work Appreciation for Youth (WAY) Scholarship Program has helped young men and women overcome severe social, emotional, and educational deficits to make successful transitions to adulthood by motivating them to stay in school and preparing them for the workplace. Support from the Fund, in addition to a grant from the U.S. Department of Labor, Employment and Training Administration, will allow The Children's Village to replicate the WAY program at three sites in the New York area and one in Philadelphia.

$10,000 Big Brothers/Big Sisters of New York City, Inc. New York Volunteer for Youth Campaign, Stephen Carey. Young people need mentors and role models in order to develop into secure, successful adults. The New York Volunteer for Youth Campaign is made up of a collaboration among New York City's youth service organizations that link at-risk youth with volunteer mentors. Fifteen organizations now participate, with 10 more preparing to join. The initiative plans to recruit up to 25,000 mentors over the next three years to serve in more than 100 community organizations throughout the city.

$10,000 Big Brothers/Big Sisters of New York City, Inc. Center for Training and Family Services, Carolyn Kennedy. Each year, the Center for Training and Family Services trains staff and volunteers from 100 youth agencies in establishing one-on-one mentoring programs in their communities. This year, the center is also assisting the New York Volunteer for Youth Campaign by training individuals from all participating organizations.

$37,000 Families and Work Institute. Development of a Guide to Video and CD-ROM Materials on Child Health and Development, Ellen Galinsky. The Families and Work Institute (FWI) is developing a comprehensive, annotated guide to videos and CD-ROM materials on child health and development for parents with children from birth to age three. The guide will serve as a resource for parents and professionals and will be distributed nationally by Healthy Steps partners and FWI's Early Childhood Public Engagement Campaign.

$30,000 Regional Plan Association, Inc. Planning Workshop on the Redevelopment of Governors Island, Robert D. Yaro and Robert Pirani. Governors Island, located in New York's inner harbor and easily accessible by ferry from Manhattan, Brooklyn, Staten Island, and New Jersey, could be an attractive waterfront destination when the U.S. Coast Guard ceases operations on the island in 1997. Among the many issues surrounding the island's disposition and reuse is the importance of preserving existing open spaces and creating new public spaces, parks, and recreational facilities to complement the further residential and commercial development likely to occur.

$99,764 Delivering Preventive Services to Women at Risk, Phase Two, Jacobs Institute of Women's Health. Innovative programs around the country that have succeeded in increasing rates of screening for breast and cervical cancer among groups of women least likely to receive preventive tests will be examined and reported on.

$344,174 Medicaid Home Care Capitation, Phase One, Health Research, Inc. Demonstration model will be developed to provide long-term care services on a partially capitated basis to Medicaid-eligible elderly people in New York and Massachusetts. If phase one is successful, the second phase would include demonstrations in the two states, funded through state Medicaid allocations, with an independent evaluation supported by the Fund.

$335,000 Developing a Health Services Strategic Plan, Meharry Medical College. Meharry Medical College will develop a strategic plan for its future and explore opportunities to develop an integrated health care delivery network to serve its community.

$400,000 The Inner City Drug Prevention Initiative, Phase Three, Partnership for a Drug-Free America. Early studies of the effect of the Partnership's New York City public advertising campaign on youngsters ages 5-15 will be analyzed and a third survey of New York City children and adolescents conducted. In addition, the Partnership will air a new round of messages, aimed at encouraging communities to provide positive alternatives to drug use and drug dealing.

$250,000 Mentoring in a National Construction Trades Youth Training Program, YouthBuild USA Inc.. YouthBuild will implement a unique mentoring model, involving national and local staff members, program alumni and participants, and volunteers. The model will enable YouthBuild, which provides training in construction skills to young people, to enhance its capacity to improve its participants' academic and leadership skills.

$25,000 Developing a Center for New York City Law, Ross Sandler, New York Law School. Start-up support will enable a journal devoted to the development and practice of law in New York City to be published by the newly established Center for New York City Law.

Directors, Officers, Trustees:

Bernard, Lewis W., Director
Craig, John, Officer
Daniels, Frank A., Jr., Director
Davis, Karen, Officer
Harkness, Edward S. (d), Donor
Harkness, Edward S., Mrs. (d), Donor
Harkness, Stephen V., Mrs. (d), Donor
Huntington, Lawrence S., Director
Kaplan, Helene L., Director
Mahoney, Margaret E., Director, Officer
Massey, Walter E., Director
O'Neil, Robert M., Director
Peri, Joseph, Officer
Perkins, Roswell B., Director
Sanders, Charles A., M.D., Director
Wilson, Blenda J., Director

William T. Grant Foundation

c/o Beatrix A. Hamburg, M.D., Pres.
515 Madison Ave., 6th Flr.
New York, NY 10022-5403
(212) 752-0071
EIN: 131624021
Source Date: 12/96

Geographic Restrictions:
Limited to New York, NY, area for community service grants.

Restrictions:
No grants for building funds, fundraising drives, operating expenses, or endowments.

To Whom:
Improve children's mental health.
Research on the development of children, adolescents, and youth: child and youth development, origins and prevention of problem behaviors and promotion of successful developmental outcomes in children, adolescents, and youth.

Research to evaluate broadly-based social interventions: interventions aimed at preventing problem behaviors in school-age children, adolescents, and youth.

Faculty scholars program, and consortia.

For What:
Research.

Financial info:
Assets: $207,385,500.
Giving: $8,899,400 for 305 grants (high: $500,000: low: $2,000).

Application info:
Applications accepted. Application to Faculty Scholars Program by nomination only. Submit inquiry letter. No deadline. Board meets in Feb., May, Sept., and Dec. Publishes application guidelines.

Recent Grants:

$45,885	Judge Baker Children's Center. "Psychoeducational Preventive Intervention for Families with Parental Affective Disorder"
$288,000	**Judge Baker Children's Center. "Adaptation and Evaluation of a Family-Based Preventive Intervention for Families with Parental Depression in a Disadvantaged Urban Neighborhood: An Initial Study"**
$200,000	University of California-San Francisco Medical Center. "Psychobiologic Reactivity and Health in Primary School Children: A Longitudinal Study"
$126,008	University of Wisconsin. "Personality Development and Mental Health in the Transition From Adolescence to Young Adulthood"
$495,994	University of Rochester. "Childhood Maltreatment, Community Violence, and Pathways to Adaptation Risk and Resilience in the Adolescent Years"
$175,000	**Children's Aid Society. "Three-year Evaluation of the Washington Heights Community Schools"**
$79,925	University of Vermont. "Consortium on Depression in Childhood and Adolescence"
$394,609	Public/Private Ventures. "Transforming Educational Communities to Meet the Needs of Youth: A Model for Linking Research and Educational Reform"
$276,313	**Institute for Research and Reform in Education. "Building the Knowledge Base for Urban Educational Reform: Research, Measurement. and Evaluation Strategies"**

$260,167	Northwestern University. "The Comer School Development Process: Assessing the Effects of up to Eight Years of Exposure in Schools that Vary in Quality of Implementation"
$388,694	University of Vermont. "How Children Learn to Resolve Conflict in Families"
$100,000	**Milton S. Eisenhower Foundation. "Evaluation of a National Corporation for Youth Investment: Community-Based Violence Prevention Evaluation"**
$66,486	University of Wisconsin. "Effects of First Birth Timing on Educational Attainment and Welfare Dependency"
$71,916	Loyola University. "Preventive Mental Health Programs for Children and Adolescents"
$442,621	University of Michigan Institute for Survey Research Pennsylvania State University. "Transition to Adulthood"
$202,214	University of Colorado Center for the Study and Prevention of Violence. "Adolescent Violence and Schools"
$114,353	University of Pennsylvania. "Effects of First Birth Timing on Educational Attainment and Welfare Dependency"
$141,037	University of Virginia. "Child Custody Mediation and Litigation: A Long-Term Follow-Up Study"
$335,702	Johns Hopkins University. "Paid Work in the Early Years"
$177,454	University of Georgia. "Functioning of Young Adults: Predictors From Early Adolescence"
$146,224	New York University. "Reconceptualizing the Special Education System in the New York City Public Schools to Improve Student Outcomes"
$38,844	New York University. A Longitudinal Study of the Academic Achievement and Family Relationships of As:an-American Adolescents"
$206,367	University of Colorado. "Preparing for Adulthood: The Transition to School and Work"
$220,000	Clark University. "Factors Influencing the Level and Characteristics of Parents' Involvement in Their Children's Schooling"
$220,000	University of North Carolina. "Mothers' Work, Welfare and Children: The Implications of Women's Employment for the Well-Being of Children in Poor Families"
$250,000	Stanford University. "Gender Specific Increase in Psychiatric Symptoms During Adolescence"
$175,000	University of Michigan. "Maternal and Child Health Among Mexican-Americans: The Role of Work Outside the Home and Father's Absence"
$205,000	Loyola University. "Family Processes and Community Contexts: African-American Family Life in Low-Income Neighborhoods"

$190,000	University of North Carolina. "Childhood Peer Rejection, Aggression, and Academic Adjustment: The Influence of Family, Neighborhood and Cultural Contexts on Developmental Pathways and Mental Health Outcomes"
$205,000	Yale University. "Modeling the Etiology and Consequences of Problem Behaviors in Adolescence"
$175,000	University of North Carolina at Greensboro. "The Relation Between Social Cognitions and Behavior Within the Family: A Longitudinal Investigation"
$250,000	Rutgers University. "Socioeconomic Differentials in Child Well-Being"
$175,000	Stanford University. "The Development of Children's Styles of Interpreting and Coping with Stress"
$250,000	Wayne State University. "School Resistance vs. Risky Behavior in Adolescence: The Role of Self"
$235,000	University of Illinois. "The Role of the Family in Preventing High-Risk Sexual Behavior"
$190,000	San Diego State University. "Maltreatment and Social Maladjustment"
$25,000	Institute for the Future. "National Survey of the Health of Adolescent Girls"
$25,000	Teachers College, Columbia University. "Jump Start Fund: Press Program/Policymakers Seminar"
$7,500	Community Service Society of New York. "Service Impacts of Budget Reductions in New York City"
$25,000	New York Academy of Sciences. "Opportunities in Science Education"
$10,000	Research Foundation for Mental Hygiene. "Eighth Annual New York State Of lice of Mental Health Research Conference"
$20,000	**Grand Street Settlement. "Evaluation of Community School District 1 Family Group Program"**
$9,000	Medical and Health Research Association of New York City. "Updating Birth Certificate/Public School Class Placement Database of New York City Children"
$5,000	American Psychological Foundation. "William Bevan Annual Lecture Series on Psychology and Public Policy"
$10,000	American Psychological Association. "Violence in America Behavioral Science Research Conference"
$10,000	New York Academy of Medicine. "Update History of New York Academy of Medicine"
$10,000	Court Appointed Special Advocates. "Advocacy Research Project"
$5,000	International Center of Photography. "Regional Secondary School Photography Contest"

$10,000	National Mental Health Association. "Dissemination of Information on the Prevention of Mental Disorders in Children"
$10,000	Fund for Public Schools. "Student Service and Philanthropy Project"

Greenwall Foundation

c/o William C. Stubing, Pres.
2 Park Ave., 24th Flr.
New York, NY 10016
(212) 679-7266
EIN: 136082277
Source Date: 12/95

Geographic Restrictions:
Primarily in New York, NY, for arts and humanities; U.S. for medical research and education.

Restrictions:
No grants for state or religious schools, individuals, building or endowment funding, operating expenses, annual campaigns, deficit financing, publications, conferences, or arts in education.

To Whom:
Medicine: Basic medical research and clinical investigation, especially in bone tumors, insulin dependent diabetes mellitus and geriatrics. Interested in the moral dilemmas of medical decision making.

Education: Assist minority and disadvantaged youth, in elementary and secondary schools, science and math education with an emphasis on bringing minorities and women into these areas of study.

Arts and Humanities: visual, performing and literary arts, libraries, museums.

For What:
Continuing support, seed money, emergency funds, equipment, professorships, research, special projects.

Financial info:
Assets: $73,992,800.
Giving: $2,621,000 for 100 grants (high: $100,000; low: $2,000).

Application info:
Applications accepted. Submit letter by Feb. 1 and Aug. 1. Board meets in spring and fall. Publishes annual report with application guidelines.

Recent Grants:

$10,000	Aaron Davis Hall (Friends of the Davis Center, Inc.), New York, NY. To support the Fund for New Works component of New Faces/New Voices/New Visions.
$2,500	Accra Shepp (New York Foundation for the Arts), New York, NY. To support creation of the photographer's artist's book, "Atlas."
$10,000	The Acting Company, New York, NY. To support commissioning and development of a new play by Lynn Nottage.
$10,000	Alvin Ailey American Dance Theatre, New York, NY. To support choreographic commissioning fees for a new work by Shapiro & Smith
$20,000	American Museum of the Moving Image, Astoria, NY. To commission a sculpture by Gregory Barsamian for the Museum's permanent core exhibition, "Behind the Screen".
$5,000	Amiel Malale Dance (Circum Arts Foundation, Inc.), New York, NY. To support development of a new work.
$5,000	The Architectural Hague of New York, New York, NY. To support the Young Architects Forum in 1995.
$7,500	The Architectural League of New York, New York, NY. Renewed support for the Young Architects Forum in 1996.
$5,000	Arden Party, New York, NY. To support the workshop and production of "Victor, or The Children Take Over."
$3,000	The Asian American Writers' Workshop, New York, NY. Renewed support for the Poetry Caravan Series in 1994/95.
$7,500	Bang on a Can, New York, NY. To support the 1995 and 1996 Bang on a Can festivals at Lincoln Center.
$4,000	Bill Young & Dancers (Hundred Grand Dance Foundation, Inc.), New York, NY. To support development of a new work, "Kindling."
$5,000	Bronx Council on the Arts, Bronx, NY. Renewed support for the Longwood Arts Project in 1994/95.
$30,000	Brooklyn Academy of Music, Inc., Brooklyn, NY. To support BAM'S Visual Arts Initiative.
$5,000	Buglisi/Foreman Dance (Circum Arts Foundation, Inc.), New York, NY. To support the company and creation of "Bare to the Wall" in 1995/96.
$5,000	The Builders Association (The Performance Zone, Inc.), New York, NY. To support a new multimedia theatrical production of"Faust."

$5,000	Celebrate Brooklyn (Fund for the Borough of Brooklyn, Inc.), Brooklyn, NY. To support a week-long dance residency during the 1995 festival.
$3,000	Chinatown History Museum, New York, NY. To support development of Jason Kao Hwang's opera, "Immigrant of the Womb."
$10,000	Circum Arts Foundation, Inc., New York, NY. To support fees for New York-based choreographers in the 1995 season of "Dance! The Circum Arts/Miller Theater Series.
$4,000	City Lore, New York, NY. To support the City Lore Festival of Film and Video in 1995.
$5,000	City Lore, New York, NY. Renewed support for the City Lore Festival of Film and Video in 1996.
$5,000	Vineyard Theatre, New York, NY. Renewed support for the Lab production program.
$10,000	Whitney Museum of Amencan Art, New York, NY. To support installations by New York artist Nari Ward in the 1995 Biennial.
$5,000	WPA Theatre, New York, NY. To support development of a new musical theatre work by Jason Robert Brown.
$7,500	The Writer's Voice (Young Men's Christian Association), New York, NY. To support First Books and the Capricorn Awards in 1994 and 1995
$30,000	American Museum of Natural History, New York, NY. To support three core teacher training programs at the Museum.
$15,000	Boys' Club of New York, New York, NY. To support the Teacher Training Institute at Camp Cromwell Summer School.
$25,000	Brooklyn Botanic Garden, Brooklyn, NY. Renewed support for teacher training in "Project Green Reach" in 1994/95.
$22,887	Brooklyn College of The City University of New York (Brooklyn College Foundation), Brooklyn, NY. To support the "Athena Math and Science Project" at the Center for Educational Change
$24,415	The City College of The City University of New York (Research Foundation of CUNY), New York, NY. To support the "Middle School Mathematics Teacher Preparation Program for Mid-Career Changers".
$98,307	The City College of The City University of New York (Research Foundation of CUNY), New York, NY. To implement a second cycle of the "Middle School Mathematics Teacher Preparation Program for Mid-Career Changers" (two-year grant).

$34,000	Columbia University, New York, NY. To support the "Summer Research Program for Secondary School Science Teachers" at the College of Physicians & Surgeons.
$50,000	Donors' Education Collaborative (Community Funds, Inc.), New York, NY. To support "Constituency Building for School Reform."
$35,000	**Fund for New York City Public Education, New York, NY. To support dissemination of the videotapes, "Approaching the Vision of the NCTM Standards," development and dissemination of accompanying print materials, teacher networking and professional development in New York City, and a formative evaluation.**
$35,000	Lehman College / New York City Mathematics Project (Research Foundation of CUNY), Bronx, NY. To support the Bronx Mathematics/Science/Technology Collaborative.
$30,000	National Action Council for Minorities in Engineering (NACME), New York, NY. Renewed support for the professional development seminars in the "TechForce Partnership for Scientific Learning."
$4,200	The New York Academy of Sciences, New York, NY. To support preparation, circulation, and maintenance of a directory and online data base for New York City teachers, "Professional Development Opportunities in Science Teaching"
$32,000	The New York Academy of Sciences, New York, NY. To support "Opportunities in Science Education: A Comprehensive Inventory of Resources, Programs, and Reform Efforts in New York City."
$25,000	New York Association for New Americans, New York, NY. To support implementation of a second cycle of "Teacher Training for Soviet Emigres."
$40,000	New York Botanical Garden, Bronx, NY. To support a new position, Manager for Teacher Enhancement Programs.
$15,000	New York Hall of Science, Corona, NY. To support the "In-Service Professional Development Program for Beginning Teachers".
$101,050	New York Hall of Science, Corona, NY. Renewed support for an expanded "In-Service Professional Development Program for Beginning Teachers".
$21,180	Queens College of The City University of New York (Research Foundation of CUNY), Flushing, NY. To support a new initiative, "Preservice and Inservice Professional Development in Mathematics for the Elementary Grades"

$35,000	American College of Obstetricians and Gynecologists, Washington, DC. Operating support for the National Advisory Board on Ethics in Reproduction.
$69,230	Baystate Medical Center, Springfield, MA. Research support: "Termination of Dialysis: The Decision to Die and the Quality of Dying"
$163,380	Choice in Dying, New York, NY. Project support: "Integrating Education About Care of the Dying Into Existing Medical School Programs".
$50,000	**Choice in Dying, New York, NY. Project support: Evaluation Component of "Integrating Education About Care of the Dying Into Existing Medical School Programs"**
$8,330	The Cleveland Clinic Foundation, Cleveland, OH. Research support: "Androgyny, Empathy, and Ethical Decision-Making Among Physicians".
$101,405	Dartmouth College / Institute for the Study of Applied & Professional Ethics, Hanover, NH. Project support: "Dreams and Dilemmas: The Practice of Family-Centered Neonatal care."
$22,500	Duke University Medical Center, Durham, NC. Research support: "How Do Expert Physicians Communicate with Their Patients About Advance Directives?"

Directors, Officers, Trustees:

Billings, Chester, Jr., Director
Bugliarello, George, Director
Cahill, George F., Jr., M.D., Director, Officer
Cassel, Christine K., M.D., Director
Donahue, Donald J., Director
Greenwall, Anna A. (d), Donor
Greenwall, Frank K. (d), Donor
Hamburg, Beatrix A., M.D., Director
Kresky, Edward M., Director
MacGrath, Andrew A., Director
MacGrath, Francis F., Director
MacGrath, Susan A.T., Director
Menges, Carl B., Director
Perpich, Joseph G., M.D., Director
Rosenblatt, Roger, Director
Salzer, Richard L., Director, Officer
Salzer, Richard L., Jr., M.D., Director
Stamas, Stephen, Director, Officer
Stubing, William Charles, Director, Officer
Vaun, William S., M.D., Director, Officer

Ittleson Foundation, Inc.

c/o Anthony C. Wood, Exec. Dir.
645 Madison Ave., 16th Flr.
New York, NY 10022
(212) 838-5010
EIN: 510172757
Source Date: 12/95

Geographic Restrictions:
U.S. giving.

Restrictions:
No grants to individuals, scholarships, internships, capital building projects, endowments, direct service programs, especially outside New York City, biomedical research, and projects that are international in scope.

To Whom:
Mental health (37% of funding): underserved populations such as elderly [seniors], poor and minority communities, AIDS and its consequences on the mental health of people.

Environment (29% of funding): educating a new generation of environmentalists, new approaches to solving environmental problems, bring out changes through policy research and add to our working knowledge through applied research.

AIDS (34% of funding): network organizations of support and care for people with AIDS.

For What:
Seed money, matching funds, professorships, special projects, research, publications, technical assistance.

Financial info:
Assets: $17,975,400.
Giving: $1,371,500 for 145 grants (high: $400,000; low: $100).

Application info:
Applications accepted. Submit letter or brief proposal. Deadline is Apr. 1 and Sept. 1. Board meets in spring and fall. Publishes annual report with application guidelines.

Recent Grants:

$25,000 AIDS Action Foundation, Washington, DC. A one-time grant for a policy document to integrate mental health perspectives into national AIDS prevention policy and community-based prevention practices with special attention focused on three groups at very high risk of HIV infection: disempowered women, young gay men, and communities of color.

$20,000 Balm in Gilead, Inc. New York, NY. For the initial development and implementation of The Black Church National HIV/AIDS Resource/Clearinghouse Center which will: (1) develop culturally relevant HIV/AIDS educational information appropriate for religious and community settings; (2) provide technical assistance to religious groups and community organizations in HIV/AIDS program planning, development and evaluation; (3) disseminate HIV/AIDS information and educational materials and referrals.

$25,000 Fund for the City of New York, The Orphan Project. New York, NY. For the preparation and distribution of the report "Orphanages Revisited: Congregate Care and Alternatives for Orphans and the HIV/AIDS Epidemic" analyzing in a historical context, if, under what conditions and with what services,"orphanages" or other congregate child care settings are appropriate options for children whose parents have died of HIV/AIDS and for other categories of children without caregiving parents.

$25,000 Iris House, New York, NY. To analyze, evaluate and document for replication the creation and performance of Iris House, the nation's first community-based organization devoted solely to the needs of HIV/AIDS women and their families.

$20,000 New York Community Trust (New York City AIDS Fund), New York, NY. To support the New York City AIDS Fund, the five year old coordinated effort to raise and pool philanthropic dollars, develop leadership and inform the philanthropic community in New York City about the AIDS epidemic. The funding priorities of the Fund in 1995 are prevention, advocacy, and organizational capacity building.

$20,000 Thirteen-WNET, New York, NY. One-time grant for the national public television documentary film: SEX and Other Matters of Life and Death profiling STAR (Sinai Teen Arts Resources) a unique theater company of teens fighting AIDS, sexually transmitted diseases, and teen pregnancy through a blend of comprehensive sexuality education and peer counseling and theater as part of the HIV/AIDS

Prevention and Treatment Program at Mount Sinai Hospital's Adolescent Health Center in New York.

$20,000 Alternatives for Comrnunity and Environment, Inc. Newton, MA. Seed money for the Roxbury Environmental Empowerment Project (REEP) an innovative, community-based model for environmental education and action for long term environmental protection in a low-income community involving neighborhood organizations, youth and a law school clinic.

$400,000 Brown University, Providence, RI. To develop a model undergraduate interdisciplinary environmental studies program which combines rigorous work in the classroom with lab work in the field, includes environmental apprenticeships; promotes a campus-wide environmental ethic through the "Brown is Green" program; and facilitates networking with other collegiate environmental programs.

$10,000 Citizens' Environmental Coalition, Albany, NY. To support the development and dissemination of a model environmental quality in schools program: "Healthy Schools' featuring technical support to develop and implement a model in New York State and the production of a manual for the national dissemination of the model.

$10,000 Coral Reef Alliance, Berkeley, CA. Seed money to launch the Coral Reef Conservation Program to address the destruction of coral reef ecosystems through the use of education, coalition building and the resources (both fiscal and other) of a national network of concerned scuba divers that they will organize and energize.

$25,000 Environmental Careers Organization, Boston, MA. To support The New England Environmental Diversity Collaboration in its efforts to diversify the membership, agenda, staff, governing boards and operating cultures of a number of New England-based environmental organizations.

$20,000 Environmental Health Network, Chesapeake, VA. One-time contingency grant for the Environmental Health Restoration Project (a collaborative effort of the Environmental Health Network, Good Neighbor Project and the Toxics Assistance Project) to create models that will assist toxics-damaged and radiation-contaminated communities in establishing local long-term strategic, technical and institutional capacity for reducing pollution, preventing disease, and restoring public health, using holistic, government-independent, reliable approaches.

$15,000	Isles. Trenton, NJ. For the Urban Site Remediation project, a model to expedite and humanize the cleanup and redevelopment process for toxic industrial sites ("brownfields") in older, low-income, minority urban areas across the country by engaging, educating and empowering residents and making them partners in the process.
$30,000	Land Trust Alliance, Inc. Washington, DC. To launch The Land Trust Alliance's Land Trust Information Center which will serve the more than 1,000 land trusts across the country and support for a model information dissemination project and related pilot programs in New York State.
$10,000	New York City Audubon Society, New York, NY. For a demonstration project in Jamaica Bay to show the feasibility of the low-cost restoration of urban wetland habitats on public parklands by a non-profit environmental group while providing and promoting public access.
$20,000	Sonoran Institute, Tucson, AZ. To support as part of a larger educational effort in partnership with the Conservation Fund, the production and dissemination of a book to provide "gateway" communities adjacent to national and state parks, wildlife refuges, and wilderness areas, effective community-driven models for managing growth adjacent to these cherished national resources.
$15,000	Development for the Disabled, Inc. Rapid City, SD. Support for a model project to demonstrate that the community-based housing needs of people with mental illnesses on limited incomes in rural areas can be addressed by utilizing the large stock of vacant historic structures found in many such communities.
$5,000	Lenox Hill Neighborhood House, New York, NY. To develop Project Crossroads, a pre-vocational training program that provides the formerly homeless, mentally ill residents of Casa Mutua, a "New York, New York" permanent residence for this population, work opportunities in their immediate community and to disseminate information on this model to others working with this population, particularly the other 49 "New York, New York" residences.
$25,000	**Montefiore Medical Center, New York, NY. To pilot, evaluate, and disseminate the HIV Mental Health Training Project, a model to provide clinical training to psychosocial staff members of inner-city community-based organizations providing HIV-related social services (case management, counseling, etc.) using the resources of academic medical center practitioners.**

$170,000	Memorial Sloan-Kettering Cancer Center, New York, NY. One-time grant from principal to support their model program for psychological intervention in women with breast cancer.
$25,000	**National Alliance for the Mentally 111 Arlington, VA A one-time grant to conduct a national study and produce and disseminate: Managed Care for Persons with Serious Mental Illness-A National Report Card, the first ever in-depth evaluation of managed care activities and practices in the U.S. as they affect people with severe mental illnesses.**
$20,000	National Center for Clinical Infant Programs Zero to Three, Arlington, VA. To develop and publish Zero to Three: Diagnostic Classification and Intervention Casebook to improve the assessment, diagnosis and treatment of infants and young children with mental health and developmental problems.
$30,000	The Gardner Group, Inc. On-Site Academy, Gardner, MA. One-time grant to disseminate and replicate the On-Site Academy's peer-driven and(clinically supported model program to assist emergency service personnel with critical incident stress (a "critical incident" being any event in the life of an emergency services provider which has unusually strong emotional impact, and jeopardizes the worker's ability to function).
$35,000	**Women in Need, Inc. New York, NY. To develop and implement a research and evaluation component for a new model program providing residential educational and vocational training for homeless women with children (the Sojourner Truth Employment Project).**
$5,000	American Cancer Society, New York, NY.
$5,000	American Foundation for AIDS Research, New York, NY.
$20,000	American Red Cross, New York, NY.
$5,000	Blue Light Theatre Company, Inc. New York, NY.
$10,000	Boys Club of New York, New York, NY.
$50,000	Brooks School, North Andover, MA.
$5,000	Cities in Schools, Inc. New York, NY.
$15,000	College Foundation at Delhi, Inc. Delhi, NY.
$50,000	College of Physicians Or Surgeons of Columbia University, New York, NY.
$5,000	Friends of the Earth, Washington, DC.
$5,000	Friends of the Family Academy, New York, NY.
$5,000	Habitat for Humanity, New York, NY.
$25,000	Housing Works, Inc. New York, NY.
$30,000	Jane Adams Hull House Assoc. Chicago, IL.
$5,000	Miracle House, New York, NY.
$5,000	Project Angel Food, Los Angeles, CA.

Directors, Officers, Trustees:

Ittleson, Blanche F. (d), Donor
Ittleson, H. Anthony, Director, Officer
Ittleson, Henry (d), Donor
Ittleson, Henry, Jr. (d), Donor
Ittleson, Lee F. (d), Donor
Ittleson, Marianne S., Director
Ittleson, Nancy S. (d), Donor
Pincus, Lionel I., Director
Sneag, Lawrence O., Officer
Syrmis, Pamela Lee, Director, Officer
Syrmis, Victor, M.D., Director
Wood, Anthony C., Director

NEC Foundation of America

c/o Sylvia Clark, Exec. Dir.
8 Corporate Center Dr.
Melville, NY 11747-3112
(516) 753-7021
E-mail: reidenbb@ccgate.ml.nec.com
Internet: http://www.nec.com/web/company/foundation/index.html
EIN: 113059554
Source Date: 3/95

Geographic Restrictions:

Programs with immediate U.S. impact, with emphasis on areas of company operations: Boxborough, MA, Mountain View, Roseville, and Santa Clara, CA, Miami, FL, McDonough, GA, Wood Dale, IL, Princeton, NJ, Melville, NY, Hillsboro, OR, Dallas, TX, and Herndon, VA.

Restrictions:

No grants to religious activities, athletic competition, fundraising or advertising, individual elementary or secondary schools or districts, individuals, equipment for individuals, endowments, capital funds, building funding.

To Whom:

Science and technology education with emphasis on secondary education, apply technology to disabled.

For What:

Conferences and seminars, general purposes, publications, research, seed money, operating budgets, special projects.

Financial info:
Assets: $9,806,100.
Giving: $285,000 for 15 grants (high: $50,000; low: $10,000).

Application info:
Applications accepted. Submit preliminary proposal (3 page limit). Deadline is Nov. 1 and May 1. Board meets in Mar. and Sept. Publishes application guidelines and grants list.

Recent Grants:

$25,000	Access Theatre, Santa Barbara, CA. For video production of the international touring, critically acclaimed stage play, STORM READING, which is based on the life of playwright/actor Neil Marcus, who has been living with a neurological disorder known as dystonia since the age of eight.
$20,000	**Adaptive Rehabilitation Technologies (ART), Marblehead, MA. For documentation, evaluation and dissemination of the TAKE CONTROL! model in order to promote the staging of these consumer awareness and training events to organizations and individuals nationwide. The goal is to spread information about assistive technology to prospective users and those who assist them.**
$25,000	Center for Excellence in Education, McLean, VA. For the Research Science Institute (RSI), a summer program held at MIT, at which the country's most gifted young math and science students who have completed their junior year of high school receive six weeks of intense academic instruction and on-site research as interns with scientists. CEE follows the progress of RSI alumnus through their undergraduate and graduate years and helps them get scholarships and career related summer employment.
$30,000	Challenger Center for Space Science Education, Alexandria, VA. Dissemination of teaching materials to accompany Encounter Earth, a new program for middle school students across the country that studies the Earth's global life-support systems: its biosphere, geosphere, hydrosphere, atmosphere and ecosphere, and the environmental hazards that threaten its inhabitants, such as volcanic eruptions, deforestation, flooding and severe tropical storms.
$7,000	Communication Independence for the Neurologically Impaired, Inc. (CINI), New York, NY . For national distribution of a resource guide to help patients and clinicians understand the roles of various professionals in ensuring successful use of technology-based communication solu-

	tions for nonspeaking individuals with disabilities related to motor-neuron diseases.
$30,000	Girl Scouts of the USA, New York, NY. Expansion of the National Science Partnership (NSP) to ten additional sites across the country. NSP establishes links between Girl Scout councils and science-technology museums in order to change the way young women view science. The program offers training to troop leaders and science "kits" on topics such as chemistry, physics and astronomy.
$15,000	The Institute for Rehabilitation & Research, Houston, TX. For a demonstration project to document the effectiveness of telecommuting as an accommodation tool for people with disabilities and for employers who underutilize the resource represented by people with disabilities.
$25,000	The JASON Foundation for Education, Waltham, MA. For Teacher Enhancement: An Innovative Approach to Preparing the Nation's Students for the Fist Century, to develop skills of elementary and secondary level classroom teachers to utilize rapidly emerging education technologies including global telecommunications systems such as Internet and World Wide Web.
$50,000	Junior Engineering Technical Society, Alexandria, VA. Expansion of the National Engineering Design Challenge academic program and competition, which engages teams of high school students in developing prototype devices to demonstrate the principles of universal design. The design specifications require that the device be usable by people with and without disabilities.
$10,000	Long Island Museum of Science and Technology (LIMSAT), Melville, NY. Toward planning of a new "hands-on" science and technology museum, to hold exhibits related to the technologies of information, the environment, biology and electronics. The facility will augment classroom learning and is expected to be a major NY State cultural attraction.
$25,000	The George Lucas Educational Foundation, Nicasio, CA. Toward major public awareness campaign related to Edutopia: Innovative Efforts Project, to include a video and resource document to promote ways that education is improving so all students will be prepared to live and work in an increasingly complex, highly technological world.
$20,000	National Easter Seal Society, Chicago, IL. To expand the Computer Assistive Technology Services (CATS) program by developing and implementing a business and marketing plan that will harness the collective value of the 14 existing CATS sites into a stronger national program

$25,000	Satellite Educational Resources Consortium, Inc. (SERC), Columbia, SC. Expansion of the audience of a distance-learning program, Math in the Middle, to nearly 15,000 deaf and hearing-impaired middle school students by adding closed captioning to this problem-solving approach which relates the functions of math to everyday experience.
$1,700	Talking Tapes for the Blind, St. Louis, MO. To purchase recorders, microphones and microphone stands to enable ten additional Volunteer Readers to tape textbooks for student borrowers.
$26,000	Vanderbilt University, Peabody College, Nashville, TN. For national expansion of the Teacher in Residence Program, which will bring outstanding classroom educators to participate in University research, teacher education and program development related to the infusion of information technology in education.
$30,300	Washington University in St. Louis, School of Medicine, Program in Occupational Therapy, St. Louis, MO. For a partnership with Gateway SeniorNet to provide computer access to older adults with disabilities, while instructing occupational therapy students in the application of assistive technology to people with disabilities.
$10,000	World Institute on Disability, Oakland, CA. For a national conference intended to increase awareness of the technology needs of people with disabilities, of existing methods for achieving increased access, and of principles of universal design within private industry, the disability community and government policy makers involved in the National Information Infrastructure (NII); and to stimulate creative solutions to access problems that may develop in next-generation technologies of the NII.

John M. Olin Foundation, Inc.

c/o James Piereson, Exec. Dir.
330 Madison Ave., 22nd Flr.
New York, NY 10017
(212) 661-2670
EIN: 376031033
Source Date: 12/96

Restrictions:

No grants for programs without significant importance for national affairs, individuals, annual campaigns, operating expenses, or building or endowment funding.

To Whom:
Public policy research: research on formulation, **implementation and evaluation of public policy in the social and economic fields**, regulatory policy, tax policy, fiscal policy, monetary policy, and welfare policy.

Strategic and international studies: relationship between U.S. institutions and the international context in which they operate, national security affairs, strategic issues, U.S. foreign policy, and the international economy.

American institutions: promote moral, cultural and institutional foundations of free government, studies of the American constitution, operation of American political institutions, and the moral and cultural principles underlying these institutions.

Law and the legal system: understanding the American judicial system and to preserve the rule of law as the bedrock of American constitutional government, public interest law, studies related to the judicial system, jurisprudence, and the relationship between law and economics.

For What
Research, publications, books, scholarly journals, conferences and seminars, professorships, institutional support, fellowships, television and radio programs, lectureships.

Financial info:
Assets: $121,670,300 (from 1995 990PF).
Giving: $18,500,000 for 150 grants (high: $2,000,000; low: $100).

Application info:
Applications accepted. Submit letter of inquiry. No deadline. Board meets quarterly with notification in 3 months. Publishes annual report with application guidelines.

Recent Grants:

$35,000	American Studies Center, Washington, DC. Radio series of perspectives from black Americans
$15,000	Atlantic Legal Foundation, New York, NY. Litigation programs
$25,000	Boston University, College of Communication, Boston, MA. Program for the Study of Disinformation under the direction of Lawrence Martin-Bittman
$10,000	The Brownson Institute, Notre Dame, IND. Translations of books by Michael Novak into Chinese, Hungarian and Polish
$189,940	California Institute of Technology, Social Science Program, Pasadena, CA. Law and Rational Choice conducted jointly

with the University of Southern California Law Center under the direction of Matthew L. Spitzer and John Ledyard

Directors, Officers, Trustees:

Flanigan, Peter M., Trustee
Furlaud, Richard M., Trustee
Gillespie, George J., III, Officer, Trustee
Knight, Charles F., Trustee
Olin, John M. (d), Donor
Piereson, James, Officer, Trustee
Simon, William E., Officer, Trustee
Williams, Eugene F., Jr., Trustee

Dewitt Wallace-Reader's Digest Fund, Inc.

c/o Jane Quinn, Pgm. Dir.
2 Park Ave., 23rd Flr.
New York, NY 10016
(212) 251-9700
Internet: http://www.dewittwallace.org
EIN: 136046680
Source Date: 12/96

Geographic Restrictions

Preference gives preference to projects with a national [U.S.] or regional impact.

Restrictions:

No grants for religious, fraternal, or veterans' organizations, private foundations, individuals, endowments, capital funds, scholarly research, or health and medical services and research.

To Whom:

Improve Elementary and Secondary Education (52% of funding): recruit more people, especially minorities, to teaching and other education professions, provide opportunities for professional development of educators, improve the capacity of schools to serve children, provide greater opportunities for students, especially minorities, to attend non-public schools.

Encourage School and Community Collaboration (10% of funding): improve collaboration between schools and community organizations to create new learning opportunities, promote family involvement in schools.

Strengthen Organizations that Serve Youth (14% of funding).
Support programs that increase career, service and education opportunities for youth (23% of funding).

For What:
Operating budgets, continuing support, internships, scholarship funds, special projects.

Financial info:
Assets: $1,077,706,800 (from 1995 annual report).
Giving: $34,054,200 for 50 grants (high: $4,000,000; low: $5,000).

Application info:
Applications accepted. Submit letter of inquiry (2 page limit). No deadline. A significant number of projects are initiated by the fund. Publishes annual report with application guidelines.

Recent Grants:

$2,400,000	Bread Loaf School of English, Middlebury, VT. To underwrite fellowships for 70 teachers of English from high schools in low-income districts for three summers of intense study at Bread Loaf campuses in Middlebury, VT; Santa Fe, NM; and Oxford, England; and to add Colorado and Georgia to the network that now includes Alaska, Arizona, Mississippi, New Mexico, South Carolina and Vermont.
$643,0000	Education Development Center (EDC), Newton, MA. To train groups of teachers from selected low-income districts in Bloomfield, MN; Boston and Cambridge, MA; Chicago; and San Francisco; to use Developing Mathematical Ideas, a pioneering professional development curriculum developed by the EDC's Center for the Development of Teaching with support from the National Science Foundation. After completing their training, teachers will organize study programs for other local school district personnel. Some 300 teachers will participate directly.
$150,000	Yale-New Haven Teachers Institute, New Haven, CT. To explore the feasibility and develop criteria for planning similar professional development programs in other cities. The model will be based on the Institute, which involves arts and science faculty from Yale in the professional development of teachers from New Haven public schools during five-month seminars.
$619,000	American Association for Higher Education (AAHE), Washington, DC. AAHE will identify 20 universities interested in changing their counseling education programs. Ten of

these universities will be recommended to the Fund's board in late 1997 for planning grants to design model programs. The balance will be assisted in developing their capacity to be future models. AAHE also will support the planning grant sites as they develop their implementation models. During the grant period AAHE also will publish results of Fund-commissioned studies on the current status of the counseling field; work with other counseling organizations to further reform efforts; and consult with national experts and monitor promising in-service practices that should be incorporated into counseling education programs.

$43,900	Rose Community Foundation, Denver, CO
$50,000	Urban Strategies Council, Oakland, CA
$50,000	Youth Futures Authority, Savannah, GA
$50,000	YouthNet of Greater Kansas City, Kansas City, MO
$50,000	YMCA of Metropolitan Minneapolis, Minneapolis, MN
$9,945	Boston College, Chestnut Hill, MA
$50,000	California State University, Long Beach, CA
$49,554	University of Utah, Salt Lake City, UT
$150,000	Fordham University and the Children's Aid Society, New York, NY
$24,589	United Way of Buffalo and Erie County, Buffalo, NY
$25,000	United Way of Genesee and Lapeer Counties, Flint, MI
$24,822	United Way of Northeast Florida, Jacksonville, FL
$24,680	United Way of Lincoln and Lancaster County, Lincoln, NE
$25,000	United Way of Greater Greensboro, Greensboro, NC
$22,751	Mesa United Way, Mesa, AZ
$25,000	United Way of Missoula County, Missoula, MO
$25,000	United Way of Southeastern New England, Providence, RI
$25,000	United Way of Southeastern Pennsylvania, Philadelphia, PA
$235,449	United Way of America (and Institute for Educational Leadership), Alexandria, VA
$450,000	Clark Atlanta University, Atlanta, GA. Scholarships to enable non-certified minority teachers currently working in the Atlanta areas school districts to complete their college coursework leading to certification.
$1,220	Apple Corps, Inc., Atlanta, GA. Library Power.
$173,990	Academy for Educational Development, Washington, DC. Assess the feasibility of staff development initiative to improve training for youth workers at the community level.
$170,002	Search Institute, Minneapolis, MN. Assess the training needs of direct service workers in youth programs based in religious institutions and to determine the feasibility of providing future training.

$50,000	CollegeBound Foundation, Baltimore, MD. Plan the National College Access Support Project, program to improve and expand local :last dollar scholarship" programs across the country.
$186,519	**Southern Education Foundation Atlanta, GA. To continue monitoring and assisting 12 DeWitt Wallace-Reader's Digest Pathways to Teaching Careers Programs throughout the South. Activities include providing technical assistance, helping programs make midcourse corrections based on evaluation findings and conducting complementary activities to further overall Pathways goals.**
$3,050,000	Lehman College, CUNY Bronx, NY. To implement a professional development program through the Institute for Literacy Studies for teachers and administrators from 27 New York City schools. In partnership with the American Social History Project at Hunter College, the City College Science Workshop Center, the Educational Video Center, the Teachers College Writing and Reading Projects, Youth Communication, and the New York City Board of Education, Lehman college will provide summer institutes, after-school courses and classroom consultations to teachers and administrators.

Ohio

Brush Foundation

c/o John J. Beeston, M.D., Pres.
3135 Euclid Ave., Suite 102
Cleveland, OH 44115
(216) 881-5121
EIN: 346000445
Source Date: 12/96

Geographic Restrictions:
U.S. and international giving.

Restrictions:
No grants to individuals, capital or endowment funding, scholarships, or fellowships.

To Whom:
Reproductive health through demographic or medical research, education,

public advocacy, litigation or delivery services, teenage sexuality education and services, freedom of choice, innovative service delivery systems, especially in developing countries, domestic family planning, international family planning.

For What:
Seed money, emergency funds, special projects, research, publications, conferences and seminars, matching funds, technical assistance.

Financial info:
Assets: $6,198,400.
Giving: $150,600 for 15 grants (high: $25,000; low: $500).

Application info:
Applications accepted. Submit letter. Deadline is Apr. and Oct. Board meets in May and Nov.

Recent Grants:

$13,500	Center for Development and Population Activities, Washington, DC, to support the Project Implementation portion of peer counseling and non-clinical family planning services at urban and rural YWCA centers in Ghana.
$13,000	Center for Development and Population Activities, Washington, DC, to help the YWCA in Ghana expand its adolescent reproductive health outreach projects. This grant covered the funds needed for a resource center.
$10,000	Center for Development and Population Activities, Washington, DC, to replicate these projects in two more sub-Saharan countries. Similar programs now are operating in 5 of 16 national YWCAs, 3 initiated by CEDPA.
$10,000	Consortium for Emergency Contraception, Welcome, MD. To help underwrite a five year effort to expand the education, distribution and use of emergency contraception pills in fifteen developing countries.
$30,000	Freedom From Hunger, Davis, CA. To help match $120,000 in funding by the Bolivian Government to design, develop and test a program to deliver family planning in rural Bolivia, using a community-based distribution system.
$22,200	Fundacion de Proyectos Fronterizos, Tijuana, Mexico. To produce a weekly radio show on health and family planning, "Recipes for a Healthy Family", designed to reach 250,000 listeners on both sides of the border.
$47,249	IPAS, Carrboro, NC. $15,000 to help establish a post-abortion care pilot program at Mulago Hospital, Kampala,

	Uganda. This grant follows ones made for projects in Zimbabwe and Ghana that appear to be successful.
$47,249	IPAS, Carrboro, NC. $32,249 to implement abortion-care training and service delivery programs in South Africa once abortion laws are liberalized.
$15,000	Orientame, Bogota, Columbia, to help strengthen the public image of Orientame (the leading provider of abortion and sterilization services in Columbia) and to increase public awareness about the need to improve women's reproductive freedom.
$10,000	Orientame, Bogota, Columbia, to help refurbish and reopen abortion and family planning clinics that had been badly damaged.
$33,000	Pathfinder International, Watertown, MA, to expand the Population Health Services' medical training program in vacuum aspiration techniques at four clinics operated by Marie Stopes International in Kenya.
$50,000	Pathfinder International, Watertown, MA, towards a $500,000 "Diversification Fund", to allow Pathfinder to develop financial support from other governments.
$25,000	Pathfinder International, Watertown, MA. For an unsolicited unrestricted grant to help offset the serious cuts in USAID funding authorized by Congress. This grant was subsequently matched by additional gifts from board members.
$19,113	Planned Parenthood of Northern New England, Williston, VT, To work with Uganda's Family Life Education Project (FLEP) in Jinja to expand service.
$10,000	Population Institute, Washington, DC, To underwrite the attendance of representatives from "Iron Curtain" countries at organizational conferences prior to the Cairo Conference on Population and Development.
$15,000	Population Services International, Washington, DC, to support a program to promote abstinence as well as condom usage among adolescents in Soweto, South Africa.
$15,000	Population Services International, Washington, DC. $20,000 to underwrite one or both social marketing programs. The first is a continuation of a Lovers Plus condom project in Soweto, South Africa. The second to help fund the first contraceptive effort in Albania, where the contraceptive prevalence rate is now seven percent, and abortion is the contraceptive of choice.
$12,500	PROSALUD, Venezuela. To produce and circulate 550,000 brochures as part of their social marketing program. Results to date have been very encouraging in the face of a population destined to double in 32 years.

$24,500	Resource Foundation, Larchmont, NY. To expand a family planning education, service and training program in Santarem, Brazil, working through Fundacao Esperanca.
$25,000	Case Western Reserve University School of Nursing, Cleveland, OH. To fund the first year's contraceptive services at the planned Nursing Health Center.
$20,000	The Free Clinic of Greater Cleveland, Cleveland, OH. For continuing support of the nurse practitioner who helps deliver family planning services in the adolescent and adult clinics.
$20,000	Johns Hopkins University, Baltimore,MD. To study contraceptive behaviors among low income, high risk women who accepted contraception after delivery 18 months ago.
$5,000	Planned Parenthood of Greater Cleveland, Cleveland, OH. to establish the Meacham Hitchcock Educational Endowment Fund for their Resource Center, recognizing his receipt of the Ellery Sedgwick Distinguished Service Award.
$10,000	**Planned Parenthood of Greater Cleveland, Cleveland, OH. to help expand and evaluate three programs aimed at young people: "Facts of Life Line" (information telephone line), "Let's Talk" (home-based sexuality education program for parents) and outreach services. Planned Parenthood of Central California, Fresno, CA 1 grant of $4,000: To purchase a human resource software package to streamline services for over 24,000 clients.**
$20,000	Preterm Cleveland, OH. For examining tables at PreTerm's new location.
$10,000	FREEDOM OF CHOICE ACLU Foundation Reproductive Freedom Project, New York, NY. To support efforts to challenge the church's role in hospital mergers which result in the curtailment of reproductive health services. Catholics for a Free Choice, Washington, DC
$15,000	FREEDOM OF CHOICE ACLU Foundation Reproductive Freedom Project, New York, NY. to support Educating and Reaching Out to the religious community.
$15,000	FREEDOM OF CHOICE ACLU Foundation Reproductive Freedom Project, New York, NY. to help underwrite a plan to challenge the Vatican on its international family planning policy.
$45,000	Center for Reproductive Law and Policy, New York, NY. For general support of the Center's legal work in the field of reproductive health, especially recent efforts to gain FDA approval of emergency contraception.

$10,000	Coalition of Labor Union Women, Washington, DC. To increase technical assistance in the Coalition's chapters for pro-choice education.
$15,000	Concentric Media, Menlo Park, CA. To produce and distribute their third film, "The Fragile Promlse of Choice".
$10,000	The Feminist Majority Foundation, San Rafael, CA. To support their Clinic Access Project. This Project assists family planning clinics in fending off efforts to shut them down. Assuming passage, it will monitor The Freedom of Access Act.
$15,000	ProChoice Resource Center, Mamaroneck, NY. To expand their "IDEA Strategy", Identify, Educate and Activate, for pro-choice supporters.
$20,000	Religious Coalition for Reproductive Choice Educational Fund (formerly RCAR), Washington, DC. Towards their educational programs.
$5,000	San Francisco's Women's Center, San Francisco, CA. To help expand circulation of "Choosing Choice", a new pro-choice publication. Voters For Choice Education Washington, 1 grant for $10,000: To support the "Pipeline to Power" project, to educate young women to become pro-choice activists.
$15,000	The American University, Washington, DC. To publish the results of a conference on how international law can be used to advance women's reproductive rights. Results will appear in "The Law Review", and be sent to Beijing conference delegates.
$6,000	Planned Parenthood and PreTerm, Cleveland, OH. To underwrite Dr. Henry Foster's visit as the speaker at a special joint meeting in Cleveland on reproductive health.
$25,584	Population Resource Center, Princeton, NJ. To organize policy discussions and bi-partisan briefing for Congress on the role of family planning services in the prevention of adolescent pregnancies.
$10,000	Advocates for Youth (formerly Population Options), Washington, DC, for: An "emergency" grant to help support AFY's Media Advisory Service.
$50,000	The Alan Guttmacher Institute, New York, NY. $25,000 to help produce and publish a follow-up to the 1981 study,. Teen Pregnancy - The Problem That Hasn't Gone Away"; A $25,000 unsolicited, unrestricted gift recognizing this organization's outstanding accomplishments in the field.
$30,000	**Advocates for Youth, Washington, DC (Formerly Center For Population Options). 3 grants totalling: $20,000 towards the costs of two additional volumes for their "Guide to School-based and School-linked Health Care"**

that Brush previously supported. Volume IV will cover program evaluation, and Volume V legal issues; $10,000 to help prepare and produce Volume VI. This volume will deal with how to amalgamate with managed care programs.

$15,000	Big Brothers/Big Sisters of Southwestern Illinois, Belleville, IL. 2 grants totalling: $10,000 to recruit, train and match 18 Big Sister mentors with 18 pregnant/parenting teens; $5,000 to help expand this program.
$10,000	Family Health of Beech Brook, Cleveland, OH. To support their Early Intervention and Sexuality Program for fifth and sixth graders in Cleveland public schools. This grant is a continuation of support started in 1992.
$40,000	New Mexico Teen Pregnancy Coalition, Albuquerque, NM. 2 grants: $30,000 to support its initial part-time staff while establishing this state-wide coalition; $10,000 as a six month challenge grant (which was met) to help broaden their base of local support.
$7,500	Planned Parenthood of Greater Iowa, Des Moines, IA. To help open a new teen clinic in the Quad Cities area.
$10,000	Sexuality Education Task Force, Unitarian Universalist Assoc. and United Church of Christ, Boston, MA. To assist in developing, field testing and implementing a Human Sexuality Education Project. Our funds are to cover the field testing portion.
$17,000	State of Florida, Health & Rehabilitative Services, Brookeville, FL. To add a family planning education and service portion to their adolescent parenting program.
$1,000	The Foundation Center, New York, NY. To help support the organization and especially the Foundation Center Library in Cleveland.
$66,342	University of Michigan, Center for Population Planning, Ann Arbor, MI. To continue the Charles F. Brush Scholarship in International Family Planning, in memory of Drs. David and William Weir, long time Brush Managers. This two year master program scholarship is awarded to an outstanding applicant who shows unusual promise of making significant contributions to the fields of population policy and family planning. The scholarship is not necessarily granted every two years.

George Gund Foundation

c/o David Bergholz, Exec. Dir.
1845 Guildhall Bldg.
45 Prospect Ave. West
Cleveland, OH 44115
(216) 241-3114
EIN: 346519769
Source Date: 12/96

Geographic Restrictions:
Primarily in northeastern OH.

Restrictions:
No grants to individuals, building or endowment funding, equipment, renovation projects, conferences, publications, operating funds, continuing support, programs for the physically, mentally, or developmentally disabled, or the elderly.

To Whom:
Education: public and private higher education focusing on improving minorities' access and retention in higher educational institutions, strengthening faculty development, elementary and secondary education primarily in Cuyahoga County focusing on improving educational programs for minorities and low-income youth, public school improvement, community and parental involvement, policy development, staff development, **program evaluation**, early childhood education focuses on strengthening the child care system in the Cleveland area, early intervention for disadvantaged preschoolers. Economic and Community Revitalization: create jobs and livable neighborhoods in the inner city Cleveland area, urban planning, design and amenity issues.

Social Services: welfare and stability of children and families in Cuyahoga County including upgrading the management of local social services, improving the economic status of women, reproductive health, prevent infant mortality, maternal and infant health, maintaining a woman's right to control her reproductivity through family planning and abortion and national [U.S.] public policy formation and local public education on AIDS;

Environmental Quality: public education, effective public policy, advocacy especially related to Great Lakes ecosystem, in U.S. for reducing the effects of climate change by creating effective energy policy, conservation and pollution prevention programs.

Arts: arts education, collaboration among arts organizations, greater cultural diversity in programming, audiences, and organizations.

Civic Affairs: strengthening effectiveness of governmental organizations, increasing citizen participation in public affairs in the Cleveland area.

For What:
Operating budgets, continuing support, seed money, emergency funds, land acquisition, matching funds, internships, scholarship funds, special projects, publications, conferences and seminars, program-related investments, exchange programs, research.

Financial info:
Giving: $20,284,300 for 390 grants (high: $500,000; low: $500).

Application info:
Applications accepted. Submit proposal with 1 page summary. Deadline is Dec. 30, Mar. 30, June 30, and Sept. 30. Board meets in Mar., June, Sept., and Dec. Publishes annual report and application guidelines.

Recent Grants:

$6,500	American Association of Community and Junior Colleges, Cleveland, OH. Urban Colleges Project.
$7,000	Akron School District Akron, OH. Total Quality Management in Urban Education project.
$95,000	Child Care Resource Center of Cuyahoga County, Cleveland, OH. Operating, scholarship and project support.
$17,275	National Invention Center, Inc, Akron, OH. "Creativity in Science" conference.
$24,566	Bellflower Center for the Prevention of Child Abuse, Cleveland, OH. Continued support for the PAST (People Abused Surviving Together) Program.
$75,000	Cleveland Works, Inc., Cleveland, OH. Beat the Streets Program for unemployed teen fathers.
$24,137	9 to 5 Working Women Education Fund, Cleveland, OH. Training programs on sexual harassment in the workplace.
$70,000	Cleveland Housing Network, Inc., Cleveland, OH. Family Development Program

Directors, Officers, Trustees:
Barber, Kathleen L., Trustee
Bergholz, David, Officer
Gund, Ann L., Officer, Trustee
Gund, Geoffrey, Officer, Trustee
Gund, George (d), Donor
Gund, George, III, Trustee
Gund, Llura A., Officer, Trustee

Pennsylvania

Howard Heinz Endowment

c/o Franklin Tugwell, Exec. Dir.
30 CNG Tower
625 Liberty Ave.
Pittsburgh, PA 15222-3115
(412) 281-5777
E-mail: info@heinz.org
Internet: http://www.heinz.org
EIN: 251721100
Source Date: 12/95

Geographic Restrictions:
Limited to southwestern PA.

Restrictions:
No grants to individuals.

To Whom:
Arts & Culture: development of a vibrant downtown cultural district, major cultural institutions, create healthy environment for small and mid-sized arts programs, promote increased access to the arts, promote the development of quality arts education programs within arts organizations and schools.

Community & Economic Development: encourage community-based revitalization efforts, including capacity-building and leadership development, stimulate private and public investment in distressed areas, especially where investment can be leveraged, strengthen targeted civic organizations that address economic issues on a regional level.

Health & Social Services: promote the healthy development of at-risk youth, children and families, improve maternal and child health, including a reduction in infant mortality, improve quality of life for adolescents, especially those more at risk of persistent poverty, build and strengthen planning, research, **and evaluation capacities**.

Environment: promote the design of urban environments in ways which eliminate inefficiency and waste, and regenerate the urban core, support the creation of environmental enterprises to protect resources and eliminate waste, promote and support an energy-efficient economy.

For What:
Seed money, special projects, building funds, equipment, research, matching funds, program-related investments, renovation projects, capital campaigns.

Financial info:
Assets: $711,810,700.
Giving: $34,600,000 for 200 grants (high: $1,500,000; low: $1,000).

Application info:
Applications accepted. Submit letter of inquiry. No deadline for letter. Deadline is Feb. 15 and Sept. 15. Board meets in the May and Nov. Publishes annual report and application guidelines.

Recent Grants:

$20,000	Allegheny County Bureau of Cultural Programs. Performing arts presentations at Hartwood Acres
$33,500	Gateway to Music and the Performing Arts. Summer Institute, Docent Training Programs, In-Service and Residency Packages, and part-time staff position
$250,000	Chesapeake Bay Foundation, Inc. Susquehanna Watershed Education Program, which provides on-the-water field studies to school students and teachers in central Pennsylvania
$20,000	Allegheny Conference on Community Development. Operating support
$300,000	Louise Child Care Center. Create Child Care Training Institute
$459,300	Carnegie Library of Pittsburgh, Homewood Branch. Expand "Project Beacon," an early intervention literacy program targeted to children, ages birth to five
$2,523,670	Children's Hospital of Philadelphia. Continuing support of pediatric nutrition education program of Nutrition Center
$280,000	Allegheny Policy Council. Open Doors, a school-community partnership to improve after-school learning opportunities for disadvantaged youth
$200,000	Education Law Center-PA. Pilot Pennsylvania School Reform Network
$100,000	Fox Chapel School District. Technology-assisted school restructuring initiative aimed at improving student achievement

Vira I. Heinz Endowment

c/o Franklin Tugwell, Exec. Dir.
The CNG Tower
625 Liberty Ave., 30th Flr.
Pittsburgh, PA 15222
(412) 281-5777
E-mail: info@heinz.org
Internet: http://www.heinz.org
EIN: 251762825
Source Date: 12/95

Geographic Restrictions:
Limited to southwestern PA.

Restrictions:
No grants for endowments.

To Whom:
Arts & Culture: development of a vibrant downtown cultural district, major cultural institutions, create healthy environment for small and mid-sized arts programs, promote increased access to the arts, promote the development of quality arts education programs within arts organizations and schools.

Community & Economic Development: encourage community-based revitalization efforts, including capacity-building and leadership development, stimulate private and public investment in distressed areas, especially where investment can be leveraged,
strengthen targeted civic organizations that address economic issues on a regional level.

Health & Social Services: promote the healthy development of at-risk youth, children and families, improve maternal and child health, including a reduction in infant mortality, improve quality of life for adolescents, especially those more at risk of persistent poverty, build and strengthen planning, research, **and evaluation capacities.**

Environment: promote the design of urban environments in ways which eliminate inefficiency and waste, and regenerate the urban core, support the creation of environmental enterprises to protect resources and eliminate waste, promote and support an energy-efficient economy.

For What:
Capital campaigns, general purposes, renovation projects, seed money, special projects, technical assistance, building funds.

Financial info:
Assets: $359,818,800.
Giving: $15,300,000 for 165 grants (high: $800,000; low: $100).

Application info:
Applications accepted. Submit letter of inquiry. No deadline for letter. Deadline is Jan. 15 and July 15. Board meets in the spring and fall. Publishes application guidelines.

Recent Grants:

$25,000	Allegheny Conference on Community Development.
$250,000	Artspace Projects, Inc.
$40,000	Carlisle Project.
$500,000	Carnegie Institute.
$50,000	Carnegie Mellon University.
$150,000	Civic Light Opera Association.
$2,000,000	Historical Society of Western PA.
$25,000	International Poetry Forum.
$60,000	Performing Arts for Children's Series, Inc.
$110,000	Pittsburgh Center for the Arts.
$30,000	Pittsburgh Chapter of Artist's Equity Association.
$250,000	Pittsburgh Cultural Trust.
$80,374	Arts on Tour Program.
$25,000	American Waterway Wind Orchestra.
$500,000	Carnegie Institute.
$85,000	Carnegie Institute, Three Rivers Arts Festival.
$350,000	Civic Light Opera Association.
$32,900	Gateway to Music and the Performing Arts.
$60,000	Historical Society of Western PA.
$50,000	I Dream a World, Inc.
$20,000	Pittsburgh Arts and Lectures.
$1,700,000	Pittsburgh Cultural Trust.
$7,500,000	Pittsburgh Cultural Trust.
$150,000	Pittsburgh Dance Alloy.
$65,000	Pittsburgh Filmmakers, Inc.
$30,000	Pittsburgh Fund for Arts Education.
$50,000	Pittsburgh Public Theater Corporation.
$66,000	Pittsburgh Symphony Society.
$400,000	QED Communcations, Inc.
$25,000	Saltworks Theatre Company.
$200,000	Shadyside Presbyterian Church.
$278,500	The Pittsburgh Foundation.
$50,000	Allegheny Clarion Valley Development Corporation
$50,000	Carnegie Mellon University
$535,400	Duquesne University

$100,000	Perry Hilltop Association for Successful Enterprises, Inc.
$525,000	Pittsburgh Partnership for Neighborhood Development, Inc.
$150,000	Pittsburgh Partnership for Neighborhood Development, Inc.
$1,000,000	Strategic Investment Fund, Inc.
$435,000	Aliquippa Alliance for Unity and Development
$100,000	Allegheny Conference on Community Development
$300,000	Braddock's Field Historical Society
$125,000	Community Loan Fund for Southwestern PA.
$650,000	Mon Valley Initiative.
$50,000	PICPA Foundation for Education and Research
$60,000	Southwestern PA Economic Development District-SPEDD.
$150,000	The Downtown Management Organization
$150,000	University of Pittsburgh Institute of Politics
$20,000	Artists Raising the Consciousness of Humanity, Inc.
$25,000	Children's Festival Chorus, Inc.
$200,000	Museum of Fine Arts, Boston, MA. "The Age of Rubens" exhibition.
$300,000	Action-Housing, Inc. Leadership grant to capitalize ACTION-Housing Development Fund.
$225,000	Alliance to End Childhood Lead Poisoning. Implement national prevention campaign.
$200,000	Center for Hazardous Materials Research. Environmental Technology Education Program.
$20,347,923	Environment Science and Economics Program. Advance study of major environmental issues and communicate findings to policy makers and public.
$300,000	University of Pittsburgh Heinz Chapel. Make Heinz Chapel accessible to handicapped visitors, primarily through installation of elevator.

Directors, Officers, Trustees:

Heinz, Andre T., Trustee
Heinz, Teresa F., Trustee
Heinz, Vira I. (d), Donor
Mackenzie, Wendy, Trustee
Mellon Bank, N.A., Trustee
Rea, William H., Trustee
Ryan, John T., Jr., Trustee
Tugwell, Franklin, Officer
Walton, James M., Trustee
Wiley, S. Donald, Trustee

Jewish Healthcare Foundation of Pittsburgh

c/o Karen Wolk Feinstein, PhD, Pres.
Centre City Tower, Suite 2550
650 Smithfield St.
Pittsburgh, PA 15222
(412) 232-6237
EIN: 251624347
Source Date: 12/95

Geographic Restrictions:
Limited to western PA.

Restrictions:
No grants to individuals, general operations, endowments, capital needs, operating deficits, scholarships, fellowships, research, or travel.

To Whom:
Seniors and Chronic Care: stimulate development of a new vision for integrated systems, provide training and incentives for community-based providers to develop wrap-around services, educate consumers and how to use the reformed health system, self-care, and prevention, **reorient professionals who serve seniors and disabled by supporting evaluation of the cost-effectiveness of current services,** strong agency strategic planning capacity, new billing and financial systems capacity, new data requirements, new linkages to the large health networks that are emerging, focus public health agencies on their roles of assessment, assurance, and policy development, introduce ethical values to cost-containment plans, build public-private partnerships.

Children's Health: improve healthy family life through education, modeling, and competent supporting organizations, teach health behaviors in settings where children and their parents congregate naturally, early detection to lessen or prevent permanent disability through outreach, early detection, and tracking, make schools violence free, explore models of managed care that integrate public health, social services, and medical care in the healthcare system.

Women's Health: review and analyze the health and social status of women in PA, examine policy, identifying research opportunities, and promote social action to improve the health of women, promote better models of health care for women in the context of healthcare reform, empower women to improve healthy behaviors and make better use of the healthcare system.

Jewish Communal: prevent falls and depression among seniors, improve nutritional status and prevent eating disorders, prevent drug and alcohol abuse, bring services to special-needs children within our communal day schools.

AIDS: access to quality, integrated care services within managed-care environments that are responsive to special-needs populations, effective prevention and outreach to reduce the transmission of the HIV virus, especially with at risk populations.

Nutrition: better understand the fundamental relationship of diet to health status and modify diets accordingly, emerging health networks will modify care pathways and reimbursement mechanisms to guarantee nutritional services to health consumers, public nutrition safety net programs for vulnerable individuals will be reinvigorated.

For What:
Matching funds, seed money, emergency funds, special projects.

Financial info:
Assets: $100,659,800.
Giving: $3,338,200 for 70 grants (high: $500,000; low: $500).

Application info:
Applications accepted. Submit preliminary letter (6 page limit, 4 copies). No deadline. Publishes annual report with application guidelines.

Recent Grants:

American Jewish Committee
American Joint Distribution Committee, Inc.
Brandeis University, Institute of Health Policy
Butler Memorial Hospital
Carnegie Science Center
City Theatre Company, Inc.
Council on Foundations
Duquesne University
Forbes Fund
Gift of Life Foundation
Grantmakers in Health
Hemophilia Council of Western Pennsylvania
Holocaust Center
Family Hospice
Fayette AIDS Task Force
Federation of Allegheny County Aging Service Providers
Funders Concerned About AIDS
Greater Pittsburgh Guild for the Blind
Heritage Health Foundation
Home Nursing Agency
Presbyterian SeniorCare
Primary Care Health Services

Radio Information Service
Regional Association of Senior Citizens and Alliances, Inc.
Pittsburgh AIDS Task Force
Pittsburgh Mercy Foundation
Pittsburgh Mercy Health System
Pittsburgh Rotary Club
Pittsburgh Trust for Cultural Resources
Renaissance Center
Cleft Palate Foundation
Community Day School
Extra Mile Foundation
Family Health Council, Inc.
Greene County Human Services Department
H. John Heinz III School, Carnegie Mellon University
Health Education Center
Allegheny County Center for the Victims of Violent Crimes
Black Women's Leadership Conference
Carlow College, Division of Nursing
Carnegie Mellon University
Chatham College
Community College of Allegheny County
Foundation of the Pennsylvania Nurses Association
Magee-Womens Health Foundation
Nursing Recruitment Coalition
Pennsylvania Organization for Women in Early Recovery
Pittsburgh Cancer Institute
Pittsburgh Research Institute
Saltworks Theatre Company

Richard King Mellon Foundation

c/o Michael Watson, Secretary & Dir.
1 Mellon Bank Ctr.
500 Grant St., Suite 4106
Pittsburgh, PA 15219-2502
(412) 392-2800
EIN: 251127705
Source Date: 12/95

Geographic Restrictions:
Primarily in Pittsburgh and southwestern PA., except U.S. giving for conservation.

Restrictions:
No grants to individuals, fellowships or scholarships.

To Whom:
Education with emphasis on elementary and secondary education, social services with emphasis on families and at risk youth, medicine and health care, civic affairs, cultural programs. Conservation of natural areas in the U.S.

For What:
Seed money, building funds, equipment, land acquisition, research, matching funds, general purposes, continuing support, operating budgets, renovation projects.

Financial info:
Assets: $1,250,592,000.
Giving: $45,848,100 for 130 grants (high: $1,000,000; low: $5,000).

Application info:
Applications accepted. Application form required. Deadline is Apr. 1 and Oct. 1. Board meets in June and Dec. Publishes annual report and application guidelines.

Recent Grants:

$125,000	Scenic America. Washington, DC, to assist with a three-year strategy to develop scenic byways in Pennsylvania (conditional)
$37,500	**Student Conservation Association, Inc. Charlestown, NH, to carry out a nationally significant evaluation of the impact of hands-on conservation education programs.**
$450,000	The Wildlife Conservation Fund of America, Columbus, OH, to help manage and coordinate its sportsmen's network which will further public education.
$14,000	Aliquippa Alliance for Unity & Development, Aliquippa, PA, toward support for two summer programs for youth of the Aliquippa area.
$200,000	Allegheny Policy Council for Youth and Workforce Development Pittsburgh, PA, toward support for the Youth Employment Alliance's summer jobs program.
$42,000	Beginnings Early Intervention Services of Cambria County, Inc. Johnstown, PA, toward operating support for Right from the Start Program.
$75,000	Big Brothers and Big Sisters of Greater Pittsburgh, Inc. Pittsburgh, PA, toward three years' support for Project Outreach.

$50,000 Big Brothers/Big Sisters of Beaver County Monaca, PA, toward two years' support to implement, manage and evaluate the Juvenile Mentoring Program.

$50,000 Boys & Girls Club of Henderson County/Hendersonville, Inc., Hendersonville, NC, toward a capital campaign to create a permanent facility for the club.

$200,000 Boys & Girls Club of Western Pennsylvania, Pittsburgh, PA, payable over two years toward program support.

$75,000 City Mission, Uniontown, PA, toward rehabilitation of men's and women's shelters and implementation of a case management program (conditional).

$40,000 Community Human Services Corporation, Pittsburgh, PA, toward two-year operating support for the Family Loan Program.

$300,000 Community Literacy Center, Pittsburgh, PA, for project support.

$100,000 Carnegie Library of Homestead, Homestead, PA, Children's Home of Pittsburgh, Pittsburgh, PA, to expand programs to help place infants in permanent homes.

$250,000 Greater Pittsburgh Guild for the Blind, Bridgeville, PA, toward three-year program support for the Access Technology Center.

$15,000 Eastside Alliance, Pittsburgh, PA, toward support of the Parent Advocacy Initiative.

$5,000 Epilepsy Foundation of Western Pennsylvania, Pittsburgh, PA, toward scholarship support for thirty lower and middle income children with epilepsy to attend summer camp.

$5,000 Fair Housing Partnership of Greater Pittsburgh, Inc., Pittsburgh, PA, toward program support.

$25,000 The Early Learning Institute, Pittsburgh, PA, toward operating support.

$100,000 Easter Seal Society of Allegheny County, Pittsburgh, PA, toward purchase of manufacturing equipment for the agency's work center which employs men and women with severe disabilities.

$300,000 Allegheny Policy Council for Youth and Workforce Development, Pittsburgh, PA, toward operating support for the Open Doors Program.

$15,000 Asset, Inc., Pittsburgh, PA, toward operating support and assistance in establishing a materials support center.

$500,000 Carlow College, Pittsburgh, PA, payable over two years toward support of the Teaching Is Caring program.

$105,000 Negro Educational Emergency Drive, Pittsburgh, PA, payable over four years toward scholarship support for five minority students.

$240,000	Negro Educational Emergency Drive, Pittsburgh, PA, payable over three years toward the general scholarship campaign.
$500,000	New American Schools Development Corporation, Arlington, VA. payable over two years to assist with Phase 3 of a strategic plan to restructure public schools (conditional).
$37,000	Pittsburgh Council on Public Education, Pittsburgh, PA, to implement the Hands Across the Campus program at Oliver High School (conditional).
$350,000	Point Park College, Pittsburgh, PA, toward a capital campaign to complete renovations of the downtown Library Center which will house both the relocated business branch of the Carnegie Library and the Point Park College Library.
$750,000	Robert Morris College, Pittsburgh, PA, payable over three years toward start-up support for a new communications skills program.
$50,000	Somerset County Campus Foundation for Allegany Community College, Somerset, PA, toward a capital campaign.
$30,000	United Negro College Fund, Inc., New York, NY, to support the first year of the Pittsburgh College Fair Program (conditional).
$700,000	University of Pennsylvania, Philadelphia, PA, to increase endowment for a professorship at the School of Veterinary Medicine.
$300,000	**University of Pittsburgh, Learning Research and Development Center, Pittsburgh, PA, payable over three years toward support for evaluation of the Pittsburgh Public Schools' Restructuring initiative**
$30,000	University of Pittsburgh Medical Center, Pittsburgh, PA, toward support for the summer internship program designed for the Richard King Mellon Foundation/NEED scholars in 1995, 1996 and 1997.
$5,000,000	Valley School of Ligonier, Ligonier, PA, matching funds for a capital campaign.
$72,000	University of Pittsburgh School of Medicine, Pittsburgh, PA, toward minority scholarship support.
$25,000	Allegheny Conference on Human Development, Pittsburgh, PA, toward support for the Transportation Agenda,a major component of the conference's economic revitalization effort for southwestern Pennsylvania
$125,000	Allegheny Conference on Human Development, Pittsburgh, PA, for the Agenda Development Fund, which supports specific projects and actuaries designed to achieve the conference's objectives

$3,000,000	Allegheny Conference on Human Development, Pittsburgh, PA, payable equally over three years toward unrestricted support
$50,000	Breachmenders, Inc., Pittsburgh, PA, far joint development projects among Breachmenders, Oakland Planning and Development Corporation and the Hill Community Development Corporation
$600,000	Carnegie Institute, Pittsburgh, PA, payable equally over three years to purchase a new automated ticketing system
$1,000,000	Carnegie Library of Pittsburgh, Pittsburgh, PA, to support an Electronic Information Network for Public Libraries in Allegheny County
$35,000	Community Design Center of Pittsburgh, Inc., Pittsburgh, PA, to provide start-up costs for the Renovation Information Network which offers design resources to individual residents (Conditional)
$100,000	Corporation for Owner-Operated Projects, Beaver Falls, PA, divided equally toward operating support and loan fund
$250,000	Pittsburgh Filmmakers, Pittsburgh, PA, toward a capital campaign (conditional)
$100,000	Pittsburgh Opera, Inc., Pittsburgh, PA, toward operating support for the 1995-1996 season
$117,000	The Pittsburgh Public Theater Corporation, toward operating support for the 1995-1996 season
$160,000	The Pittsburgh Symphony Society, Pittsburgh, PA, toward annual operating support.
$617,960	The Pittsburgh Trust for Cultural Resources, Pittsburgh, PA, toward capital support.
$200,000	QED Communications, Inc., Pittsburgh, PA, toward general operating support.

Directors, Officers, Trustees:

Mathieson, Andrew W., Trustee
Mellon, Richard K. (d), Donor
Mellon, Richard P., Officer, Trustee
Mellon, Seward Prosser, Officer, Trustee
Miltenberger, Arthur D., Officer
Scully, Arthur M., Jr., Trustee
Taber, George H., Officer, Trustee
Turcik, John J., Officer
Walsh, Mason, Jr., Trustee
Watson, Michael, Officer

Vermont

Vermont Community Foundation

c/o Judy E. Dunning, Grants Mgr.
P.O. Box 30
Middlebury, VT 05753
(802) 462-3355
EIN: 222712160
Source Date: 12/93

Geographic Restrictions:
Limited to VT.

Restrictions:
No grants for religious purposes, individuals, annual campaigns, building funds, continuing support, deficit financing, equipment and materials, endowments, land acquisition, operating funds.

To Whom:
Arts, humanities, education, seniors, disabled, health, social services, civic affairs, youth, community development.

For What:
Conferences and seminars, consulting services, exchange programs, internships, program-related investments, publications, renovation projects, research, scholarship funds, fellowships, seed money, student loans, technical assistance.

Financial info:
Giving: $1,286,400 for grants.

Application info:
Applications accepted. Application form required. Deadline is Apr. 1 and Oct. 1. Board meets bimonthly. Publishes annual report with application guidelines.

Recent Grants:

$2,000	Center for Creative Healing. To provide funding for children's grief support services in Windham County (McClure Motivation Fund)
$3,000	Franglais Enterprises. To support teacher training sessions to develop an interdisciplinary Franco-American curriculum for Spaulding High School in Barre
$2,000	Intervale Foundation. To support the Intervale Land Restoration and Market Expansion Program, a 3-year project

to restore the soil of 225 acres of Burlington farmland and to develop markets for agricultural products that can be grown there

$3,000 K.I.D.S. Place. Inc. To support hiring a college-age supervisor who will work with teen volunteers to implement recreational programs for younger children (McClure Motivation Fund)

$1,000 Land Trust Alliance. Inc. To support the Land Trust Alliance's ninth National Land Trust Rally, which will take place in Burlington on October 17-19, 1996 (VCF Fund)

$1,800 Leicester Central School. To create a summer reading incentive program, circulating books through home delivery to children and families in rural Leicester, Vermont (Wister Fund)

$5,000 Minority Business Association. Inc. To support expansion of the People's Food Stamp Co-op in Burlington (Rhodebeck Fund)

$2,000 Mount Independence Coalition. To provide support for an Archaeological Management Plan for Mount Independence in Orwell, Vermont

$1,500 Peace and Justice Center. To support a marketing campaign and logo to solidify and strengthen the organization's image in the community and to broaden its base of support (McClure Motivation Fund)

$500 Starksboro Public Library/Project READ. To support and expand the Starksboro Bookwagon project, a program to circulate books from the elementary school library in the summer to rural children (VCF Fund)

$3,000 STOP IT NOW! To support year 2 of a pilot media campaign encouraging sexual abusers of children to get treatment - focus will be on program evaluation (McClure Motivation Fund)

$2,000 Technology Resources for Education and Community. To support a project to refurbish computers through a system of volunteers and by establishing refurbishment centers in high schools (McClure Motivation Fund and VCF Fund)

$3,000 United Way of Chittenden County. To support the Champlain Initiative strategic planning project

$2,500 Vermont Council on the Humanities. To support a series of reading/discussion groups for teen parents (Wister Fund)

$1,000 Vermont Folklife Center. To support an expanded edition of VISIT'N, a collection of first-hand accounts of Vermonters about their lives and traditions (VCF Fund)

$2,500 Vermont Literacy Resource Center. For the purchase of two Adult Learning Differences and Disabilities Teacher

	Resource Kits, and for training workshops on their effective use (Rhodebeck Fund)
$3,000	Visiting Nurse Association. To support volunteer management and training for the Family Room (Rhodebeck Fund)
$3,000	Watershed Center. To develop a plan for education programs and managing the future nature center (McClure Motivation Fund)
$4,000	Woman Centered. Listening Partners project, a rural outreach program targeting women in the Central Vermont region (Better World Fund, Nichols Fund, Global Village Fund, VCF Fund)

Washington

Laird Norton Endowment Foundation

c/o Patrick de Freitas, Pres.
Norton Building, 13th Flr.
801 Second Ave.
Seattle, WA 98104-1516
(206) 464-3851
EIN: 916339917
Source Date: 12/95

Geographic Restrictions:
Limited to U.S.

Restrictions:
No grants for political groups, building projects, endowments, operating expenses, or general purposes.

To Whom:
Funding efforts are directed toward distinctive programs in conservation, resource management, sustainable development or economic development to renew natural resources, **combine resource evaluation with education,** environment, and forestry education.

For What:
Special projects, publications, internships, scholarship funds, matching funds, equipment, land acquisition, lectureships, research, seed money.

Financial info:
Assets: $3,344,800.
Giving: $563,600 for 165 grants (high: $20,000; low: $50).

Application info:
Applications accepted. Submit preliminary letter (2 page limit) with application form. Deadline is Mar. 31 and Sept. 30. Board meets in Nov. and May. Publishes annual report with application guidelines.

Recent Grants:
American Rivers, Seattle, WA. American Rivers' participation in consensus-based restoration program in Yakima River valley of central WA.
American Wildlands, Englewood, CO. On-site technical assistance to Montana landowners so they may develop site-specific sustainable timber management plans.
Defenders of Wildlife, Lake Oswego, OREG. Pilot program for Oregon Biodiversity Project. Project will provide public and private land managers with understanding of resources and long-term management goals.
Eastside Conservation Ontology, Bend, OREG. Four workshops on economics of resource management for upper Columbia River basin east of Cascade mountains.
The Energy Environment and Resources Center, Knoxville, TN. Production of video designed to address complex issues of flood control and wetlands management resulting from extensive damage to Mississippi River valley.
Environmental Policy Center, San Francisco, CA. Sustainable Cities Initiative for Seattle, WA. Initiative helps community leaders identify and implement programs and policies to conserve resources and protect city's environment.
The Doyon Foundation, Fairbanks, AL. Career development program in natural resource management.

Directors, Officers, Trustees:
Berger, Margie B., Director
Cameron, Mary M., Director
Clapp, James N., II, Director
de Freitas, Patrick S., Director, Officer
Helmholz, Elizabeth L., Director
Mentor, Marie B., Director
Parks, Allison, Officer
Storm, Anne M., Director, Officer
Sullivan, Jeffrey W., Director
Vorhies, Todd, Officer

Appendix D
Resources

Books, Directories and Guides

Corporate Foundation Profiles, 9th Edition profiles 235 of the largest corporate foundations in the United States. Features include contact information, purpose and grant restrictions, application guidelines and a list of key officials. The 778-page directory is $155 from the Foundation Center, 79 Fifth Ave., New York, NY 10003, (800)424-9836, fax (212)807-3677; http://fdncenter.org.

Corporate Giving Directory, 18th Edition contains information on the 1,000 largest corporate giving programs. Features include biographical data on corporate and foundation directors, officers and trustees; recent grants; historical data; and application information. The 1,873-page directory is $410 from The Taft Group, P.O. Box 33477, Detroit, MI 48232-5477, (800)877-TAFT; http://www.gale.com/taft/1taft.html.

Corporate Giving Yellow Pages, 12th Edition is a contact guide that lists the names, addresses, and phone and fax numbers of nearly 3,500 corporate giving programs. The 340-page book is $99 from The Taft Group, P.O. Box 33477, Detroit, MI 48232-5477, (800)877-TAFT; http://www.gale.com/taft/1taft.html.

The Directory of Corporate and Foundation Givers *1996* lists more than 8,000 of the leading U.S. funding sources. Features include biographical data on foundation directors, officers, trustees; recent grants; historical data; and application information. The 4,114-page directory is $235 from The Taft Group, P.O. Box 33477, Detroit, MI 48232-5477, (800)877-TAFT; http://www.gale.com/taft/1taft.html.

The Foundation Directory, 1997 Edition contains information on more than 7,900 foundations that hold assets of at least $2 million or distribute $200,000 or more in grants each year. The 2,068-page directory is $215 for hardcover or $190 for softcover from the Foundation Center, 79 Fifth Ave., New York, NY 10003, (800)424-9836, fax (212)807-3677; http://fdncenter.org.

The Foundation Grants Index, 1997 Edition lists over 70,000 recent grant descriptions from 1,000 of the largest independent, corporate and community foundations in the U.S. The 2,266-page directory is $160 from the Foundation Center, 79 Fifth Ave., New York, NY 10003, (800)424-9836, fax (212)807-3677; http://fdncenter.org.

Foundation Reporter, 29th Edition provides all the important contact, financial and grants information on the top 1,000 private foundations in the U.S. The 1,969-page directory is $390 from The Taft Group, P.O. Box 33477, Detroit, MI 48232-5477, (800)877-TAFT.

Government Online helps you access government—federal and state—information via the Internet, phone and fax. The book is $15 from HarperCollins Publishers, 10 East 53rd Street, New York, NY 10022.

Grants for At-Risk Youth contains information on approximately 200 funders of at-risk youth programs. Includes a special introduction written by Dr. Daniel Kaczyniski and Dr. John Platt and a disk containing application forms. The 342-page book is $119 from Capitol Publications Inc., P.O. Box 1453, Alexandria, VA 22313-2053, (800)655-5597; http://www.grantscape.com.

Grants for School Technology is an unique one-of-a-kind resource to assist administrators and education grantseekers tap into more than 200 public and private funding sources. The 436-page book is $99 from Capitol Publications Inc., P.O. Box 1453, Alexandria, VA 22313-2053, (800)655-5597; http://www.grantscape.com.

The Grants Development Kit. You'll use this three-ring binder over and over again as you copy the forms and checklists to streamline the grantseeking process. Includes an idea development form, grant development timeline, outline of basic proposal elements and much more. $45 per kit from Capitol Publications Inc., P.O. Box 1453, Alexandria, VA 22313-2053, (800)655-5597; http://www.grantscape.com.

The Grants Management Kit. As a companion to ***The Grants Development Kit***, this three-ring binder has forms, charts, checklists and outlines to help grantees manage a funder's money efficiently. Contains a grants management checklist, outline for preparing financial and project reports and more. $43 per kit. Both kits are available as a set for $76 from Capitol Publications Inc., P.O. Box 1453, Alexandria, VA 22313-2053, (800)655-5597; http://www.grantscape.com.

The Grantseeker's Guide to Project Evaluation. This step-by-step guide shows you how to plan and design an evaluation; collect and analyze evaluation data; manage an evaluation; and write a complete report. Contains a glossary of terms, sample evaluation plans, a description of statistical methods and a bibliography of additional resources. The book is $49 from Capitol Publications, Inc., P.O. Box 1453, Alexandria, VA 22313-2053, (800)655-5597; http://www.grantscape.com.

The Grantseeker's Handbook of Essential Internet Sites lists 250 Internet addresses for people looking to get money from corporations, foundations, associations and government agencies. Web sites for research organizations serving nonprofit groups are also included. The 163-page book is $75 from Capitol Publications Inc., P.O. Box 1453, Alexandria, VA 22313-2053, (800)655-5597; http://www.grantscape.com.

The National Directory of Corporate Givers, 4th Edition lists over 2,600 corporate foundations and direct giving programs The 1,092-page directory is $195 from the Foundation Center, 79 Fifth Ave., New York, NY 10003, (800)424-9836, fax (212)807-3677; http://fdncenter.org.

Outcome Funding: A New Approach to Targeted Grantmaking promotes a new concept for grantmakers and grantseekers—buying results with grant funds and not just services. The grant proposal thus because a targeted plan with defined outcomes for funders to invest in, and the grantwriter becomes an entrepreneur. The book is $21 from the Rensselaerville Institute, Rensselaerville, NY 12147, (518)797-3783.

Raise More Money for Your Nonprofit Organization: A Guide to Evaluating and Improving Your Fundraising contains information on the necessary first steps before launching a development campaign. The 51-page book is $14.95 from the Foundation Center, 79 Fifth Ave., New York, NY 10003, (800)424-9836, fax (212)807-3677; http://fdncenter.org.

Sources of Operating Grants. Discover more than 500 hard-to-find sources for personnel, administrative and other operating expenses. The 500-page book is $99 from Capitol Publications Inc., P.O. Box 1453, Alexandria, VA 22313-2053, (800)655-5597; http://www.grantscape.com.

Successful Grants Program Management. Learn how to evaluate your grants system, boost success rates, establish consistent district-wide policies and more. The 272-page book and CD-ROM is $24.95 from Classroom Connect, 1866 Colonial Village Lane, P.O. Box 10488, Lancaster, PA 17605-0488, (800)638-1639, fax (717)393-5752; e-mail, connect@classroom.net; http://www.classroom.net.

Writing Grant Proposals That Win, Second Edition! This step-by-step guide shows you how to assemble a winning grant proposal with concise explanations and solid examples to help you through every phase. You'll learn how to condense your entire proposal into a compelling abstract; describe project dissemination and continuation plans; write a solid boilerplate proposal first, then fit it to different situations and funders. The 200-page book is $85 from Capitol Publications Inc., P.O. Box 1453, Alexandria, VA 22313-2053, (800)655-5597; http://www.grantscape.com.

Winning Grants Step by Step: Support Center's of America's Complete Workbook for Planning, Developing, and Writing Successful Proposals. The workbook provides information on how to create a proposal that fulfills important criteria grantmakers demand from a successful request. The 127-page book is from Jossey-Bass Publishers, 350 Sansome Street, San Francisco, CA 94101, (800)956-7739, ext. 520.

Periodicals

Chronicle of Philanthropy. The Newspaper of the Non-Profit World keeps you up-to-date on the latest news, fundraising techniques, IRS regulations and recent foundation and corporate grants. Bi-monthly: $67.50 for 24 issues from The Chronicle of Philanthropy, P.O. Box 1989, Marion, OH 43306, (800)728-2819; http://www.philanthropy.com.

Corporate Giving Watch. Monthly updates on grantmakers, key trends, statistics, and recent grants of corporate givers. Monthly: $149 from Taft Group, P.O. Box 33477, Detroit, MI 48232-5477, (800)877-TAFT; http://www.gale.com/taft/1taft.html.

Federal Grants and Contracts Weekly. Helps readers find and win federal grants and contracts. It flags the latest funding opportunities in all areas across all agencies and tells how to pursue them. The newsletter alerts readers early to future funding, signaling specific solicitations often months in advance, unveiling agency grant plans in progress, tracking trends and forecasting areas of funding growth. Articles pass on advice from the experts, help readers calculate their chances and locate key prospecting resources. 50 issues per year, $389 from Capitol Publications Inc., P.O. Box 1453, Alexandria, VA 22313-2053, (800)655-5597; http://www.grantscape.com.

Foundation and Corporate Grants Alert. Foundation & Corporate Grants Alert helps grantseekers find and win private and corporate support. It provides comprehensive coverage of available national and local funding well in advance of deadlines, and reveals proven techniques and inside information on how to win more money. 12 issues per year, $289 from Capitol Publications, Inc., P.O. Box 1453, Alexandria, VA 22313-2053, (800)655-5597; http://www.grantscape.com.

Foundation Giving Watch. Monthly updates on grantmakers, key trends, statistics, and recent grants of foundations. Monthly: $149 from Taft Group, P.O. Box 33477, Detroit, MI 48232-5477, (800)877-TAFT; http://www.gale.com/taft/1taft.html.

For a list of general fundraising and grantseeking resources, go to Amazon.com's listing of books on "Fund Raising And Grants (General)" at: http://www.amazon.com/exec/obidos/subject-combination/0568-5163501-951535

Software

FC Search: The Foundation Center's Database on CD-ROM covers over 43,000 U.S. foundations and corporate givers in a fully searchable CD-ROM format. $1,195 single-user, $1,495 multi-user from the Foundation Center, 79 Fifth Ave., New York, NY 10003, (800)424-9836, fax (212)807-3677; http://fdncenter.org

Grants on Disk contains profiles of more than 250,000 recently awarded grants from more than 5,200 independent U.S. foundation and corporate funders. $695 for single-user, $895 for multi-user from The Taft Group, P.O. Box 33477, Detroit, MI 48232-5477, (800)877-TAFT; http://www.gale.com/taft/1taft.html.

GrantScape: CFDA has the most complete listings of federal funds available and how to apply to the funding agencies. Considered to be the "yellow pages of federal money," each listing includes program objectives, federal agency authorization, types of assistance and more. Updated annually. $175 from Capitol Publications Inc., P.O. Box 1453, Alexandria, VA 22313-2053, (800)655-5597; http://www.grantscape.com.

GrantScape: Corporate Foundations and Giving contains information on more than 4,000 corporate foundations and direct giving programs. Updated annually. $295 for single-user, or $395 multi-user from Capitol Publications, Inc., P.O. Box 1453, Alexandria, VA 22313-2053, (800)655-5597; http://www.grantscape.com.

GrantScape: Sources of Foundations is a national database that puts more than 13,000 private and corporate foundations at you fingertips. Features include over 63,000 names of directors, officers and trustees; contact names and numbers; application information; recent grants awarded; application forms (when available) and more. Updated annually. $495 single-user, $695 multi-user from Capitol Publications Inc., P.O. Box 1453, Alexandria, VA 22313-2053, (800)655-5597; http://www.grantscape.com.

GrantWrite: A Step-by-Step System for Writing Grant Proposals that Win walks you through the proposal-writing maze to prepare concise and compelling arguments for your projects. Available in DOS, Macintosh and Windows for $149 single-user and $199 multi-user from Capitol Publications Inc., P.O. Box 1453, Alexandria, VA 22313-2053, (800)655-5597; http://www.grantscape.com.

Prospector's Choice gives you more than 10,000 profiles of the top private foundations and corporate giving programs. Each entry provides contact information; financial summary; giving officers; application information and more. $849 for single-user, $1,045 for multi-user from The Taft Group, P.O. Box 33477, Detroit, MI 48232-5477, (800)877-TAFT; http://www.gale.com/taft/1taft.html.

9 780834 217607

Printed in Dunstable, United Kingdom

88190718R00205